BALKAN SOCIETY IN THE AGE OF GREEK INDEPENDENCE

Balkan Society in the Age of Greek Independence

Edited by
Richard Clogg

BARNES & NOBLE BOOKS
TOTOWA, NEW JERSEY

First Published in the U.S.A. 1981 by
BARNES & NOBLE BOOKS
81, Adams Drive, Totowa,
New Jersey, 07512
ISBN 0–389–20024–7

Printed in Hong Kong

CONTENTS

PREFACE

The papers brought together in this volume were originally delivered at a symposium organised in October 1977 by the Department of Byzantine and Modern Greek Studies at King's College to mark the 150th anniversary of the Battle of Navarino. This battle, the last great battle of the age of sail, witnessed the destruction of the Turco-Egyptian fleet by a combined British, Russian and French fleet in the Bay of Navarino in the Southern Peloponnese. This somewhat improvised intervention by the Great Powers was to ensure that some form of autonomous or independent Greece would come into existence. The movement for Greek independence and the war itself having been covered in an earlier symposium held in 1971 (and published as The Struggle for Greek Independence. Essays to mark the 150th anniversary of the Greek War of Independence, Macmillan 1973) it was decided to broaden the emphasis of the Navarino symposium into a considera- tion of early 19th century Greek society within its Balkan context. It is hoped that this collection of papers will afford the opportunity of making some tentative comparative analysis of Serbian, Montenegrin, Romanian, Bulgarian and Greek society in the age of national awakening.

It is a pleasure to thank the various participants in the symposium for the willingness with which they prepared their papers for publication and to acknowledge the valuable contribution of those that attended the symposium to the ensuing discussions. A particular debt of gratitude is owed to three successive secretaries of the Department, Kate Blade, Jackie Willcox and Adrianne Bradshaw, for the cheerfulness, patience and efficiency with which they have prepared the typescript for publication. The editor apologises for certain inconsistencies in transliteration which have arisen for technical reasons.

Lastly it is with great sadness that I have to record the death of one of the contributors to this volume, Alan Ferguson. Although so young, he had already shown great promise as a historian of the South Slavs, as his chapter on Montenegro amply demonstrates. This volume is dedicated to his memory as a token of our affection and respect for a scholar, a colleague and a friend.

Richard Clogg
1 July 1980

1

THE 'UNTOWARD EVENT': THE BATTLE OF NAVARINO 20 OCTOBER 1827

C. M. WOODHOUSE

The shortest and most celebrated account of the battle of Navarino was written by the Duke of Wellington. He inserted the following sentences in the speech from the throne at the Opening of Parliament on 29 January 1828:

> In the course of the measures adopted with a view to carry into effect the object of the Treaty,[*] a collision, wholly unexpected by His Majesty, took place in the port of Navarin, between the fleets of the Contracting Powers and that of the Ottoman Porte. Notwithstanding the valour displayed by the combined fleet, His Majesty laments that this conflict should have occurred with the naval force of an ancient ally: but he still entertains the confident hope, that this untoward event will not be followed by further hostilities, and will not impede that amicable adjustment of the existing differences between the Porte and the Greeks, to which it is so manifestly their common interest to accede.

The Duke's view of the matter was not widely shared in Parliament. Both in the House of Lords and in the House of Commons, the debates on the Address showed a strong tendency to question the Duke's judgment. His use of the word 'untoward' was thought particularly untoward. Of course, when a government faces a major crisis, its opponents tend to be more vocal than its supporters, so it must not be supposed that the Duke had no support. But he was certainly in an embarrassing situation. It was so embarrassing that his predecessor, Lord Goderich, who had been Prime Minister at the time of the battle, had quickly resigned in the hope of escaping into oblivion. His hope was fulfilled. No one but the Duke could have been strong enough to handle the crisis.

---

[*] The Treaty of London, signed by Britain, France and Russia on 6 July 1827.

1

Before we look at the reasons why the Duke was so upset, let us see first what he was upset about. The beginning of the drama of Navarino could be located at many different points. One point would be the outbreak of the war of independence of the Greeks against the Ottoman Empire in March 1821. Another point would be the formation of Philhellenic Committees in western Europe, followed by the arrival of money and volunteers in Greece: most notably of course Lord Byron in January 1824. Another point would be the recognition of the Greeks as belligerents by the British government in 1823, under the influence of George Canning as Foreign Secretary. Another point would be the first of the successive appeals by the Greek leaders to the British government, culminating in the Act of Submission in July 1825. Another point would be the Protocol of St. Petersburg, signed by the British and Russian governments in April 1826, which proposed mediation between the Greeks and the Turks without providing any sanction to make it effective. Yet another point would be the Treaty of London in July 1827, which reinforced the Protocol of St. Petersburg by the inclusion of France as a signatory and by provision, in the last resort, for the use of force to impose a truce on the two combatants.

But the more I study all these dates, the more I am convinced that the origin of the battle of Navarino cannot be sought in mere chronology. Its origins lay in the psychology of those involved. The contest between the Greeks and the Turks was psychologically impossible to resolve by any kind of compromise. To the Sultan, the Greeks were simply rebellious subjects. In their own eyes, the Greeks were a European people under an Asiatic tyranny, whose continuation they would not accept in any conceivable circumstances. Upon this scene of irresoluble conflict there came a number of strong personalities, whose characters as well as the orders which they had received made it impossible for them to accept that the conflict was irresoluble. I will start with the two most remarkable of these personalities: Ibrahim Paşa , the son of Mehmet Ali, the Albanian-born Paşa of Egypt; and Vice-Admiral Sir Edward Codrington, KCB, the Commander-in-Chief of the Mediterranean fleet.

Ibrahim was 35 years old when he sailed from Alexandria in July 1824 to take control of his newly-created Paşalik of the Peloponnese, Crete and adjacent islands. He was described by Codrington's son, a midshipman in his father's flagship, the

Asia, as a man 'not more than 5 foot 7 inches high' and 'not at all good looking, but with heavy features, very much marked with small-pox, and fat as a porpoise'. On land, Ibrahim was commander-in-chief, and imposed his control with brutal efficiency, first in Crete and then, from January 1825, in the Peloponnese. At sea he shared the command with a Turkish admiral. He detested the first holder of this appointment, and procured his removal in January 1827. His successor was Tahir Paşa, with whom Ibrahim was also on bad terms; but having no naval experience himself, he was obliged to leave operations at sea in Tahir's hands.

Ibrahim had his headquarters at Modon (in Greek, Methoni) on the south-west tip of the Peloponnese, about eight miles due south of Navarino. He gained control of Navarino in May 1825 by capturing the fort guarding the entrance to the bay. This was one of a succession of Ottoman victories which reduced the Greeks to the last extremities in the years 1824-27. The islands of Kasos and Psara, on which much of the Greek navy was based, were captured and devastated in the summer of 1824, and most of Crete in the following winter. Navarino fell in May 1825, Mesolonghi in April 1826, Athens in June 1827. On the mainland the Greeks held only Nauplia and its surrounding territory. Of the few remaining islands in their hands the most important was Ydra, now the principal base for their ships. It was the main target for the next attack by Ibrahim, who used to refer to it as 'little England'.

The desperate situation did not stop the Greeks from holding National Assemblies and quarrelling among themselves. Their first two National Assemblies had met in 1821 and 1823. The third, in 1826, was adjourned on the news of the fall of Mesolonghi. By the time it was re-convened in March 1827, it had fallen apart into two rival Assemblies. But the rival groups were persuaded to come together again by the imminent arrival of important foreign visitors. Chief among them were General Sir Richard Church and Admiral Lord Cochrane, who had accepted appointments as Commanders-in-Chief of the Greek army and navy respectively. It must be admitted that their contribution to the actual liberation of Greece was small. Cochrane, though perhaps the finest naval tactician since Nelson, was irresponsible, intemperate and mercenary. Church was an excellent soldier and accustomed to the command of irregular troops. He had raised and commanded a Greek force called the Duke of York's Greek Light

Infantry for service in the Ionian Islands in the war against Napoleon. But he was unable to achieve much in mainland Greece until after independence was won. The Greeks already had serving with them a number of freelance philhellenes who were much more useful than Church or Cochrane, notably the French Colonel Fabvier and the English naval Captain Frank Hastings. But the arrival of men with the high professional reputations of Church and Cochrane did much to revive Greek morale.

In fact, their arrival quite overshadowed that of another newcomer to the scene. Admiral Codrington took up his command at Malta in February 1827. He was 57 years of age and a veteran of Trafalgar. He was correct, stubborn, undiplomatic, rather unimaginative, a strict disciplinarian, and highly competent. He came from a Gloucestershire family with intellectual interests: one of them had founded the Codrington Library in Oxford. He himself carried a pocket edition of Thucydides around with him, from which he no doubt studied the topography of Navarino, but it would not have taught him much for the conformation of the bay had changed since the fifth century B.C. He always insisted that he was not what he called 'a philhellenist': he had no personal feelings towards the Greeks or the Turks, and was guided, he said, 'solely by my duty as an English officer'.

When Codrington took up his command in February 1827, there was no reason to expect an armed intervention between the Greeks and the Turks, for the Treaty of London was not signed until five months later. The only specific instruction he received relating to the struggle was a document handed over by his predecessor, Sir Harry Neale. This dealt with what was known in London as 'the Barbarisation Project'. It was a supposed plan attributed to Ibrahim Pasa, of systematically destroying or removing the Greek population of the Peloponnese and re-settling it with Muslims from Africe and Asia. Admiral Neale had been instructed in February 1826 to ensure that this did not take place, by intercepting suspicious ships. He had extracted from Ibrahim an assurance that he had no such intention, and there the matter rested. But he passed on the instruction to Codrington in case of a recurrence of the supposed project.

Meanwhile the Greeks and their foreign supporters caused Codrington more anxiety than Ibrahim. Towards the end of April Cochrane landed an irregular force at Piraeus and led a charge on the Acropolis armed only with a telescope. The consequences were disastrous, but Cochrane sailed blithely away to Alexandria, no

doubt dreaming of singeing the Paşa of Egypt's beard but with
no success. The Greeks concluded that he was mad, and Codrington
took pains to make it clear that Cochrane was no officer of his,
and that his actions were the sole responsibility of the Greek
government.

Codrington's first contacts with the Greeks and the Turks
would probably have predisposed him towards the latter. In July
he visited Nauplia, the Greek capital, to find a bitter quarrel
in progress between the government and a rebel faction, which he
was invited to suppress. After reluctantly intervening to restore
a semblance of order, he sailed on to Izmir, the administrative
centre of a prosperous and peaceful Turkish province. Codrington
had no reason to be aware that the prosperity derived entirely
from the Greek population, but he could appreciate that the
peace was entirely due to the Turkish government.

His main reason for visiting Izmir was that it was a
convenient point of communication with Istanbul. He had learned
at Nauplia of the signature of the Treaty of London, and that
instructions were on their way to him through the British
Ambassador at Istanbul. The Ambassador was Stratford Canning,
a cousin of George Canning, who had become Prime Minister a few
months earlier. Both George and Stratford Canning had the
reputation of being philhellenes, and Stratford effectively showed
it; but George died tragically on 8 August 1827, only a month
after the signature of the Treaty, to be succeeded by the feeble
Lord Goderich.

The consequence was that Codrington had to rely mainly on
Stratford Canning for his understanding of the Treaty of London.
He received a copy of it on 7 August, accompanied by a number of
Annexes containing detailed instructions on various contingenc-
ies, some addressed to Stratford Canning and some to himself. He
also received a letter of interpretation from Stratford Canning,
who had himself received a private letter from his cousin the
Prime Minister along with the Treaty.

To analyse the Treaty, the Annexes and the letters in detail
would take inordinately long. A summary of the essential points
must suffice. The declared purpose of the Treaty was to bring
about a 'reconciliation' between the Greeks and the Sultan. (I
need only pause to point out that a 'reconciliation' was
inconceivable, so the Treaty was based on a mirage from the
first.) To achieve this reconciliation the three signatories of
the Treaty, (Britain, France and Russia) offered their mediation.

They envisaged an 'immediate armistice' followed by 'negotiation'. The three Ambassadors at Istanbul were to inform the Sublime Porte of the plan, the three Admirals were to inform the Greeks. As it happened, there were only two Admirals in the Mediterranean at the time: Codrington and the French Count de Rigny. De Rigny had been there five years longer than Codrington and had a shrewd understanding of the problems ahead. In April he had actually sailed to Alexandria on his own initiative, in a vain attempt to persuade Mehmet Ali to withdraw Ibrahim's forces from the Peloponnese. The third Admiral, in command of the Russian fleet, was Count Heiden, a Dutchman who had formerly served in the Royal Navy. He left Kronstadt only in mid-June, arrived at Portsmouth on 21 August, and joined Codrington on 13 October, a week before the battle.

The Admirals' instructions laid down the procedure to be followed if both belligerents accepted the proposed mediation. With this we need not be concerned, because they did not. A second instruction laid down the procedure if either party refused mediation. Again it is only relevant to consider the procedure if the Turks refused, because the Greeks in fact accepted. In the case of a Turkish refusal, the Ambassadors were to inform the Porte that they would still do their utmost to secure the aims of a truce; they would prevent Turkish or Egyptian supplies from reaching Greece; and they would 'treat the Greeks as friends'. But the Admirals were sternly ordered to do all this 'without taking part in the hostilities betwixt the contending parties'. The intention of the Powers was still reconciliation, and 'every hostile proceeding would be at variance with the pacific ground which they have chosen to take'. Force must not be used unless the Turks 'persist in forcing the passages which they(the Admirals) have intercepted'.

All this was sincerely meant by George Canning. His letter to his cousin reaffirmed that 'the spirit of the agreement was peaceful interference recommended by a friendly demonstration of force'. At the same time he sent an emissary, Major Cradock, to Alexandria on a secret mission to Mehmet Ali, to try to persuade him to recall his son and to dissuade him from hostilities. But events frustrated his pacific plans.

First, the Treaty of London was leaked in The Times. The leakage included a secret clause to the effect that if the Turks did not accept mediation within a month, the Powers would appoint Consuls to Greece. This would clearly be a step towards formal recognition, and must have suggested to the Turks that the Powers were not acting in good faith.

Next, Major Cradock arrived at Alexandria on 8 August to find that a new Egyptian fleet had left to join Ibrahim three days before. Another fleet was being prepared at Istanbul. These forces not only showed a determination to resist but also assured Ibrahim of superiority in numbers and fire-power to the allied fleets which were being assembled at the same time.

Thirdly, Codrington's personal inclination to settle the whole matter by what he called 'one strong act of coercion' was reinforced by two further letters which Stratford Canning sent to him from Constantinople on his own authority. In the first, dated 19 August, he told Codrington that he was authorised to interpose his forces between the belligerents and 'to keep the peace with your speaking trumpet if possible; but, in case of necessity, with that which is used for the maintenance of a blockade against friends as well as foes; . . . I mean force.' Canning underlined the word 'force' himself. In the second letter, dated 1 September, he told Codrington that he was not to act 'in a hostile spirit', but his orders were 'ultimately to be enforced, if necessary; and when all other means are exhausted, by cannon shot'.

Such were the instructions and advice which Codrington received. Against this background of diplomacy and politics, it may be helpful to follow the story from the beginning of August 1827 in a chronological sequence of events as they might appear in ships' logs or Embassy diaries.

1 August. Codrington and de Rigny met for the first time at Izmir . Codrington regarded de Rigny with suspicion: he thought him more a diplomat than a sailor. Neither of them yet had definite orders about the overall command, except that Codrington had orders not to subordinate himself to de Rigny. Codrington wondered 'what the deuce I shall do with a set of tallow eating Russians' when they arrived.

5 August. Egyptian reinforcements sailed from Alexandria under Muharrem Bey, Ibrahim's brother-in-law.

7 August. Codrington received his instructions.

12 August. A second meeting between Codrington and de Rigny at Izmir went better than the first. De Rigny had useful information about the movements of Egyptian and Turkish ships. He had learned of the departure of Muharrem Bey's fleet from Alexandria a week earlier. Also one of his frigates had seen a Turkish

squadron off Cythera on 6 August, moving towards Navarino.
Since this cannot have been the fleet from Alexandria, which
sailed only one day earlier, it must have been another reinforce-
ment from Istanbul.
16 August. The three Ambassadors at Istanbul delivered their
first message to the Reis Efendi, or Secretary of State. He gave
them no reply. As the text of the Treaty had already been leaked
in London, the deadline for reply was reduced from a month to
fifteen days.
17 August. Codrington and de Rigny visited Nauplia together to
advise the Greeks to put their house in order.
19 August. Stratford Canning wrote his letter of advice to
Codrington, hinting at the use of force.
20 August. The dragoman of the French Ambassador sounded the
Reis Efendi on the prospect of a reply from the Sultan, but
received no satisfaction. It was suspected, correctly, that the
Austrian Ambassador, under instructions from Metternich, was
urging the Sultan to stand firm.
21 August. Codrington and de Rigny separated at Nauplion and did
not meet again for a month. On the same day the Russian fleet
under Heiden arrived at Portsmouth.
26 August. De Rigny received orders to serve under Codrington
in the event of naval action.
27 August. The Sultan discussed the proposed mediation with his
advisers and decided to reject it. On the same day reinforcements for de Rigny sailed from Toulon.
30 August. The dragomans (interpreters) of the three Ambassadors
sought a reply from the Reis Efendi, pointing out that the time
limit would expire on the following day. They were rebuffed.
31 August. The dragomans were again rebuffed.
1 September. Stratford Canning wrote his second letter of
private advice to Codrington, speaking of 'cannon shot'.
2 September. Codrington and de Rigny each sent a Captain,
together with a Russian official, to Nauplia to notify the Greek
government of the terms of the proposed armistice. On the same
day Codrington sent Captain Richards in the Pelorus to Alexandria
on another mission to persuade Mehmet Ali to desist from the
hostilities.
3 September. The Greek government accepted the armistice.
4 September. The Ambassadors wrote a Protocol to their respective Admirals on the enforcement of the Treaty in the light of the
Turks' stubbornness. The Protocol defined the area in which the

Treaty was to operate as lying south of a line drawn from the Gulf of Volos to the mouth of the River Aspropotamos, including the Peloponnese and adjacent islands. It pointed out that since the armistice could only be enforced at sea, and since the Greeks were already operating a blockade, the Admirals would in effect be acting as allies of the Greeks. This was justified by the fact that the Turks had refused the armistice and would certainly continue hostilities on land.

8 September. Stratford Canning forwarded the Ambassadors' Protocol to Codrington, with comments of his own emphasising the difficulty of the operation. On the same day Muharrem Bey arrived at Navarino with the Egyptian reinforcements.

9 September. The Turkish reinforcements from Istanbul arrived at Navarino. On the same day the Reis Efendi again refused to give any reply to the three dragomans.

11 September. Stratford Canning sent Codrington a further elucidation of the Ambassador's Protocol. It was clear that he was extremely worried, and that the three Ambassadors were not in perfect agreement.

11/12 September. During the night Codrington stationed himself off Navarino. He had only 12 ships mounting about 460 guns, against the Turco-Egyptian fleets' 60 ships mounting at least 2000 guns. Actually over 100 ships were in the bay, the surplus being accounted for by transports, fire-ships and neutral vessels, including a number of Austrians.

19 September. Codrington wrote to the Ottoman Admiral, Tahir Paşa, warning him against aggressive action. Tahir refused to receive the letter, which he forwarded to Ibrahim at Modon (Methoni). Codrington suspected that Tahir intended to sail out of Navarino and attack Ydra, off the south-east corner of the Peloponnese.

21 September. Part of the Turco-Egyptian fleet put to sea from Navarino. Codrington's fleet was not strong enough to force it back, but providentially de Rigny arrived in the nick of time to help him do so. No shots were fired.

22 September. Codrington sent a letter of warning to Ibrahim.

23 September. Captain Richards of the Pelorus reported from Alexandria that his efforts to dissuade Mehmet Ali had been unsuccessful. On the same day de Rigny had a private meeting with Ibrahim, which was also fruitless.

24 September. Codrington received the Ambassadors' Protocol elucidating his instructions.

25 September. Codrington and de Rigny held a formal meeting
with Ibrahim at the latter's camp overlooking the bay. The
British and French accounts agree that Ibrahim undertook to
seek fresh orders from Istanbul, and in the meantime not to move
his ships out of the bay. Ibrahim later said that the Admirals
had agreed to allow him to send ships to supply his garrison in
Patras, at the north west tip of the Peloponnese.
26 September. Ibrahim complained to Codrington that Lord
Cochrane had attacked Patras. Codrington forbade him to move in
response, but sent a remonstrance to Cochrane, and also to
Church, who was marching on Patras at the head of his Greek
troops. On the same day de Rigny left Navarino for Cythera,
where he had ships undergoing repair.
29 September. Captain Hastings, in command of his powerful
steamship Karteria (Perseverance), sank nine Turkish ships in the
Gulf of Corinth. The Karteria, which fired red-hot cannon-balls,
was the most advanced ship in the Mediterranean. It was in the
service of the Greek government and therefore not under
Codrington's control, so he could do nothing about it.
1 October. The Turco-Egyptian fleet again began to move out of
Navarino bay, to carry supplies to Patras. A number of Austrian
supply ships accompanied the fleet.
2 October. The British fleet followed and interposed itself
between the Turco-Egyptian fleet and the entrance to the Gulf of
Corinth.
3 October. More ships moved out of the bay, but the whole Turco-
Egyptian fleet returned to Navarino at nightfall.
4 October. The Turco-Egyptian fleet sailed from Navarino again
at nightfall, and anchored off Cape Papas at the entrance to the
Gulf. Codrington fired shots across their bows, whereupon they
retreated southwards again. A severe storm scattered them
during the following night.
6 October. Codrington anchored off Cape Papas to make sure that
the Turco-Egyptian fleet did not try to approach Patras again.
7 October. Most of the Turco-Egyptian fleet was back in Navarino
bay again.
9 October. The Sultan received Ibrahim's report of his meeting
with Codrington and de Rigny on 25 September. He decided against
any change of policy, and sent instructions to Ibrahim to
continue to reject the armistice. These instructions, despatched
only on 19 October, came too late to have any influence, but in
fact Ibrahim conformed to them.

10

12 October. Ibrahim wrote a pessimistic letter to the Sultan, implying that defeat was certain as a result of the policy which he was ordered to follow. On the same day, de Rigny returned to Navarino from Cythera. On the same day also Captain Richards of the Pelorus, who was still at Alexandria, sent a further message to Codrington. The message had no bearing on the battle, but one interesting point about it deserves to be mentioned. Richards sent the message by two routes, one in cipher by a Turkish brig and the other en clair by a French brig. The version carried by the Turk was delivered on 19 October, the day before the battle; the version carried by the French brig was delivered on 28 November, nearly six weeks after the battle.

13 October. The Russian fleet under Heiden arrived off Navarino. Codrington found that Heiden was not a tallow eating Russian but an agreeable Dutchman, ex-Royal Navy. After a brief meeting, de Rigny left for Zakynthos to buy stores.

14 October. The commanders of the fleet in the bay were engaged in forming their dispositions, in a horse-shoe line of ships at anchor. They were advised by French officers in Ibrahim's service, whom Codrington referred to as the 'renegadoes'. At his request, de Rigny repeatedly ordered them to leave, but they would not do so until their dispositions were completed. The strength of the Turco-Egyptian fleet consisted of 3 ships of the line carrying 74 guns each, 20 frigates, 32 corvettes, 7 brigs or sloops, and 5 fire-ships.

15 October. De Rigny returned to Navarino. The three Admirals met to discuss their tactics. All agreed that their object was to force the Turkish and Egyptian fleets to leave Navarino and return to their respective home bases in Istanbul and Alexandria. De Rigny was the most militant of the three: he argued that it would be necessary to enter the bay and, if the Turkish and Egyptian commanders disobeyed, to attack them immediately.

16 October. Codrington received reports of the devastation by Ibrahim of the Peloponnese. The source was Captain Hamilton, of the Cambrian, well known for his philhellenic sympathies, who had just returned from a reconnaissance at Kalamata. On the same day Codrington visited Heiden in his flagship. Heiden, who knew the aggressive mood of the Tsar, told Codrington that the Tsar had probably already declared war on Turkey.

17 October. De Rigny visited Codrington in his flagship. He told Codrington that he saw no alternative but to enter the bay

11

and anchor alongside the Turco-Egyptian fleet, since there was
no chance of blockading Navarino from outside the bay through
the winter. He had succeeded at last in compelling the French
officers to leave Ibrahim's fleet. Codrington sent a ship into
the bay with a final warning to Ibrahim, signed by all three
Admirals; but it was not delivered because Ibrahim was absent
at Modon (Methoni).

18 October. The allied fleets were completed, apart from three
or four late-comers. The totals were 27 ships of the line and
frigates: 12 British, with 456 guns; 8 Russian, with 490 guns;
7 French with 352 guns. In smaller ships, the allied fleet was
greatly outnumbered: the Turco-Egyptian fleet had a fire-
power of about 2,000 guns against about 1,300. On the same day
the three Admirals met to draw up a Protocol defining their
intentions. Their purpose, they said, was to enforce the Treaty
and put an end to Ibrahim's barbarities. They had three possible courses: (1) to blockade Navarino throughout the winter;
(2) to enter the bay and by a 'permanent presence' there to
prevent Ibrahim from further action; (3) to enter the bay and
'renew to Ibrahim propositions' in the spirit of the Treaty.
They decided that the third course was the only one which could
succeed 'without effusion of blood and without hostilities, but
simply by the imposing presence of the squadrons'.

19 October. The Admirals and their Captains met to receive
Codrington's orders. He proposed that the British squadron
should enter the bay first in line ahead, followed by the French
and Russians parallel to each other and also in line ahead, the
Russians to the leeward of the French. The ships of the line
and the frigates were to anchor alongside the Turkish and Egyptian ships within the horse-shoe. No shot was to be fired except
on his signal, unless the other side fired first. The smaller
ships, under the command of Captain Fellowes of the Dartmouth,
were to attack and remove the fireships. Codrington's last
words to his colleagues were a quotation from Nelson: 'No
captain can do very wrong who places his ship alongside that of
an enemy'.

20 October. In Istanbul a Turkish official remarked to the
dragoman of the British Ambassador: 'We shall have war! You
believe it and so do I! At this very moment it has perhaps
already begun!' He was in fact perfectly right.

The allied fleets cleared for action at dawn. On the
lower decks there was no doubt that a battle was about to take

place. The weather was fine, with a light breeze, which became stronger during the morning and then flagged. About noon Codrington's flagship, the Asia, led the way towards the bay, entering it at 2.00 p.m. The Egyptian commander, Muharrem Bey, in his flagship, the Warrior, sent him a message asking him to withdraw. Codrington replied that he had come to give orders, not to receive them. At 2.10 he anchored alongside the Warrior. Other British ships followed and also anchored. The French were still entering the bay, and the Russians had not yet begun to do so, when a fatal incident occurred between 2.25 and 2.30.

Captain Fellowes in the Dartmouth saw the Turks apparently preparing a fireship for action. He sent a pinnace under his first lieutenant to bid them stop. So anxious was he not to provoke hostilities that he ordered a midshipman in the pinnace, who had drawn his sword, to sheathe it again. When the small boat reached the fireship, the first shots were fired by the Turks, killing the coxswain and wounding other sailors. Captain Fellowes then sent another boat to tow away the fireship. Again the Turks fired, killing the Lieutenant in command. Then other shots were fired on both sides. The action soon became general.

The battle of Navarino was no Trafalgar. No tactical lessons could be derived from a battle in which many of the ships engaged were firing at anchor, broadside to broadside. It was a holocaust sprung from a single act of folly. Clearly neither the Turkish nor the Egyptian Admiral intended a battle, for both avoided committing their flagships until the action had become general. It was simply what the Duke of Wellington would have called 'hard pounding, gentlemen' for three and a half hours, from 2.30 to 6.00 p.m. When night fell at least 60 enemy ships had been destroyed, but none of the allied fleet was more than severely damaged: such was the disparity in skill and gunnery. The total casualties on the allied side were 174 killed and 475 wounded. On the other side casualties were estimated at 6,000 killed and 4,000 wounded. Some of these casualties were Greeks and other impressed men of various nationalities, including, according to Codrington, some British and American sailors, presumably captured by pirates. Some of the bodies found float- ing in the bay had been chained to their posts.

On the allied side there were also a few Greeks, but not in chains. Each of the Admirals had Greek interpreters and pilots. Codrington's interpreter was called Petros Mikelis, known to the sailors as Peter Mitchell. He was sent aboard the Egyptian

13

flagship at an early point in the battle, with a British
officer, to try to ensure Muharrem Bey's neutrality. An enemy
officer, who recognised the Greek, shot him through a port-hole
as he went on board. He is the only Greek known to me by name
who died in the battle which won his country's independence.

All night long the Turkish and Egyptian ships were explod-
ing in flames. The next day the Turkish Admiral, Tahir Paşa,
boarded Codrington's flagship. It was not clear what he came
for, but what he received was another tirade from Codrington,
chiefly about Ibrahim's breach of faith. Tahir, who detested
Ibrahim, was probably not sorry to hear the blame placed there.
The three Admirals also sent another joint letter to Ibrahim,
who returned from Modon to Navarino overland the same afternoon.
They blamed him for the battle and warned him against renewing
it. But of that there was no risk. It was plain that Ibrahim's
surviving ships neither would nor could fight any more. A few
weeks later Codrington allowed them to leave Navarino unmolested.

News of the battle reached Malta on 29 October, Istanbul
on the same day, Alexandria on 2 November. It reached London,
Paris and St. Petersburg a week later, and was published in an
extraordinary edition of the London Gazette on 10 November.
Reactions to the news were paradoxical. The three Ambassadors
in Istanbul thought it only decent to express their regrets to
the Sultan, and this gesture led him to believe that he was in a
strong position. He demanded compensation and denounced the
Convention of Akkerman, by which friendly relations had been
established with Russia in 1826. In December he issued a proclamation foreshadowing a Holy War, but went no further for the
time being.

His subordinates, however, were less put out by their
defeat. Ibrahim went on to a successful military career, chiefly
against his own master, the Sultan. When Ibrahim's father,
Mehmet Ali, heard of the defeat, his only comment was: 'It was
to be!' As a matter of fact, the battle contributed almost as
much to the independence of Egypt as to that of Greece. Tahir
Paşa also took a stoical view of his defeat. Some years later,
when he was Governor of Izmir, he received a visit from the
son of Admiral Codrington, by this time himself a senior naval
officer. The former Turkish Admiral proudly showed young
Codrington an oil painting of the battle, embraced him warmly
and exclaimed: 'Figlio di Codrington, figlio mio!'

On the European side, the victory had a mixed reception.

14

The Tsar was delighted, and took the opportunity to go to war with Turkey: a war which did not go too well at first, but finally ended with the Treaty of Adrianople in 1829, by which the Sultan at last agreed to recognise the independence of Greece. Metternich, who had been doing his best to bolster the Ottoman Empire, called the battle of Navarino 'une epouvantable catastrophe': even stronger words than Wellington's. The French government fell at a General Election; the British government fell from a lack of will to survive, and its successor was in a state of shock. The Duke of Clarence, as Lord High Admiral, insisted on awarding Codrington the Grand Cross of the Order of the Bath, but the Duke of Wellington was determined to remove him from his command.

The first step against Codrington was the despatch to him from the Foreign Office of a number of questions designed to suggest that he had exceeded his instructions. But Codrington answered them all without difficulty. Then a question was asked in the House of Commons about his allowing Ibrahim's ships to withdraw from Navarino carrying a number of Greek women and children. The fact was that most of the women went voluntarily, but it could be made to look as if Codrington had failed to carry out the orders passed on to him by his predecessor to frustrate the so-called 'Barbarisation Project'. In the end Codrington was recalled in June 1828, after holding his command for barely 18 months. No one ever gave him a clear reason for his recall. All that the Duke of Wellington would tell him was: 'You seemed to understand your orders differently from myself and my colleagues, and I felt that we could not go on.'

Even the Duke of Clarence failed to back Codrington any further. In protest, Codrington refused to pay the fees for his promotion in the Order of the Bath. Clarence, by then King William IV, retaliated by refusing to invite him to dinners of the order. The government also victimised Codrington by refusing to pay compensation to himself and his men for their personal losses in the battle, on the ground that 'hostile proceedings were not contemplated in the instructions'. Codrington then got himself elected to Parliament to present his case. He finally won his last battle in July 1834 when another government decided to award £60,000 in compensation. The Greeks naturally took a different view of the battle. They could not afford material rewards, but they created a new order of gallantry, in which the first three holders of the first class were Codrington, de Rigny and Heiden.

It remains to consider why Wellington was so upset by the untoward event. It is possible to suggest several reasons, both political and strategic. He regarded the Russians as a threat to British interests in the Mediterranean, and consequently further East in India, where he had himself fought his first campaigns and his brother had been Governor-General. The attempt to impose peace between the Greeks and the Turks had resulted in the arrival of a Russian fleet in the Mediterranean and the threat of the total destruction of the Ottoman Empire. If this were to occur, and if the Russians were to capture Istanbul, then the main bulwark against Russian expansion southwards and east-wards would be destroyed. These were not idle fantasies in the circumstances of 1828.

So far Wellington's probable line of reasoning was not so much anti-Greek as pro-Turkish. But he was also anti-Greek. He distrusted Capodistrias, whom he had known as the Tsar's principal adviser on foreign policy at the Congress of Vienna in 1814-15, and who was now the president-elect of Greece. He was worried about the security of the Ionian Islands, where the Greek population would undoubtedly demand the end of the British protectorate and union with Greece. He was convinced that Greece would be a continuing source of uncontrollable disorder both on land and sea. Moreover, Wellington was a member of the Protestant ascendancy in Ireland, like Castlereagh before him; and he was presumably not blind to the argument that the subjection of the Irish to Britain was not very different from that of the Greeks to Turkey.

Put more generally, Wellington was a supporter of the European system created, or rather restored, after the defeat of Napoleon. It was a system best managed by a small number of super-powers. The emergence of small nation-states in the inter-stices between the super-powers was bound to cause irritation and even upheaval. So convinced was Wellington of the merits of the system of super-powers, and so alarmed by the prospect of Russian expansion, that when he was finally convinced that Greek independence was inevitable , he offered the remarkable suggestion that a Greek Empire might be created to replace the Ottoman Empire. He might thus be claimed by the Greeks as the first progenitor of what they called the Megali Idea, the Great Idea of restoring the old Greek Empire of Byzantium.

However, I must not stray too far into speculation.

Returning to Navarino, I will end with another anecdote about
Codrington, told in his daughter's memoir. One day after his
return to England

     ' . . . he met an acquaintance in the street, a country
     gentleman of that sort to whom foreign events or public
     interests are a blank, who, seeming only to associate
     the thought of him with turnip fields and pointers,
     greeted nim with, 'How are you, Codrington? I have not
     met you for some time; have you had any good shooting
     lately?' He merely answered, 'Why, yes, I have had some
     rather remarkable shooting;' and passed on.'

2

GREEK SOCIETY ON THE EVE OF INDEPENDENCE

YANNIS YANNOULOPOULOS

Perhaps the most welcome outcome of recent historical writing on the Tourkokratia - the long centuries of Ottoman rule - has been a growing realization that the only way that one can meaningfully explore the nature of pre-independence Greek society is through a study of its relations to two much larger totalities: European economic interests in the Levant, with which the Greeks increasingly came into contact, and the Ottoman social formation of which they were an integral part. However, if placed in this wider context, the subject becomes vast to the point of being unmanageable. The many aspects of Ottoman society in decline which have to be taken into account add not only to its size but even more to its complexity.

In dealing with the lands which constituted in the 1830s the nucleus of the Greek Kingdom and the regions outside these lands where the Greek element was preponderant or substantial, one is faced with a multitude of case histories - whether surveying specific geographical areas or different economic sectors. Each of these case histories changed according to circumstance, local, regional or general, in the last fifty years or so before the Greek War of Independence. This being the case, it is not always safe to summarize arguments and to generalize on the basis of certain enduring common features of Ottoman economy and society during this period. The second, more important, preliminary point is that we are dealing with questions many of which are still wide open and are likely to remain so for some time to come. The recent interest in the last phase of the Tourkokratia has not yet produced that basic information (quantitative or other) necessary for a thorough examination of at least the material basis of the eighteenth century Greek society. The same is true for Ottoman society as a whole.

Despite this fact, and sometimes because of it, there seems to be no lack of enthusiasm in offering fully elaborated theories as to the articulation of Greek society to its

European and Ottoman contexts, and the direction in which it developed, or failed to develop, in the years leading up to 1821. A unifying element of these theories is the degree of emphasis placed upon the European 'factor'. A number of contemporary Greek writers claim that the Ottoman Empire during the later eighteenth and early nineteenth centuries was the object of intense exploitation of its natural resources by the leading commercial nations of the West. This type of large scale, colonial or semi-colonial, exploitation had annexed the Empire for good to the orbit of a Euro-centred nexus of trade relations, assigning to it the role of exporter of agricultural products. European economic penetration thus prevented the local non-Muslim element, possessors of considerable commercial capital, from gradually eroding and breaking down the prevailing feudal relations by their own 'autonomous' action. It prevented in other words the Balkan and in particular the emergent Greek middle class, from transforming and developing the geographical areas of their operations - perhaps the Ottoman 'periphery' as a whole - in competition with these more advanced countries forcing them instead to adopt an intermediate or 'comprador' position in relation to foreign traders.[1] It is true that the exchange of manufactured commodities for agricultural products, which was the basis of the trade of the Empire,[2] cannot be considered as anything other than an unequal exchange. It is true also that a clear breakthrough of the existing 'feudal' conditions did not occur at that time. Foreign colonial exploitation was a contributing factor, but was it the determining one?

The first question that has to be answered is whether the Ottoman Empire was important enough economically to be exploited by the commercial and 'industrial' capital of Europe. Great Britain had by the beginning of the nineteenth century taken the lead in trade relations with the Ottoman Porte, yet the annual amount of her import/export trade with the Empire as a whole during the second half of the eighteenth century and the first two decades of the nineteenth, amounted to approximately 1 per cent of her total foreign trade.[3] (We naturally take trade as our indicator since capital exports to the Levant is a later phenomenon). The amount of British shipping annually involved in this trade was a small fraction of 1 per cent.[4] For France who had held the leading position throughout the eighteenth century there are no comparable sets of complete figures. According to one estimate the Levantine markets of France in the

1780s represented about 5 per cent of its total trade,[5] a
percentage consideralby larger than that of England but still
marginal to French commercial interests on a global basis,
particularly in view of its steady decrease during the first
quarter of the nineteenth century.

This may dispose of the claim that the Ottoman Empire was
an area of vital economic importance for the West in the period
under discussion.[6] However, it is not the main issue. A much
more interesting question is the size of the external trade
sector in an underdeveloped agricultural economy such as the
economy of the Ottoman Empire in the late eighteenth century.
What part of the total Turkish produce was exported and what
part of domestic consumption was covered by foreign imports?
Figures which can help towards providing a definite answer to
these questions are largely lacking and those that are available
are not always reliable.. It is perhaps possible roughly to
estimate the total value of foreign exports from specific areas
or that of specific products,[7] but indices for the total production of the country are extremely difficult to construct. As
far as foreign imports were concerned estimates of their value
and volume have been suggested[8] but again there can naturally be
no such thing as total consumption figures for any part of the
Ottoman Empire.

However, despite the scarcity of numerical data, we are
not entirely in the dark on this point. Diplomatic and consular
reports, travellers' accounts and the works of other observers
of the Ottoman scene, provide sufficient evidence, even after
allowing for local variations, that the Ottoman economy outside
the big cities was largely based on local consumption and exchange. Indeed it was the foreign merchants themselves exporting goods to the Levant who complained of a small, inelastic
market.[9]

Thus in summary, one may say, with the help of whatever
indicative figures are available, that the external trade
sector of the Ottoman economy was perhaps not insignificant but
small,[10] too small at any rate for the alleged disarticulation of
the whole economy that it is supposed to have produced, particularly in the areas that were to constitute the Kingdom of
Greece, areas which ranked among the least economically important
parts of the imperial dominions. If European economic penetration is over-emphasized, it is the Ottoman 'factor' which, as a
consequence, is understated: the extent to which the Ottoman

state aimed to control the production and distribution process and to channel economic and social developments away from the mercantilistic paradigm of Western Europe and back into their traditional, peculiarly Ottoman, mould, whenever internal or external market demands (or both) brought the pressures of economic laws into play.

Any detailed investigation of the nature of Ottoman society, raises a number of highly complex and certainly much wider issues: the variety of evolutionary patterns of pre-industrial societies, the primary or secondary importance of international trade in the dissolution of feudal relations in the West, the controversial notion of the 'Asiatic' mode of produc-tion and its applicability to the Ottoman social formation and many others, including the meaning of the term 'feudalism' itself.[11] It will suffice to say that whenever the effects of European economic penetration are over-stressed, this is accompanied by a tendency to over-estimate the degree of openness of the Empire to processes that might have allowed the commercial capital of its merchants - let alone that of foreign merchants - to create conditions capable of altering its socio-political, cultural and religious basis.

The Ottoman state was the expression of a society organized along military/corporate lines and geared to conquest; a despotic theocracy, immensely bureaucratic and what was perhaps most important, technologically backward and isolated by the end of the eighteenth century. Its backwardness and isolation was not due to the 'nature' of the East, as many Western thinkers of the time self-confidently assured their public with a certain measure of relief, but to a culturally determined lack of receptiveness - an Islamic 'defence' to the realities of military decline.

In principle, all land and other sources of wealth belonged to the Sultan/Caliph. All political and social institutions and all types of economic activity were regulated to preserve and promote his power.[12] With a persistent emphasis on centralized control,[13] the absence of a hereditary nobility, a nominally free peasant class, a powerful infra-structure of local guilds which were generally hostile to large scale interregional and foreign trade, no concept of 'civil society' based on collective property rights, and with towns devoid of any kind of a corporate civic identity, Ottoman 'feudalism' in its juridical and political principles stood in direct opposition to the feudal societies of

21

Europe.

In the years of its ascendancy through ideology and in the years of its long decline through ideology and neglect, the Ottoman state, without opposing accumulated wealth or merchant capital as such (welcome sources of taxation and, occasionally, of confiscation), antagonized the type of trade expansion, capital accumulation and investment which is associated with the genesis of mercantilism and industrial capitalism.[14] It is within this framework that our main questions arise in relation to the nature of pre-independence Greek society. To what extent had the Greek middle classes (a necessary plural) come of age? Were any of the conditions necessary for this to happen present or emerging by the end of the eighteenth century? Or did the Greek middle classes (and those of the other non-Muslim groups) manage by their own activities, which were intertwined with those of European trade in the Levant, to create and then to solidify and extend such conditions?

In any attempt to provide an answer to these questions, production and distribution of labour have to be considered. During the later phases of the Tourkokratia certain important changes occurred in agriculture which was the dominant sector of production. The timariots of the early centuries, with their strictly regulated income corresponding to the number of armed men that they were required to supply to the Porte, had gradually given way to powerful landlords of large, export oriented çiftlık estates. These were to acquire a de facto possesion of their lands. The number of vaqfs also increased considerably - mainly in Macedonia, Thrace and Bulgaria. The vaqfs were nominally corporate religious estates (i.e. the only form of land property not ultimately 'belonging' to the Sultan). In essence however, they constituted what one author has called a camouflaging device to render land hereditary in a single family entrusted with its administration.[15]

It is known that the çiftlık properties expanded during the eighteenth century, not only in Greece but throughout the Balkans, and that a general tendency towards land concentration became increasingly manifest in the last quarter of that century. We also know that some of the big landlords were Greek primates, particularly in the Morea (Peloponnese). What is much less clear is the mechanism behind all these changes and the ratio between çiftlık estates and other forms of land tenure.[16]

The principal produce of the Greek lands was grain and

other cereals and there is clear evidence that the value and
volume of Greek exports was rising in the second half of the
eighteenth century. Cereal trade appears to have been an important feature of this 'export drive'. Its overall effect, however,
on the Greek economy cannot be assessed without regard to two
basic questions. What was the volume of this trade and what was
its nature? The total volume of cereal exports from Greece is
simply not known and since reliable, let alone reliable and
diachronic, production figures are hard to come by, the first
question can only be answered indirectly and tentatively. In the
absence of any pronounced increase in the agricultural population
or of technological advances in cultivation, the rise of grain
exports in the peak years must be attributed to underconsumption
and non-economic forms of violence rather than to a consistently
expanding production.[17]

This, however, could have operated as a limiting factor only
on the volume of cereal exports. The manpower necessary for
their production had to be fed and cereals constituted the basis
of their diet. If, as it has been suggested,[18] maize of different varieties had taken the place of grain as the staple food of
the peasantry in certain areas, grain production in these areas
must have dropped. An additional limiting factor was that grain
producing areas had to use a sizeable part of their surplus
produce to pay for a variety of goods and services including
seasonal agricultural labour.[19]

The nature of the trade was erratic, depending on the
conjuncture of European demand and (relative) internal abundance.
Shortages of grain in the towns, a bad harvest, or war meant
that the standing prohibition of its export at all times,[20]
along with that of other essential foodstuffs, was more rigidly
enforced, albeit only in the areas where the Porte had the power
to enforce it. In other areas, however, exporters and conniving
officials had to take into account the reaction of the local
population in times of grain shortage. Exports did take place
even then, although not without risk.[21]

To sum up the answer to both questions, these activities
do not seem to amount to the type of enterprise which produces
and reproduces a relatively stable, large scale, commercial
agriculture geared to exports, nor the social type of landlord/
merchant who was supposed to have figured prominently in the
Greek agricultural sector by the end of the eighteenth century,
complete with a 'capitalist' mentality and an anti-Western,

anti-Ottoman 'national' consciousness.[22] That there was capital left in the hands of big landlords, both Christian and Muslim, there can be little doubt. After all, in addition to cereals a number of other exportable crops were produced: cotton, tobacco, currants and silk.

Again however, the question arises how much capital existed and how was it used. As to how much, there can be no certain answer. But some of the constraining factors mentioned in the case of grain production and grain exports applied also, albeit in varying degree, to other crops. As for the use of available capital, a part of it was conspicuously consumed or spent on armed retainers, a part invested in the acquisition of lucrative tax-farming contracts, another part invested in trade (mainly in shipping) or lent at interest, and a considerable part was hoarded in readiness for the uncertainties of life in the Ottoman Empire.[23]

In the manufacturing sector production and distribution was regulated by the state-sponsored Muslim, Christian and Jewish esnafs or guilds, corporate organizations in every trade which aimed at eliminating free competition. The profit margins of their members were strictly controlled, the volume of their production normally limited to cover the needs of the local or regional market (unless they worked on bulk government orders for the provisioning of the army), as was the range of their products.

Outside the towns however, in the rural areas and in the numerous Greek and Vlach mountain villages, manufacturing production often tended to assume the organizational form of a community based 'company' rather than that of a guild.[24] The effective range of these companies was again limited both geographically and economically since home manufacturing for self-consumption purposes covered nearly all the needs of the vast majority of the population: the peasants. There was little that a peasant could afford to buy with money and this meant a chronically weak internal base for Greek manufactures.[25]

Yet some of these communities managed to extend their business further afield and to attain a degree of concentration of production and a level of prosperity unknown to town artisans. The most celebrated example of this type of enterprise, the 'co-operative' of Ambelakia in Thessaly, became a major exporter of spun red cotton to the markets of Austria and Germany with considerable assets deposited in Vienna and trade representatives in a number of European cities, in Istanbul and in Izmir.[26]

24

But the decline of Ambelakia, brought about by internal dissent and increased British competition in the central European markets, shows clearly both the limitations of such large scale ventures from the organizational point of view as well as the slender possibilities, within the Ottoman economic structure, of their further expansion in the face of foreign competition. Other manufacturing activities such as soap making and silk weaving were rather small scale, often ephemeral, affairs of only local significance with the exception of the soap making manufacture of Crete which was largely controlled by the local Muslims.[27]

It was the trade and shipping sector which was the most advanced in pre-independence Greece. Foreign merchants in the principal ports of the Empire, even those who were not unfamiliar with the languages and customs of the Levant, were naturally obliged to rely to a considerable extent on the local non-Muslim elements in order to build up the necessary infrastructure for their commerce. The Greeks made use of this opportunity, such as it was, to develop trading activities which they had maintained throughout the Tourkokratia.[28] As protégés of foreign commercial establishments with capitulatory privileges, intermediaries, minor partners or independent operators, they nearly always found themselves within the orbit of European trade. Their subordinate role was written into the conditions of their new, more prosperous, existence. It was, initially, a fact of life that developed into a way of life and they never quite outgrew that role, despite the expansion of their businesses and the challenge, however limited, which they sometimes were able to offer to the powerful trading nations of the West towards the end of the eighteenth century.

Greek business activity comprised two main branches: first, the carrying trade from Thessaly, Epirus and Western Macedonia northwards into the Balkan interior and on to Austria, Hungary, southern Germany, the Danubian principalities and southern Russia; and second the maritime trade of the Aegean islands, which gradually expanded to include the Italian ports, the Black Sea, and, to a certain extent, the western Mediterranean.[29]

Starting from small beginnings the overland Thessalo-Macedonian traders (Greeks, hellenized Vlachs and Macedonian Slavs) acted as carriers of, and armed guards for, local produce, extending their operations both in economic and geographical terms to become commission agents and merchants themselves. As imports from across the Austrian border could not be absorbed by

the Balkan market, save for the purchasing power of local landlords, and as the demand for raw materials (mainly wool and
cotton) which they exported rose steadily during the second half
of the eighteenth century, there was a considerable cash balance
left in their hands.[30] Where did they invest their accumulated
wealth? In their own trading activities and those of other
traders, fellow-villagers and preferably relatives, in commercial
ventures between Austria and Italy,[31] in moneylending which sometimes took the form of loans to the wretched Balkan peasantry
who were thus obliged to sell their crops at cut prices in anti-
cipation of the harvest, and finally in banking enterprises in
Vienna.[32] What money came back into the land of their origin
was mainly in the form of donations for building, renovation
and decoration of churches and monasteries, of cash remittances
to relatives, and of funds for the rebuilding of the family
house, for charity, for the establishment of schools and the
provision of scholarships or for the construction of works of
public utility.[33]

The rise of successful traders from rags to riches completely bypassed the manufacturing sector. They did not depend on
it at any stage of their career, except perhaps for its starting point, and in the absence of an adequate internal market
and of security of property in the Ottoman Empire they did not
invest in the manufactures of their localities.[34] On the
contrary their local economic links, in a more general sense,
grew weaker. The further away they moved from their often
humble beginnings, the further away the centre of their commercial activities and the source of their wealth shifted from the
highlands of Epirus and Macedonia, and eventually the most
prosperous of them, with their business assets, settled in the
Habsburg Empire, to the economic history of which they basically
belong from this point onwards.

Shipping was, without doubt, the most important and profitable area of economic activity for the Greeks under Ottoman rule.
There is a considerable body of literature on the Greek merchant
fleet of the time, but few, if any, of the basic questions relating to its size, its relative importance in the Levant trade,
and its diverse functions, have yet been tackled.[35] The basic
problems, and these are not limited to the Greek merchant
marine alone, are twofold. First, the flag of a ship and its
relation to the ship's owner(s) and/or its place of registration; second, the bulk value and kind of merchandise carried,

the place of origin and the destination of the cargoes. These
are problems which, unless examined on the basis of information
from different ports and/or the private archives of shipowning
families, become almost impossible to solve on account of the
invariably false manifests (i.e. descriptions of a ship's
cargo) deposited at the main customs houses of the Ottoman
Empire.[36] There is also the problem of the necessary ground
work, that still remains to be done, on the different measures,
weights and currencies in use in each part of the Empire and
their changing ratio vis-à-vis those of Europe.

Other difficulties, however, arise from the general
tendency, which has already been mentioned, to talk of the
emergence of some sort of advanced capitalist relations in
certain sectors of the Greek economy by the end of the eighteenth
century. It is in this context that the size, strength and
cohesion, both economic and ideological, of the Greek middle
classes during the last phase of the Tourkokratia is inflated
out of true shape, particularly in relation to shipping which
was the most dynamic sector of Greek enterprise.

There are a number of reasons for this but the most
frequent one is the failure to distinguish between the diaspora
Greek shipowners established outside the Ottoman Empire (those of
southern Russia and the Italian ports for instance) and the
indigenous shipowners of the Aegean. The same applies in
relation to the Greek merchants and bankers resident in Austria
or in other European countries.[37] This is neither a formal
question of nationality nor indeed of national consciousness. In
this last respect the opposite seems to have been the case. The
sense of nationality was generally far more pronounced in the
Greek diaspora communities of the late eighteenth century than
amongst the Greek-speaking Christian subjects of the Porte.
From the point of view of the economy, however, it is important
to look specifically at the nature of the mercantile activity of
the diaspora Greeks and to look at what part of it, if any, was
related to the economy of the Greek lands and in what ways.
Another method that leads to the same result, the overrating of
the shipowning class in pre-independence Greece, is the failure
to probe into certain rather obvious problems or to at least
acknowledge the existence of the corresponding questions.

There is little doubt that the Greek element was not only
important but, at times, perhaps indispensable to the maritime
trade of the Levant. References by foreign observers of the

27

Ottoman scene that bear this out frequently occur, in different
formulations, in contemporary documents and books. Equally
often, however, they are quoted either out of context or with
little regard to who says what, when and why. The question here
is what part of this attested importance should be attributed to
Greek owned shipping and what part to the need for Greek crews in
Russian, Austrian and other ships.[38]

What part of the growing business of the indigenous Greek
shipowners combined transport and commerce, - that is to say they
owned their cargoes, - and what part was work for freight or
commission? As in the first question there can be no certain
answers in the absence of specialized studies. But the frequency
of references, in the British documents at least, to the
chartering of Greek ships, seems to suggest that until the
continental blockade of 1807 the latter was quite frequently the
case.[39]

Further unanswered, and to a certain extent unanswerable,
questions, given the present state of research, arise if one
attempts to place the importance of the Aegean merchant marine in
context. How did the fleets of the Archipelago compare (both in
type and bulk of business) with, for instance, the fleets of Ragusa,
Sardinia and the Ionian Islands? These other flags were not very
dissimilar in terms of numbers or of the average size of ships
that they employed. They competed for the same markets, they
rose into prominence roughly at the same time,[40] and their
operations were guided by the same more or less business
mentality. Was there a rota of good and lean years for each or
everyone concerned? With the southeastern Mediterranean and the
Black Sea taken as a whole, was a certain flag during the period
under discussion prevalent in one major port for a few years or
for a specific year at the price of being absent from others?

The increasingly important Black Sea trade,[41] and in
particular the key grain trade, in the words of an early
nineteenth century observer, was carried out in a 'mysterious,
variable and hazardous way'.[42] It has often been claimed that
the Greek Aegean fleet enjoyed the lion's share of this trade and
that, at times, even monopolised it under the protection of the
Russian flag. The treaty of Küçük Kaynarca of 1774 is usually
reckoned to have been the starting point of this process.[43]
But the peace settlement of 1774, which incidentally did not
provide for any special privileges to the merchant marine of the
Greek islands, failed to 'open the Black Sea' to the Russians.[44]

This is what ought to have happened, at least according to the letter of article 11 of the treaty. The Porte however simply refused to implement this provision and to allow the free passage of goods through the Straits. It took another ten years and the threat of another Russo-Turkish war over the similarly unresolved Crimean issue to force the Sultan to concede this right to the Russian flag (Treaty of Constantinople, ratified in January 1784) and to the Austrians in May 1784.[45]

Like any other ban or prohibition in the Ottoman Empire of the late eighteenth century, trade restrictions applied only to the extent that the Ottoman government was able or willing to resist pressures for their circumvention. There is evidence to suggest that wheat from southern Russia did travel down the Straits at infrequent intervals during the decade of 1774-1784 and that Greek ships had a share in its transport. But the quantities involved were generally small. Even after the 1783 treaty and until the beginning of the second war between Russia and the Ottoman Empire (1787-1792) the Porte continued to resist by all possible devices the export of Russian wheat, a form of trade which tended to deprive Istanbul of cheap grain supplies and was therefore highly unpopular with the janissaries, the ulema and the populace of the Ottoman capital.[46] Only after the renewed defeat of Turkey in the Russian war which ended with the treaty of Iaşi (January 1792) did the wheat trade from the Black Sea to the Mediterranean assume considerable proportions. Between 1792 and 1815/6, the year that marks the beginning of a long period of depression in the Greek shipping sector,[47] account must be taken of the third Russo-Turkish war (1806-1812) during which the Russian flag would have been of very little use, as far as the Black Sea trade was concerned, to the Russians, the Greeks or indeed anybody alse. Thus, instead of the allegedly close and steadily growing association of the Aegean fleet with the lucrative wheat trade of Russia during the last fifty years or so before 1821, what emerges from a closer look at the dates is a period of prosperity covering less than twenty years; a period which coincided with the generalised upheaval of the Napoleonic wars.

A further important aspect of the Black Sea trade, one that tends to be totally overlooked, is that between the treaty of Küçük Kaynarca and the Greek War of Independence the Russian flag was not conferred on the Greek shipowners as a matter of course and certainly not only to them. Where large cargoes were

29

involved the much larger French, English and other European ships were normally preferred, at least until the beginning of the nineteenth century when these powers finally managed to acquire from the Porte the right to trade in the Black Sea in their own colours.[48]

On account of the difficulties that have already been mentioned concerning the financing of Greek maritime operations, the value and kind of merchandise carried, the frequency of flag changing (sometimes at different ports of call during the same journey)[49] the equally frequent sales of ships (including fictitious sales) usually resulting in a change of their name or place of registration, and finally on account of the scarcity of published data from several ports over a long period of time, it is not yet possible to present an adequate picture of the activities of the Greek merchant marine before Independence.

It is clear however that on the whole these activities have been very much overrated. All that can be said with certainty is that the Greek ships did hold a sizeable part of the internal Ottoman market and an equally large share of the Black Sea trade under the Ottoman flag not only after but also before the treaty of 1774.[50] Bulk trade and that of valuable cargoes between the Levant and the major ports of the western Mediterranean and north-western Europe, both before and after the wars of the French Revolution (for during the wars there was not much trade of this kind), remained firmly in the hands of the European maritime powers.[51] One of the main functions of the Aegean merchant fleet seems to have been the relocation of foreign imports and exports to and from the lesser ports of the Empire and the Black Sea.[52] It reached the peak of its strength during the Napoleonic wars by quick and extremely profitable blockade running operations in which the Hydriots, who, according to a number of contemporary accounts, were perhaps the best sailors in the Levant, figured very prominently. It declined steadily following the re-establishment of general peace in 1815.

The questions relating to the way in which the Greek shipowners disposed of their money assets can at present only be dealt with in broad outline.[53] They basically invested it back into their own shipping business or that of others,[54] engaged part of it in money lending and kept what they could not invest in 'hard' currency. Their cosmopolitan activities had little relation to the agricultural or manufacturing production of the Greek lands, except in the following three ways. They naturally

traded in Greek produce; they made some use of the capital of
local landlords, Christian or Moslem, state officials and other
traders (Chiot merchants of Izmir for example) to finance their
operations;[55] and lastly, and most importantly, they gave rise to
a local ship-building industry. But information regarding the
labour force involved, the way in which it was paid and the ratio
of ships locally constructed to those built abroad or bought for
ready cash, is still very insufficient.[56] What is certain is
that the industry followed the declining fortunes of the Greek
shipowners after 1815.

The level of social division of labour in the Greek lands
was very low. Wage labour did exist but only in certain areas of
economic activity and, even there, wages were usually supplemented
by payments in kind. Work in the shipyards may prove to have
been one of the few 'clear' cases. In the first place there were
not that many potential wage labourers around. So far as the
areas with substantial Greek-speaking population are concerned,
there is no evidence of large scale expropriations other than
those carried out by Ali Paşa of Jannina.[57] But there is little
doubt that, by the second half of the eighteenth century, the
non-economic pressures on the peasantry went on increasing amid
conditions of widespread anarchy and maladministration in the
Ottoman provinces. Faced with these pressures the peasant had
two radical options: to cross the border of the law or that
of the Empire. There were other somewhat less exciting
possibilities, namely to accept conditions as they were; to
switch to sheep breeding or to seek better terms and a quieter
life under another landlord, sometimes very far away from his
birthplace. This, for example, was what many Moreots decided to
do when in the 1770s they left their province devastated by
Albanian bands, and crossed to Asia Minor to work in the domains
of Karaosmanoğlu.[58] In other words, any displaced or surplus
agricultural population was mainly absorbed within the agricultural sector.

A part of them must have drifted to the big cities and
towns of the Empire. That much is clear from the measures taken
by the first reforming Sultan, Selim III (1789-1807), who set
out to reverse the trend.[59] We know that these measures were
only partially successful. What we do not know is whether this
immigration was meant to be permanent and what numbers were
involved. It is possible for this trend to have mainly affected
the areas of the second Russo-Turkish war (areas without

31

substantial Greek-speaking inhabitants), in which case an additional reason for the flight to the cities could well have been the attempt by the Moslem peasants to avoid military service, since the right of exemption was normally granted to city dwellers. Be that as it may, even if there were some potential wage labourers amongst the displaced peasantry, the Ottoman cities, and in particular the small urban population centres of the Greek lands, would have had a very limited need for them. There was no manufacture to make use of their labour and no possibility of expansion in this direction, given the control that the esnaf maintained over the production and distribution of goods and the provision of services. Any circumstantial local needs were adequately covered by the itinerant 'companies' of artisans and labourers. Agriculture used a certain number of labourers, but on a seasonal basis and wages were not unusually paid wholly or partly in grain or other foodstuffs.[60] As for the Greek and Greco-Vlach manufacturing production outside the constraint of the esnaf, there existed a system of relations which minimised the need for wage labour (this was also the case in the shipping sector); a system based on the participation of one's labour in the expected profit from the selling of the product in which this labour was invested.[61]

Finally a brief word on the towns and their function.[62] Not unlike their medium size counterparts in other Ottoman provinces, the towns of pre-independence Greece served mainly as administrative centres and focal points for regional trade. Their 'agrarian' features were quite pronounced since most of their inhabitants were incompletely separated (economically and socially) from the surrounding countryside. Their role as centres of craft production was secondary to that of being centres of consumption.[63] The town did not predominate over the countryside by subjecting its agriculture to a pattern of new economic relations; on the contrary it lived off the latter's surplus which was directed toward the provincial capitals in the same fashion as the surplus from the provinces was capital city oriented.[64] Due to the multitude of toll-duties and local taxes, the hazardous communication and, above all, due to the limited volume of esnaf production, manufactured goods available in the town market rarely travelled beyond the boundaries of the province. Given such constraints, maintained by state intervention at every level of the economic process, the Ottoman towns as centres of manufacturing activity were bound to remain weak and isolated.

The degree to which capitalist production was compatible with 'Ottoman feudalism' is a separate, wider issue, as are the relations in general between capitalism and Islam. Suffice it to say that these relations have never been characterised by immobility. The two have always interacted at different times and under different circumstances to give rise to a variety of social formations, the nature of which has often proved a subject of controversy. What concerns us here is something more specific: the state of play in the case of the Greek provinces of the Ottoman Empire, at a particular period of time, - the end of the eighteenth and the beginning of the nineteenth century. The evidence adduced in this paper points to the conclusion that the necessary preconditions for the emergence of capitalism proper in pre-independence Greece were for the most part conspicuous by their absence. What we have observed is the non-existence of a free labour market; zones of money economy - ports, towns and certain areas where commercial agriculture had developed - surrounded by, if not submerged in, a vast agricultural hinterland, the economy of which was based on cereals and cereal surpluses, self-consumption and a limited, mostly local, transfer of resources; manufacturing activity of a small range capable of expansion only within prescribed limits set by its institutional framework and, in the case of craft production outside the esnaf, by the lack of elementary state protection, let alone positive support; and lastly, an overgrown trading sector, dynamic, outward looking and cosmopolitan with little relation to local production: a commercial bourgeoisie which grew up and attained its maturity and wealth as the intermediary link between the foreign trader and the Levant market.

1. To mention only some of the better known and more influential recent works, see N. Psiroukis, To neoelliniko paroikiako phainomeno (Athens 1974), V. Kremmydas, Eisagogi stin istoria tis neoellinikis koinonias (1700-1821) (Athens 1976), K. Moskof, I ethniki kai koinoniki sineidisi stin Ellada (1830-1909) (Thessaloniki 1972) and K. Vergopoulos, To agrotiko zitima stin Ellada (Athens 1975). The last two essentially accept the basic premise that European demand was responsible to an ever increasing degree for the shaping of the structure of production in the Greek lands and in the Ottoman Empire as a whole and that the Greek middle class (or part of it) had substantial economic power and ideological cohesion as this process got under way.

2. Board of Trade records, class 6, vol iii (hereafter BT 6); Board of Customs and Excise records, class 3 (hereafter Cust. 3); Virginia Paskaleva, 'Contribution aux relations commerciales des provinces balkaniques de l'Empire Ottoman avec les états européens au cours du xviiie et la première moitié du xixe siècles', Études Historiques iv (1968) 265-92.

3. Cust. 3, vol 17; BT 6, vol 185.

4. BT 6, vol 185.

5. Ralph Davies, 'English Imports from the Middle East, 1580-1780', in M. A. Cook, ed., Studies in the Economic History of the Middle East, from the Rise of Islam to the Present Day (London 1970) 193-206. The figures cited by Cesar Moreau, Tableau comparatif du commerce de France avec toutes les parties du monde avant la révolution et depuis la restauration (London 1827), if they are accurate, suggest a somewhat higher percentage. They do confirm, however, the dramatic decline in French trade in the Levant after 1815. It is worth noting that in the late sixteenth century the Levant accounted for 50 per cent of the trade of France, Davies, op. cit., 205.

6. Psiroukis, op. cit., 55-8; Vergopoulos, op. cit., 46-7; Kremmydas, op. cit., 27.

7. N. Svoronos, Le Commerce de Salonique au xviiie siècle (Paris 1956) 239-326; V. Kremmydas, To emporio tis Peloponnisou sto 18 aiona (1715-1792) (Athens 1972) 144-205.

8. F. Beaujour, Tableau du commerce de la Grèce (1787-1797) (Paris 1800) ii 163; Svoronos, op. cit., 220-239.

9. BT 6, vol 180; Beaujour, op. cit., ii 268.

10. Ralph Davis, Aleppo and Devonshire Square. English Traders in the Levant in the Eighteenth Century (London 1967) 27-40.

11. Eric Hobsbawm introduction to Marx's Pre-Capitalist Economic Formations (London 1964); R. Hilton, ed., The Transition from Feudalism to Capitalism (London 1976) reproduces the debate between M. Dobb, P. Sweezy, K. Takahashi and C. Hill originally published in Science and Society in the early 1950s, together with a number of subsequent contributions to the debate. On the related question of the importance of international trade see I. Wallerstein,

The Origins of the Modern World System (New York 1974) and the critique of
R. Brenner, 'The Origins of capitalist development: a critique of neo-
Smithian Marxism', New Left Review no 104 (July-August 1977) 25-92. The
literature on the 'Asiatic' mode of production is equally extensive. See
M. Godelier, 'La notion de "mode de production asiatique"', Les Temps
Modernes, xx (1965) 2002-27, S. Divitcioğlu, 'Essai de modèles economiques à
partir du M/ode/ P/roduction/ A/siatique/', Recherches internationales à la
lumière du marxisme, nos 57-8 (1967) 204-89; M. Sawer, 'New Directions in
historical materialism', The Australian Journal of Politics and History, xxii
(1976) 243-257 provides a short and extremely informative, if not always fair,
account of this particular debate so far.

12.   H. Inalcik, 'Capital formation in the Ottoman Empire', Journal of
Economic History, xxix (1969) 97-140.

13.   The increasing inability of the Porte to cope with its rebellious
provincial governors during the later part of the eighteenth century did not
affect the structure or the rationale of the Ottoman state. The rebels did
not challenge such principles. They rather aimed at creating small replicas
of the Sultan's administration in their areas, and to bargain with the central
government from a position of strength.

14.   P. Anderson, Lineages of the Absolutist State (London 1974) 361-431;
S. Mardin, 'Power, Civil Society and Culture in the Ottoman Empire',
Comparative Studies in Society and History xi (1969) 258-81; Inalcik, op.cit.

15.   Anderson, op. cit., 386.

16.   It is not only the scarcity of data that renders such questions very
difficult to answer but, as one author rightly points out, also the fact that
the very concept of land ownership was complex and ambiguous under the
Ottoman system of mixed forms of landholding and shared rights in land,
W. M. McGrew, 'The land issue in the Greek War of Independence' in
N. P. Diamandouros et al. eds., Hellenism and the First Greek War of Liberation (1821-1830): Continuity and Change (Thessaloniki 1976) 111-129. Works
referring to the landholding regime in the Balkans include, H. Inalcik, 'Land
problems in Turkish history', Muslim World xlv (1955) 221-8; B. Cvetkova,
'L'évolution du régime féodal turc de la fin du XVIe jusqu'au milieu du
XVIIIe s.', Etudes Historiques i (1960) 171-207; V. P. Mutafcieva and
S. Dimitrov, Sur l'état du système des timars des XVIIe-XVIIIe ss. (Sofia
1968); and Traian Stoianovich, 'Land tenure and related sectors of the Balkan
economy, 1600-1800', Journal of Economic History xiii (1953) 398-411.

17.   Svoronos, op. cit., 365-6, singles out underconsumption as the principal
reason for the increase in grain exports from the region of Thessaloniki, on
the basis of several unpublished French consular reports and the observations
of Beaujour.

18.   Stoianovich, op. cit., 403-5; Stoianovich, 'Le mais dans les Balkans',

Annales xxi (1966) 1026-39; Kremmydas, To emporio 7.

19. Moreot wheat for example was exported to the Ionian islands and used in lieu of cash payments to Zantiot seasonal workers. Memo by Spyridon Foresti, 22 June 1790 in FO 42, i.

20. There were cases of landlords who managed through powerful connections in the capital to obtain official sanction for the export of grain, but this was the exception rather than the rule.

21. G. Baldwin to R. Lee, Alexandria, 18 June 1795, FO 24, i; Francis Werry to Stratford Canning, Smyrna, 9 December 1810, FO 352/i(9); Svoronos, op. cit., 273-4.

22. Kremmydas, Eisagogi 54; Vergopoulos, op. cit., 68-70 simply refers to bourgeois landlords.

23. On the different types of capital investment in eighteenth century Greece, Sp. Asdrachas, 'Economia' in Istoria tou Ellinikou Ethnous xi (Athens 1975) 159-188.

24. Ibid., 165.

25. V. Panayotopoulos, 'O eidikos rolos tis georgias sti diamorphosi ton scheseon polis - ypaithrou ton 18° aiona', O Politis 7 (1976) 30-36; F. Thiersch, De l'état actuel de la Grèce 2 vols. (Leipzig 1833) (Greek translation /Athens 1972/ i 296-7).

26. A. Vacalopoulos, Istoria tou Neou Ellinismou iv (Thessaloniki 1973) 531-548.

27. V. Kremmydas, Oi sapounopoies tis Kritis sto 18° aiona (Athens 1974); Y. Triantafyllidou, 'L'industrie du savon en Crète au XVIIIe s.: aspects économiques et sociaux', Etudes Balkaniques XI/4 (1975) 75-87.

28. P. Masson, Histoire du commerce Français dans le Levant au XVIIIe siècle (Paris 1911); G. L. Maurer, Das Griechische Volk 2 vols. (Heidelberg 1835) (Greek translation /Athens 1976/ i 39-40).

29. T. Stoianovich, 'The Conquering Balkan Orthodox Merchant', Journal of Economic History xx (1960) 234-313.

30. Sp. Lambros, 'Selides ek tis istorias tou en Oungaria ke Austria makedonikou Ellinismou', Neos Ellenomnemon, vol. 8 (1911) 257-300; W. M. Leake, Travels in Northern Greece vol. i (London 1835) 307 ff.

31. Stoianovich, 'The . . Balkan . . Merchant, 283-4.

32. ibid., 300-305.

33. A. Vakalopoulos, Oi Dytikomakedones apodimoi epi Tourkokratias (Thessaloniki 1958) 9, 14, 17.

34. Stoianovich, 'The . . Balkan . . Merchant, 306.

35. Kremmydas, Eisagogi, 116 n.1. G. B. Leon, 'The Greek Merchant Marine (1453-1850) in S. A. Papadopoulos (ed.), The Greek Merchant Marine (Athens 1972) 13-52, is the best and most comprehensive study of the subject to date which makes use of all the important, yet hardly sufficient, published

material available, while Kremmydas' own contribution, <u>Archeio Hadjipanayoti</u>, vol. i (Athens 1973) makes available extremely useful new evidence on certain aspects of the financing of Greek maritime operations and other related topics.

36. See for instance FO 78, vol. 136, Reports from Levant Consuls (1821-1825); vol. 112 f.314-52 'Effects of Greek war on the trade of the Levant C^{o}', unsigned memorandum dated 10 October, 1822 which traces the history of the Black Sea trade back to 1783.

37. On the methodological questions posed by the existence of a large and prosperous Greek diaspora, the importance of these distinctions and their wider implications for the comparative study of pre-independence and post-independence Greek society see G. Dertilis' excellent introductory chapter (11-29) to his Ph.D thesis, <u>Social change and military intervention in politics: Greece 1881-1909</u> (University of Sheffield 1976) published in Greek (Athens 1977) in a slightly different form. Would it not be misleading, asks Dertilis, to consider the Jewish diaspora as part of the Israeli middle class? Or, one may add, the Greeks of Ethiopia or Zaire as part of the Greek middle class of today?

38. On the significant contribution of Greek crews to the Levant trade see FO 78 vol. 112, ibid; vol. 96, undated /1821/ and unsigned /Francis Werry, the Levant Company's consul in Smyrna 1794-1825/ 'Memoir on the political and commercial relations of Great Britain with Asia Minor'; FO 95, vol. 23, Robert Liston to FO, Constantinople 10 September, 1814.

39. See for instance, COL/5 (Vice-Admiral C. Colingwood Papers, National Maritime Museum, Greenwich), Consul's Letters (1806-7); BT.6 vol. 180, unsigned memorandum on British Trade with the Ottoman Empire, dated 13 October, 1790; FO 42, vol. 2, Sp. Foresti to FO, Zante 16 October, 1793; vol. 3, Foresti to FO, Zante 12 April, 1799.

40. As far as Ragusa was concerned the case was, needless to say, of a natuical power coming back into prominence.

41. In addition to the memoranda mentioned in notes 38, 39 and 42, 46 below, see C. C. de Peyssonnel, <u>Traité sur le commerce de la Mer Noire</u>, 2 vols (Paris 1787); H. A. S. Dearborn, <u>A Memoir on the Commerce and Navigation of the Black Sea, and the trade and maritime geography of Turkey and Egypt</u>, 2 vols, (Boston 1819); the review article by /Jacques/ Peuchet on the 'Essai historique sur le Commerce et la Navigation de la Mer Noire' published anonymously (Paris 1805) in <u>Le Moniteur Universel</u>, nos 197 and 199 (7 and 9 April 1805); undated (1806) and untitled memorandum (on the navigation and trade of the Black Sea) in Ad.Ms. 33554 (Bentham Papers, vol XVIII) ff. 144-146; 'Notes respecting the Commerce of the Black Sea and the Sea of Azoff, more especially as regards the Trade of Wheat', unsigned and undated (1827) in Ad.Ms 38749 (Huskisson Papers, vol XVI) ff.12-51.

42. FO 352 (Stratford Canning Papers) Bundle 2B, file 9, unsigned memorandum on the Black Sea Trade, dated Pera 5 June, 1812.

43. See, for instance, K. Paparrigopoulos, Istoria tou Ellinikou Ethnous, 2nd ed., (Athens 1885-7) vol 5, 587-8; Psiroukis, op. cit., 74-5; Moskof, op. cit. 37, 84-6; Kremmydas, Eisagogi . . 125-6; To emporio . ., 95-6; Leon, op. cit. 27, 32.

44. As claimed, among many others, by Moskof, op. cit., 84.

45. PRO 30/26, vol. 72 'Sir Robert Ainslie's letters to the . . Levant Company' 1776-1792; SP97, vol 55, ff.5, 157, 244.

46. PRO 30/26 vol 72; FO 78, vol 6, ff.8, 14, 30-1; FO 352, Bundle 11, file 5; J. Bland Burges Papers (Bodleian Library, Oxford) file 58, ff.1-43, 'Report by W. Lindsay (Secretary of the British Legation at St. Petersburg) on the Black Sea' dated 1791.

47. Kremmydas, Eisagogi . ., 122.

48. SP 105, vol 126, ff.274-5; vol 188 (British Chancery Records, Constantinople, 1782-9); FO 78 vol 4, ff.6, 128-9; vol 6, f.184; Dearborn, op. cit., vol 1, 115.

49. FO 359 (Odessa)/1; FO 42/2, Sp. Foresti to FO, 27 November, 1793.

50. Peyssonnel, op. cit., i, 22, 223-4, ii, 212; BT6 vol 180, memorandum cit.

51. Asdrachas, op. cit., 182-3.

52. Bentham Papers, vol. cit.; E. Habesci, The Present State of the Ottoman Empire, (London 1784) 426-7; Asdrachas, op. cit., 183.

53. Research in this field is almost non-existent, the one important ` exception being Kremmydas, To archeio.

54. ibid., 79-104.

55. Stoianovich, 'The . . Balkan . . Merchant', 275; Kremmydas, Eisagogi . ., 128; Leon, op. cit., 28-9.

56. Kremmydas, Eisagogi . ., 128-143, 179; Some useful figures about ship construction in Mesolongi and Anatoliko in Western Greece during the third quarter of the eighteenth century are provided by Leon, op. cit., 29.

57. Panayotopoulos, op. cit.

58. Richard Clogg, 'Aspects of the Movement for Greek Independence' in Richard Clogg, (ed.), The Struggle for Greek Independence, (London 1973) 5.

59. S. J. Shaw, Between Old and New. The Ottoman Empire under Selim III, 1789-1807 (Cambridge, Mass. 1971) 75-76, 83-84, 175.

60. See note 19 above; Asdrachas, op. cit., 168. It is interesting to note that at least as late as the 1860's the practice of paying farm labourers in agricultural produce had not died out in certain regions of the Balkans (FO 83, vol 334, Report from the British Consul at Monastir, 23 Novebmer, 1869).

61. Asdrachas, op. cit., 168.

62. The papers of two conferences on the Balkan town held in Moscow (1969) and Venice (1971) were published respectively as La ville Balkanique, XVe -

XIXe siècles, (Sofia 1970), Studia Balcanica, No.3 and Structure Sociale et Développement Culturel des villes sud-est Européennes et Adriatiques aux XVIIe - XVIIIe siècles (Bucharest 1975). Prof. N. Todorov's many important contributions on this subject, focusing on the Bulgarian urban centres, have been collected in a separate volume entitled La ville Balkanique aux XVe - XIXe siècles (Sofia 1972). In all these works there is very little reference to the Greek towns during the latter part of the Tourkokratia. This is yet another area where, as far as Greece is concerned, specialised studies are virtually non-existent. Certain aspects of the city-countryside relationship in the eighteenth century are briefly touched upon by V. Panayotopoulos, op. cit. See also V. Filias, Koinonia kai Exousia stin Ellada (Athens 1974), 23-26.

63. The degree of differentiation of town inhabitants in terms of wealth, which is all that the eighteenth century Kadi records from Vidin, Sofia and Ruse clearly show, cannot by itself be considered as evidence of an emerging capitalism. Todorov seems to advocate a different view. Cf. La ville . . Ch. VII, 'La différentiation de la population urbaine au XVIIIe s. d'après des registres des cadis de Vidin, Sofia et Ruse'.

64. Gonul Tankut 'The spatial distribution of urban activities in the Ottoman city' in Structure Sociale . ., 245-265.

3

STATE AND SOCIETY IN THE IONIAN ISLANDS, 1800-1830

GEORGE YANNOULOPOULOS

The Ionian Islands are situated off the western coast of Greece. They are seven in number and Corfu, furthest to the north, is opposite Albania while Cerigo, furthest to the south, is to be found between the southeastern tip of the Peloponnese and Crete. They cover an area of 2,300 square kilometres approximately and their population in the period under discussion was just over 200,000 people.

The Ionian Islands like many other parts of the Balkan peninsula were gradually detached from the Byzantine Empire when the latter began its long decline in the eleventh century. In the centuries that followed they became the prize of incessant feudal and dynastic wars which convulsed the eastern Mediterranean. They were occupied by marauding Norman barons, Byzantine princes, Italian adventurers, Venetian soldiers of fortune and, in the case of some of them, even by the Turks. The first island to come under permanent Venetian occupation was Corfu in 1385. Zante (Zakynthos) and Cephalonia followed and the cycle was finally closed in 1684 when Lefkas or Santa Maura as it was then known, was taken from the Turks.

Until the fall of <u>Serenissima</u> in 1797 the Venetians were the absolute masters of the islands. In order to maintain their possession they had to defend them against repeated Turkish attacks from the mainland which culminated in the unsuccessful siege of Corfu in 1716. Meanwhile they introduced an aristocratic system of government which was broadly modelled on the system that obtained in Venice itself. They also encouraged the settlement of Christian families primarily from mainland Greece and the Italian peninsula, promoted trade and above all the production of olive oil and currants, the two cash crops from which the islanders secured their livelihood.

The gradual decline of Venice meant the loss of her overseas possessions to the Turks. Cyprus and Crete fell and by the end of the eighteenth century the proud Republic had only

managed to hang on to the Ionian Islands and a few outposts
along the Dalmatian coast. The islands were thus saved from
the Turkish menace only to be lost to the most unlikely
conquerors: the French, the Russians and the British. This
unexpected turn of events was the result of the Napoleonic
wars. The Treaty of Campo Formio lifted the veil which had
hitherto covered these rather obscure Venetian possessions at
the entrance to the Adriatic and suddenly the Ionian Islands
became pawns on the vast chessboard of Europe.

The first to fill the vacuum were the French,[1] naturally
enough since they were the ones who created it. In June 1797
a French expeditionary force took over from the demoralised
Venetian authorities and proceeded to plant the tree of liberty
while the Ionian crowds looked on with mixed feelings. The
French administrators, still fired with revolutionary fervour,
preached equality,[2] did little to implement it but did enough
nevertheless to antagonise certain sections of the population,
especially those who thought that their social position and
their religion was threatened by the godless Jacobins of
France. There was little popular support for the French when
the Ottoman Empire and Russia decided to patch up their quarrels
and intervene. After the battle of Aboukir a joint Russo-
Turkish armada attacked and occupied the islands one by one,
the last being Corfu which fell in February 1799 following a
siege that lasted four months and bitter fighting.

A period of confusion began. The islanders, under a
virtual Russo-Turkish protectorate in which the Russian admiral
held the upper hand, tried to devise an administrative system
for their 'free' country. In other words they decided to
draft a Constitution. A provisional charter was hastily drafted
and implemented[3] while delegations were despatched to St.
Petersburg and Istanbul in order to finalize the constitutional
arrangements. This they managed to do eventually after lengthy,
confused and quarrelsome negotiations or rather intrigues.
But the so called 'Byzantine Constitution' of 1800,[4] which
introduced a semblance of independence and fully restored the
political privileges of the Ionian aristocracy as though
nothing had happened in the intervening three years,[5] was not
well received. One island after the other displayed strong
centrifugal tendencies generated by a variety of factors:
localism, particular economic interests, factionalism - all
against a background of class fears and aspirations.[6] In

Zante the inhabitants raised the Union Jack and placed themselves under the protection of the British who were their main
trading partners. In Cephalonia fighting broke out between
feudal chiefs and their followers. The peasants of Santa
Maura rose in revolt and in Cerigo (Cythera) the leaders of
the aristocratic party were murdered. The most serious
rebellion took place in Corfu where the 'vulgar' people gained
the upper hand over the patricians and proceeded to frame
another Constitution, this time of Jacobin inspiration.[7] The
Ionian Islands were proving a nuisance in indirect proportion
to their size. At that point the allies intervened. First a
British naval detachment managed to impose law and order in
Corfu and then the Russians, whose departure had given the
signal for the civil strife, resolved to play a more active
part in the protection of their unruly co-religionists. In
1802 Count Mocenigo, an Ionian nobleman who had distinguished
himself in the service of the Czar, was despatched to the
Islands as Russian plenipotentiary, accompanied by a sizeable
number of Russian troops and men-of-war.[8] Mocenigo with
cunning, intelligence and the threat of Russian bayonets, soon
became the undisputed master of the islands. In 1803 he
drafted and put into effect another Constitution,[9] the third in
succession, which took into consideration the irreversible
political changes that had ocurred and broke the stranglehold
of the nobility over the state apparatus, the main beneficiary
being himself and to a lesser extent the middle classes. Three
years later in 1806 Mocenigo dictated a series of material
amendments to his Constitution in order to correct its alleged
shortcomings and strike the right balance between the legislature and the executive by increasing the powers of the latter.[10]
But by then it was too late. Following the treaty of Tilsit in
1807, the Russians handed the islands to the French whose
second occupation was not to last very long. This time the
British decided to take a hand. In 1809 a detachment of Lord
Collingwood's Mediterranean fleet occupied the three southern
islands and worked their way up to the north slowly but steadily.
The French garrison in Corfu finally capitulated in 1814 on the
orders of Louis XVIII.

Thus began the British occupation of the Ionian Islands
which was to last for half a century. The British right of
possession was confirmed and legitimized on 15 November 1815
by the Treaty of Paris after haphazard and confused negotiations

42

in Vienna and Paris, which need not concern us here.[11] The
important point was that the Treaty of Paris proclaimed the
islands a free and independent state and then contrived to put
them under the exclusive protection of Great Britain which was
given virtual carte blanche to organise their internal administration while taking over completely the management of their
defence and foreign affairs. The Treaty of Paris created the
British protectorate over the United States of the Ionian
Islands.[12]

    The first British Lord High Commissioner was Sir Thomas
Maitland,[13] a seasoned campaigner. His appointment proved
extremely significant. Operating within the broad guidelines
laid down by the Treaty of Paris and the cabinet in London, but
motivated chiefly by his autocratic tendencies and the utter
contempt in which he held his 'subjects', for this was what the
Ionians had become, he proceeded to dictate the Constitution of
1817.[14] It was unanimously approved by an Ionian Assembly hand-
picked by Maitland himself and lasted for thirty years until
1847 - thirty years which must have seemed like eternity to
the mercurial Ionians. Maitland, through the Constitution and
the policies he implemented, often in violation of it, created
almost single-handed a relatively stable and viable state
structure.

    The object of this paper is to examine the social struc-
ture and the state in the Ionian Islands in the first third of
the nineteenth century. The limited space at our disposal and,
perhaps more to the point, the right approach to such an
enterprise, demand that certain assumptions be laid down. First,
that any analysis of the social and political aspect of life in
the Ionian Islands can only be grounded in the mode of production which prevailed in the islands. And secondly, that the
mode of production in question was feudal. A lot has been
written about the feudal mode of production in general, and in
particular about feudalism in the Ionian Islands. It is of
course impossible to make a critical survey of this vast material. Therefore the use of the term in this paper must be
explicitly defined. The term 'feudal mode of production' implies
that the individual producers were not separated from the means
of production, that surplus labour was extracted by a group of
non-labouring landlords who were not directly involved in the
production process, and that the means whereby that was achieved
were not economic but chiefly political and ideological. This

43

leads us to the formation of the state which is seen as a relatively autonomous level which secures the conditions of existence of the dominant mode of production. In other words, the terrain on which the various groups, defined as social classes by the role they played in the production process and their position vis-à-vis the extraction of surplus labour, pursued their basic antagonistic interests thus giving the state at each stage its concrete form.

Let us now examine the available evidence which, it is hoped, will support or at least not contradict the foregoing assumptions. But before we do so a few introductory remarks. Some of the Ionian Islands, unlike any other part of what is now Greece, escaped the Ottoman rule and had the good fortune, if good fortune it be, to be administered by a Christian western power. One of the consequences was that the records of the Ionian government and other extremely valuable archival material have survived almost intact. Not only in Venice but in the islands themselves there are literally millions of documents of all kinds which may one day become the raw material for the historians of the islands. Unfortunately that day lies in the future. With the exception of Professor Andreadis'[15] book on the finances of the Venetian administration no systematic attempt has ever been made to utilize the available material. The sheer bulk of it seems to have been the main obstacle. This has a particular bearing on our investigation. Any analysis of the social structure requires quantitative data on land tenure, commerce, price fluctuations, demographic changes etc. and these are simply lacking. What is of course available is the relevant historical literature, some of it dating from the period in question. Unfortunately the preoccupations of historians have changed with time. The various histories of the islands were written in order to answer questions which are no longer considered important, whereas other aspects which have become the focus of current attention are hardly touched on or are omitted altogether as common or unnecessary knowledge. It is therefore obvious that any conclusions to be drawn about the social structure and the state in the Ionian Islands must inevitably be of a highly tentative nature.

In order to tackle the problem at hand we must go back in time. The foundations of the Ionian society and state had been slowly laid during the four centuries of Venetian domination.[16] The swift changes that took place during the thirty years under

44

examination can be rendered meaningful only if seen as a transformation of a determinate social and political structure. If
we are to start from the prevailing mode of production the best
approach would be through the question of land tenure. Khiotis
in his monograph on the feudal estates of Corfu[17] writes that
the first feudal grants were made by the Byzantine Emperor
Alexios in the eleventh century. The practice was naturally
continued and given much wider scope by the Norman and Italian
conquerors of the islands. According to Marmora[18] the Angevins
of Sicily divided Corfu into 24 baronies which were somehow
later reduced to 12, and according to Lunzi[19] the same system
was subsequently introduced to the remaining islands. The
relations between the feudal overlord and his feudal vassal
were broadly based on the western European model and need not
concern us here. The relations, however, between landlord and
tenant were much more complex and also much more significant
because they provide the key to the relations of production
which remained in force long after the medieval state structure
had become obsolete. Khiotis[20] writes that the feudal owners of
the land would lease it out to the peasants against the payment
of ground rent, either labour rent or rent-in-kind. In the
case of uncultivated land one fourth of it would become the
property of the tenant, the lease on the remaining portion would
be perpetual and the rent due to the landlord rather small. The
terms of the leases differed when cultivated land was involved;
the duration of the lease would normally be five years and the
lease would be renewable. The introduction of this system is
aptly described by Khiotis. Land was not given to the peasants,
he writes. On the contrary the cultivators were deprived of
their right to it. 'Only those in whom the feudal property was
vested were deemed owners of land. Consequently the former free
owners having lost their title to the land could, if they so
wished, stay on as tenants and the same applied to their
agricultural labourers who could also stay in their employ'.[21]
He also remarks that 'those receiving land which was part of a
feudal estate were not free to sell, convert or exchange the
land without the intervention or permission of the landlord . . .
they could, however, bequeath the land to their heirs or give
it as dowry to their daughters.'[22] This practice coupled with
the fact that the landlord could not object to this change of
tenant implies a significant departure from the principles of
Roman law.[23] A further complication was the diritto del lavoro

as described by Napier,[24] according to which no change in the cultivation could be effected without the consent of the tenant.

Two questions arise concerning the nature of the ground rent. The first relates to its nature and the second to its size. There is evidence which supports the view that when first introduced Ionian feudalism was much closer to the typical western model. Some documents talk of peasants tied to the soil[25] and there is also evidence that the barons exercised almost exclusive jurisdiction over their tenants and that the form of labour rent predominated. The _timar_ of the Gypsies in Corfu[26] which survived into the nineteenth century can be seen as a relic of a not so distant past when the 'classical' features of the feudal system were much more marked and widespread. It is impossible to chart the slow changes which gradually led to the abolition of most feudal dues other than rent-in-kind.[27] However it would not be inaccurate to say that by the end of the eighteenth century, when our story begins, the greater part of cultivated land in the Ionian Islands was owned by landlords who used hired labour on their rather small _demesne_ estates while the rest was leased out to tenant farmers against the payment of ground rent-in-kind. In the absence of any detailed research on the conditions of land tenure it is impossible to determine with any degree of accuracy the size of the rent in precise quantative terms. There certainly were wide variations due to a number of factors; the fertility of the land, the kind of crop raised, the conditions of supply and demand of manpower which prevailed when the land was leased out, and even political considerations. Any firm answer to this crucial question must wait for more detailed research.

Next we must turn to the antagonistic nature of the relations of production and locate the points of friction between landlord and tenant and the form this clash assumed. There is ample evidence of discontent on the part of the peasants which was either channelled to the Venetian authorities through petitions or led to open insurrections.[28] However there is no adequate and systematic documentation on the complaints of the peasants. It may be assumed that the landlords were eager to secure better terms for themselves by forcing the lessees to agree to them or by evicting them and leasing out their land to more co-operative or needy tenants. Another extremely important factor must have been the creation of debts. The most significant feature of the economy of the islands was that they

produced commodities for export. Their olive oil, currants and
wine were the principal source of income for the peasants.
Locally grown grain in most of the islands was enough for only
three or four months consumption,[29] therefore grain and other
important items like meat had to be imported and then bought by
the peasants. The international prices for oil and currants did
of course vary but the main danger came from the nature of the
crop. Both olive oil and currants are highly speculative;[30] it
is impossible to calculate in advance the yield of an olive tree
and in the case of currants a few days of rain at the wrong time
can destroy the labour of a whole year. The peasant would then
have to borrow money under terms which were highly unfavourable
to him[31] by offering his tenancy as security and this would
inevitably lead to a further subdivision of property. The
opinion of the British in the nineteenth century was that the
property relations in the islands resembled a veritable jungle.[32]
Another weapon in the hands of the landlords was the control of
certain resources vital for the production process or the
marketing of the produce.[33] For example both olive trees and
vineyards require a certain amount of irrigation which put the
owners of streams or the land through which an elaborate
system of ditches had to pass in a very strong position. Under
the same heading come the abuses connected with the _seraglia_,
the warehouses for the storing of currants, which are colour-
fully described by Napier in his book.[34]

The dominant position of the land-owning class, however,
was consolidated and maintained not by economic but mainly
political means, and this brings us to the state and its function. It has already been pointed out that the system of
internal organisation in the islands was broadly based on that
which obtained in Venice. Here we must add that there were two
important differences; the first was the very presence of the
Venetian officials who were the ultimate source of authority.
The second, and much more significant, was that the Ionian
patricians, unlike their Venetian counterparts, were landowners
and looked upon any form of mercantile activity with unrestrained aristocratic contempt.[35] For the rest, both the origin and
the subsequent development of the oligarchic system in the
islands closely followed that of Venice.[36] Initially the sovereign body in each island was the grand assembly of the inhabitants which was open to all. Gradually it became more and more
difficult to attend and the grand assemblies of the islands

finally closed their doors to the vast majority of the community echoeing the _Serrata_ of 1297 in Venice.[37] Membership of the assembly became hereditary and the names of the nobles were inscribed in a book called the _Libro d'Oro_, thus settling once and for all the question of who was to be included in the small body of privileged citizens who constituted the state. The nobles would gather once a year to elect in a democratic manner the leaders of the community, the judges and the rest of the officials who, together with the Venetians, were responsible for the administration of the islands.[38]

It is clear that the political organisation of the islands was based on the principle of exclusion. This led to an unambiguous and rigid differentiation between those who part- icipated in the administration and those who did not.[39] The disenfranchised majority was further subdivided into the _civili_ or _cittadini_ who were the middle class, and the _popolari_ who were placed at the bottom of the social ladder. It is relatively easy to calculate the degree of social mobility from the middle class to the nobility on the basis of the bourgeois families who periodically replaced in the grand assemblies aristocratic lineage that had died out. Two important points emerge: first, that mobility within the political system did not reflect accurately the shift in the socio-economic balance of power between the two classes. The land-owning aristocracy managed to hang on to their political privileges on the strength of their possession of land whose nominal value was kept artificially high by legislation.[40] In other words the patricians being the only section of the population with access to the state were able to enlist the support of the state in maintaining their political domination, and in this way they managed to perpetuate the dis- enfranchisement of the middle class. But the interests of the two classes which clashed head on in the political field were not exactly mutually exclusive when it came to the social rel- ations of production. Many members of the middle class were themselves small or medium size landowners, and so long as the feudal mode of production remained dominant the extraction of surplus labour from the tenant farmers continued to be the main source of income of the non-labouring classes which included both the nobility and the upper strata of the bourgeoisie.

The second point relates to the 'rising bourgeoisie'. It is a phrase that has been very often used when talking about the eighteenth century. In fact it has achieved the enviable status

of a commonplace. A commonplace, however, has a very slippery
surface and the best way to avoid it is by asking some simple
and obvious questions: Why was there a bourgeoisie and who were
its members? Did it actually rise and, far more important, why
did it rise? At the outset it must be pointed out that the term
bourgeoisie when applied to the Ionian Islands implies a
strictly political differentiation vis-à-vis the nobility. A
cittadino was a person whose name was not inscribed in the
Libro d'Oro and was not a peasant. It is very likely that when
the original differentiation was crystallized the patricians
were the wealthy, or rather the wealthier people in the islands,
in other words the big landowners. After the Ionian Serrata
this distinction was maintained in two ways. First in terms
of the families who became members of the grand assemblies, and
secondly, in terms of what these families could or could not do.
The nobility's code of behaviour, falling foul of which resulted
in expulsion from the assembly and loss of franchise, laid down
that the nobles could not engage in trade, and this is probably
the key to our problem. The implications of such a rule are
obvious. First of all it explains the existence of the
bourgeoisie; the material reproduction of life which included
the circulation of goods was made possible through certain
'services' which the nobility could not render even if they
wanted to. This enables us to say that there was a bourgeoisie
in the strict sense of the term. It is also reasonable to
assume that a non-noble person could amass wealth outside purely
commercial activities. The interesting point about the political
arrangement was that whereas the nobility could not become
merchants, there was no corresponding ban on the non-nobles
acquiring or enlarging their property in land or real estate
in general. True, the legal system as formulated by those who
could legislate, i.e. the nobles, did discourage the transfer of
land ownership but this does not mean that it was impossible for
a wealthy man to augment his estate or acquire an interest in
someone else's estate through marriage, inheritance, usury or
even the purchase, at an inflated price, of a nobleman's estate,
provided that it was not one of those officially designated as
baronies, which as such could not be sold.[41] Therefore when we
speak of the bourgeoisie in the Ionian Islands at the end of the
eighteenth century the term comprises all those people who were
not nobles but had become wealthy enough through commerce,
usury, tax farming, small scale manufacture, landholding or a

combination of all these.

This brings us back to the initial question. Did the bourgeoisie rise and why? In the present state of research this question cannot be properly answered, although there are indications which suggest that it did. Any attempt to treat them as conclusive evidence can only indicate a lack of awareness of the specificity of the problem. Instead we should try to draw the broad outlines of an interpretation that will establish the conditions necessary for and the likelihood of certain processes to have taken place. Needless to say, such an enterprise is a mere guidance for the processing of historical data and must be discarded when it proves useless as a means of assimilating evidence.

The cardinal point is that the middle class families, despite their disenfranchisement, were, at least in theory, in a better position to take advantage of existing opportunities for relative enrichment. Unencumbered by the disabilities imposed on the patricians, a bourgeois family could diversify in agriculture, commerce, carrying trade and even the professions, thus achieving increased efficiency and maximization of profit. According to Ansted[42] in Santa Maura the members of a family would specialize in the different sectors of the production and circulation process. One of them, usually the eldest, would look after the estate and the rest would occupy key positions in the town and abroad as commercial agents.

Another way of approaching the same question would be to explore the possibilities of the successful investment of a surplus. Again we find the wealthy commoner in an advantageous position vis-à-vis the nobility. There was no law which prevented the bourgeoisie from undertaking purely speculative commercial ventures, usury or tax farming. On the other hand the noble landowners were more or less obliged to invest their surplus in their estates or simply consume it, the latter being far more likely given the system of land tenure which effectively barred the way to agricultural improvement. This of course does not mean that the line which divided the activities of the nobles and the rest of the population was clear. We know that some patrician families engaged in tax farming and we can also assume that some landowners, perhaps the bigger ones, could undertake commercial ventures indirectly through agents. Unfortunately the lack of detailed research into individual estates and the vicissitudes of their fortunes does not allow us to suggest any answers based on hard evidence.

The general remarks about the possibility of a middle
class ascendancy do not necessarily mean that the introduction
of a new social system through political reform or revolution
was the accurate reflection of the conscious policy pursued by
the rising bourgeoisie. The basic elements of the concrete
conjuncture are sadly missing and without them any attempt to
reconstruct the specificity of the situation would inevitably
lapse into a crude model of social classes acting in full
accordance with their interests as conceived today with hind-
sight.

Let us now look more closely at the major events of the
period which started with the fall of Venetian colonialism and
the introduction of the French revolutionary principles in the
Ionian Islands and ended with the establishment and consolidation of the British protectorate.

The effects of the French occupation were, in the short
term, only political but their long term repercussions went
far deeper than the political surface and cannot be over-
estimated. The French did not stay long, but it was long
enough for the Libro d'Oro to be ceremoniously burned and the
tree of liberty to be planted. Thus the political privileges
of the aristocracy were abolished at a stroke and the place of
their grand assemblies was taken by municipal committees in
which all the social classes, i.e. nobles, the bourgeoisie,
peasants and even Jews were for the first time represented.
This was the measure of the change. The presence of the French
encouraged some extraordinary notions on the part of a few
fanatical Ionian democrats[43] but the French failed or did not
have the time to do anything about the grievances of the
peasants which were not strictly political. The relation
between landlord and tenant did not change and the juridical
domination of the aristocracy continued, the only difference
being that it could not be enforced with the previous ease and
impunity by the courts. Meanwhile the French kept real
authority firmly in their hands. They did not make any serious
attempt to create a unitary Ionian state through the establishment of centralised political institutions. In each island a
municipal council was set up and the only thing that united all
the seven islands was the presence of the French occupation
forces.

The expulsion of the revolutionary French by the Russo-

51

Turkish fleet raised high hopes in aristocratic circles. When the islanders were asked to send delegations to St. Petersburg and Istanbul their hopes were translated into action. The state structure envisaged by the so-called Byzantine Constitution of 1800 was a loose federation with the restored grand assemblies of the nobles in each island electing all the local functionaries and the Senators who resided in Corfu and formed the only organ of centralised authority. There was also a General Treasury but the money allocated to it was fixed by the local assemblies whose approval was required for any extra expenditure. But the most controversial clause was that which related to the membership of the reconstituted aristocratic assemblies. The constitution decreed that there should be no extension of franchise - the hegemony of the nobility would continue.[44]

The plans misfired for two reasons: first, the attitude of the disenfranchised Ionians had become far more militant, and secondly, there was no coercive state apparatus to enforce the political system the nobles had devised. The nascent Ionian Republic had no army. The Russians withdrew for reasons of international diplomacy, despite the exhortations of the nobles, and social discontent which had been simmering while they were still there came suddenly to the boil. The political and social dislocation seemed complete. The bourgeoisie were trying to regain their right to be part of the state and 'those who worked in the fields refused to return the lands they had occupied during the siege of Corfu (by the Russo-Turkish fleet) or pay the landlords their share of the crop according to the tenancy agreements.'[45] Mavrogiannis goes on to say that 'this general and persistent rebellion was principally caused by the plot which the Ionian nobles had hatched and executed and which resulted in the people loosing their political rights.'[46] The departure of the Russians had made the radicals more bold. The nobles in Corfu watched on anxiously and helplessly while the peasants and the middle class elected 64 deputies who formed the Onoranda Deputazione. The Onoranda, as it became known, regarded itself as the only lawful body to execute the wishes of the protecting powers, which in effect meant that the bourgeoisie and the peasants claimed the right to arrange the system of government according to their views through a new constitution. The provisional system of government that they devised laid down that all sovereignty resided

in the so called 'Aristocratic Council' which comprised 240
representatives of all social classes. The villages and the
town suburbs provided 140 deputies and the rest came from the
town of Corfu in the following proportion: 40 nobles, 40 members of the professions, 14 merchants and 6 artisans. The vote
was given to all male adults and any Corfiot who was at least
thirty years of age and possessed property worth at least 6,000
ducats or had a 'virtuous and sterling' character could be
elected. The Ionian democrats following the example of their
patrician opponents seemed to leave no room for a unitary state
with a strong central government. The emphasis was placed on
the sovereign body in each island, the only difference between
the two approaches being the extent of franchise.

The policy of Count Mocenigo, the Russian Plenipotentiary,
proved to be a significant departure from both aristocratic and
Jacobin principles and, at the same time, a compromise between
the two. His policy can be reduced to two fundamental objectives: first, the qualified extension of the franchise and
secondly, the creation of a unitary state with a strong central
government which would faithfully toe the line laid down by the
representative of the protecting power. Mocenigo introduced the
so-called 'constitutional nobility' which in effect meant that
the franchise was extended to those who possessed a certain
amount of annual income or a university degree. The enlarged
assemblies in each island, composed of the 'old nobles' and the
'constitutional nobles' were to elect directly the 40 members
of the Legislative Body and the 17 members of the Senate, the
name given to the executive. The two bodies were reasonably
well balanced, the judicary was independent, at least in theory,
and the Russian plenipotentiary, on whose presence, let alone
functions, the constitution was completely silent, assumed the
real responsibility of government.

Mocenigo's position was unofficially very strong, but
officially it was vulnerable to the wishes of the electoral
bodies, which wishes could be expressed through the election
of legislators and senators. In the beginning Mocenigo made
sure that nothing like that would happen by blatantly rigging
the elections. Three years later, in 1806, when he put forward
his major constitutional amendments, that became known as the
constitution of 1806, Mocenigo solved the problem with the
introduction of the notorious 'double lists', an ingenious
device that the British subsequently used to their advantage.

According to the new arrangement the Ionian electors were asked
to choose their representatives from a list which contained
twice as many names, and was prepared, in theory, by the out-
going administration, but in fact by the Plenipotentiary of
the protecting power.

Mocenigo's constitutional principles were implemented and
carried to their limit by Sir Thomas Maitland, the first
British Lord High Commissioner. The question of British policy
in the Ionian Islands is extremely complicated and cannot be
examined here in any detail. Suffice it to say that the factors
which shaped it were many and varied: the diplomatic, strategic
and economic interests of Britain, the treaty of 1815 which
established the protectorate, the constitutional practice in
the islands up to that time, the unsuccessful attempts by the
British to introduce the principles of parliamentary government
in Corsica and Sicily, the successful experiment in Malta,[47]
the current ideology in Britain about government, colonialism
and 'the lesser breeds without the law', and, last but not
least, the personality of Sir Thomas Maitland. The Lord High
Commissioner used Mocenigo's devices in order to secure absolute control of the state, and the Constitution of 1817 which
he almost literally dictated proclaims his omnipotence. Nothing
could be done without his direct or indirect approval. The
franchise of 1803 was retained and at the same time rendered
meaningless by the operation of the 'double lists'. The Ionian
electors would gather merely to give their approval to the
appointments made by the Lord High Commissioner.

The first two decades of the nineteenth century were
undoubtedly the most eventful period in the history of the
Ionian Islands. The frequent changes of foreign master was
more than matched by the alterations in the system of government which can be traced through the successive constitutions.
If we try to put this veritable heap of events into some kind
of perspective there are two vantage points from which such an
enterprise can be approached; the state structure, primarily
as reflected in the constitutions, and the social relations of
production, as expressed through legislation, the concrete
policy of the administration in relevant matters and the reactions of the groups whose role in the process of production
and the allocation of surplus labour assigns them the status
of social class.

First, a few words about the state. There seems to be a

clear tendency away from the principle of loose federation, and toward the creation of a unitary state with a strong government. As far as the foreign protecting power was concerned the reason is not difficult to find. Colonial government had to be centralised for mainly administrative purposes. A small number of foreigners could run a country, only if they managed to keep the reins of power firmly in their hands by means of a central agency. On the part of the Ionians things were more complicated. In the absence of any detailed study on the matter, we may assume that ideological reasons (i.e., the Ionian and by extension the Greek identity) strengthened the ties between the islands. Also some importance may be ascribed to the slow movement in the direction of economic integration (rationalization of inter-island trade tarrifs, quarantine regulations etc.). The fact that the business of government was taken over by foreigners was the main reason for the strengthening of the executive at the expense of the legislature. Both Mocenigo and Maitland were very sensitive on this point. The parliaments they created had virtually no power to initiate legislation or block it – this was the task of the executive which was in effect appointed by the representative of the protecting power. This loss of sovereignty was of course in a way the result of international rivalry between the big powers which pursued their conflicting interests on a global scale by extending their political, commercial and military authority. From the point of view of the Ionians, however, foreign intervention operated in a different way. After the unsuccessful attempt by the nobles to maintain, unaided, their social and political supremacy through the constitution of 1800, and the equally unsuccessful attempt by the lower classes to gain the upper hand in 1802, an indispensable element for the creation of a stable state structure - coercive force in the shape of an army - had to be imported from abroad. This gives us the opportunity to open a very brief parenthesis on the subject of nationalism in the Ionian Islands before Greece became independent. Neither the nobles nor their opponents displayed any marked appetite for nationalism. The nobles implored the Russians in 1801 not to leave and welcomed them with open arms when they returned a year and a half later. The same can be said of the middle class whose hopes were firmly pinned on France. What both classes had come to realize was that neither of them could win without the support of the foreigners. The task of maintaining order in the face of open class strife in seven islands scattered along the western coast of Greece required the power of an efficient state mechanism which was far beyond the capabilities of the Ionians.

The foreigners of course controlled the islands because this was what they had gone there to do in the first place. But foreign occupation, whether French, Russian or British, could not be imposed from a safe distance. The conquerors of the islands had to take a positive stand on the issues that divided their Ionian subjects, and their stand was determined primarily by the political ideologies which prevailed in the countries in question at the time, mediated through their representatives on the spot. · This means that every major shift in the Ionian political and social balance during the period under discussion may be seen as the result of two factors: the internal, i.e., the conflicting interests of the Ionian social actors, and the external, i.e., the determinate policy of the protecting power. It was such a combination, with one or the other element being dominant, that produced the collapse of the aristocratic regime in 1797, its partial restoration under Mocenigo and the colonial state structure of the British protectorate.

What is of greater interest to us, of course, is the internal factor. Bearing in mind that we are entering territory that historical, sociological and economic research has not yet charted adequately, we must proceed to make certain observations.

The first observation is that the many changes that occurred in the period we are examining were almost exclusively political. In other words the social infrastructure, the social relations of production remained virtually unchanged. The tenant farmers went on working the land and paying their dues to the landlords, and the members of the middle class went on about their business as merchants, shopkeepers, lawyers, doctors etc. If we want to answer the question why certain things did not happen, one possible approach would be to consider what conditions would have been necessary for structural changes in the social relations of production to have taken place, and it then becomes immediately apparent that there was no other viable alternative so long as the Ionian Islands remained an autonomous political, social and economic unit. In the absence of any raw materials for manufacture, the Ionians could not but go on producing agricultural commodities for the

56

international market. The laws on land tenure perpetuated the
fragmentation of property which, in its turn, frustrated the
attempts of the British to promote efficient agriculture. We
are dealing with small insular communities where almost every-
body had some kind of right in a plot of land or a couple of
olive trees.[48] The introduction of new radical legislation
could either expropriate the landlords and turn the peasants
into small landholders or drive the peasants from the land when
they had nowhere to go.

   This means that the economy of the islands remained
stagnant. Its salient feature, as we have seen, was the small
scale production of agricultural commodities by tenant farmers.
So long as this persisted no major improvement could have taken
place. In an essentially feudal economy the level of productivity could not rise much above the average productivity of the
individual small farmer[49] despite the efforts that were made by
some enlightened landlords to introduce new agricultural
techniques in their demesne estates. Some Greek Marxist
historians imply that the real obstacle to progress were the
landlords[50] who were inefficient and deeply in debt to the
bourgeoisie, but somehow managed to hang on to their land, thus
eliminating any chance of development. This interpretation
seems to ignore the fact that what really stood in the way of
capitalist agriculture were not the landlords but the rights
that the tenant farmers had in their land. If the estate of
inefficient nobleman X came under the hammer and was bought by
efficient capitalist Y, that would merely mean a change of owner,
since capitalist Y could not change the terms of the tenants
leases. Efficient capitalist agriculture meant necessarily
driving the peasants from the land and using hired labour in
their place. This, apart from all the other difficulties,
would have involved a political decision on the part of the
legislator, i.e., the British colonial authorities which they
could not and did not make. Therefore the factors that
determined the prosperity of the Ionian Islands were either
purely contingent, like the failure of the crop due to weather
conditions or the destruction of vineyards and olive trees in
continental Greece during the War of Independence, or fiscal,
for example the rise or fall of import duties on olive oil or
currants in England and elsewhere or the increase of taxation
for the repair and maintenance of the fortifications of Corfu.

   Another observation relates to the diminishing import-

ance of politics and the increasing rapprochement between the
nobility and the middle class. During the first three years of
the nineteenth century the two opponents fought themselves to a
standstill. More important than exhaustion though, must have
been the realization that the intervention of foreigners had
taken away the prize – the control of the state, which had
previously been the main friction point. In the event the
foreigners solved the problem by becoming the state. There is
no evidence that during the first fifteen years at least of the
protectorate, the landowners or the bourgeoisie made any serious
or persistent efforts to win over the British or influence their
policy to their advantage, for the simple reasons that their
interests were not seriously threatened by the protectorate or
by the other class. It is interesting to note that only the
peasants tried to enlist the support of the British for the
defence and improvement of their social position.

Finally a few comments about the objectives of the
British colonial administration. The British tried to create an
efficient administration[51] which, they thought, would be in the
interests of both parties. In order to achieve that they simply
abolished politics and, anticipating a trend that was to become
fashionable a century and a half later, entrusted the running
of the country in the hands of a small group of allegedly
disinterested and efficient technocrats - themselves. The main
thrust of their social policy was rationalisation. At the same
time they firmly suppressed the excesses of the landlords,which
traditionally assumed the form of extra-exploitation of the
peasants and illegal possession of church property through the
manipulation of the judiciary, and the creation of feudal clans
and private armies. All this offended the sense of justice of
the British administrators and, at the same time, posed a threat
against the supremacy by creating rival centres of power.

A number of Ionians, a number which continued to grow,
were not exactly happy with the situation. The presence of the
British frustrated the ambitions of the would be political
élite of the country. They, like the rest of the fellow
islanders tried, in true Greek fashion, to secure employment by
the government[52] in order to obtain a much needed additional
income and, mainly, in order to manipulate the state to their
advantage. The British by assuming complete control assumed
also, at least in the eyes of the Ionians, total responsibility
for whatever happened or did not happen. And this leads us to

the force that eventually brought down the protectorate, but chronologically lies outside the period we have been examining: Nationalism.

1. Ermanno Lunzi, Storia delle Isole Ionie sotte il Regimento dei Republicani Francesi (Venice 1860).

2. Gerasimos Mavrogiannis, Istoria ton Ionion Nison (Athens 1889) i 88-9.

3. Mavrogiannis, 266-71.

4. Mavrogiannis, 312-4.

5. Mavrogiannis, 314.

6. Mavrogiannis, 443 et seq.

7. Piano Constituzionale Formato dalla Deputazione della Cita, Borghi e villa di Corfu (Li XXI Ottombre MDCCCI, Corfu).

8. For Russian policy in the Ionian Islands extremely useful information is contained in the series Vneshniaia Politika Rossii XIX i nachala XX veka, Ministervstvo Inostrannykh Del SSSR (Moscow 1960-).

9. Katastasis tis Eptanisou Politias (Trieste 1804).

10. C.O. 136/385 part 2 contains a very interesting and detailed memorandum on the differences between the two constitutions.

11. Some interesting aspects of the debate on the fate of the Ionian Islands are included in the Richard Church Memorandum (1813) Brit. Mus. Add. MS. 36,543, The Memorandum by George Foresti, Observations upon the project for the cession of the Seven Islands to Austria, Aberdeen Papers, vol clxxix Brit. Mus. Add. MS. 43,217 f224, and the Capodistria Memorandum, Brit. Mus. Add. MS. 27,937 f.62.

12. W. E. Filpot, The Origins and growth of the Protectorate System, M.A. Thesis (University of London 1934) 234-39.

13. For a rather jingoistic account of the personality and policies of Sir Thomas Maitland see Walter Frewen Lord, Sir Thomas Maitland (London 1898). A much more detailed account is contained in C. Willis Dixon, The Colonial Administration of Sir Thomas Maitland (London 1939).

14. C.O. 136/7, copy of the Constitution with candid comments by Maitland.

15. Andreas M. Andreadis, Peri tis Oikonomikis Doiikiseos tis Eptanisou epi Venetokratias (Athens 1914).

16. For a brief and comprehensive account of the Venetian rule in the Ionian Islands see William Miller, Essays on the Latin Orient (Cambridge 1921) and The Latins in the Levant (London 1908). The best Greek source is Ermanno Lunzi, Peri tis Politikis Katastaseos tis Eptanisou epi Veneton (Athens 1969).

17. P. Khiotis, Istoriki Ekthesi kai engrapha peri ton Timarion tis Kerkyras (Zante 1865) 3.

18. Andrea Marmora, Della Historia di Corfu (Venetia 1672).

19. Lunzi, 263-74.

20. Khiotis, 2.

21. Khiotis, 2-3.

22. P. Khiotis, Istorika (Zante 1849) iii 400.

23. Anna Cosmetatos, British Social and Economic Policies in the Ionian Islands (Report for the Degree of Master of Science, London School of Economics 1976) 12.

24. Charles J. Napier, The Colonies, treating of their value generally, of the Ionian Islands in particular (London 1833) 262.

25. Lunzi, 264.

26. Lunzi, 259-62.

27. According to Kiotis, Istoriki Ekthesi 14, serfdom was abolished in 1660.

28. Konstantinos Sathas, To en Zakyntho archontologion kai i popolari (Athens 1867). Also Marmoras, op. cit., 259, 283-4.

29. Napier, 262.

30. D. T. Ansted, The Ionian Islands in the year 1863 (London 1863) 51; J. Davy, Notes and Observations on the Ionian Islands and Malta (London 1842) i 335; for olive culture in general see Lewis A. Bernays, The Olive and its products (Brisbane 1872).

31. On usury see Memorandum of 1822 in C.O. 136/444/5.

32. Lord Nugent to Lord Goderich, 3 January 1833 in C.O. 136/65. Also Ansted, 59 and Davy, 324.

33. Barry Hindess and Paul Hirst, Pre-Capitalist Modes of Production (London 1975) 239-40.

34. Napier, 344 and 563.

35. Leonidas Zois, Istoria tis Zakynthou (Athens 1955) 130.

36. Miller, Essays . . . 205.

37. Frederikos Alvanas, Peri ton en Kerkyra Titlon Evgenias kai peri ton Timarion (Corfu 1894) 3-4.

38. Lunzi, 124-30.

39. Dionysios Romas, 'I polis tis Zakynthou prin kai meta tin Enosin', Khronika Zakynthou (Athens 1964) 153-75.

40. Memorandum on land valuation in C.O. 136/154, December 1853.

41. Lunzi, 263 et seq.

42. Ansted, 199-200.

43. Ioannis P. Loverdos, Istoria tis nisou Kephalinias (Cephalonia 1888) 202-3.

44. Mavrogiannis, 314.

45. Mavrogiannis, 302.

46. Mavrogiannis, 414.

47. For a detailed and illuminating account of the British views on the problem of Malta see Malta Report in C.O. 158/19.

48. Ansted, 456; Napier, 298.

49. Hindess and Hirst, 246.

50. K. Porphyri, 'I Eptanisiaki kai idios i Zakythini koinonia stin periodo tis Anglokratias', Khronika 80-1; in the same issue of Khronika, A. I.

61

Liveris, op. cit, puts forward the theory that the relations of production
were 'bourgeois' or 'civil' (the word being the same in Greek) even before
the collapse of Venice, and justifies his contention by asserting that they
were relations between 'individual producers'. This seems to be completely
wrong. 'Bourgeois' relations of production (an extremely obscure term)
could exist only where wage labour predominated. This clearly not being
the case in the Ionian Islands the mode of production in question was feudal
since the landlord appropriated the surplus labour of the peasants and not
the surplus value which they did not create, not being wage labourers.
51. For an example of British efficiency see, Memoir relating to the
Revenue and Expenditure with state of the commercial duties of the Ionian
Islands from 1801 to 1820 inclusively, C.O. 537/147.
52. Ansted, 451.

4

THE GREEK INTELLIGENTSIA 1780–1830: A BALKAN PERSPECTIVE

PETER MACKRIDGE

During the late eighteenth and early nineteenth centuries, while the spiritual centre of the Greek world was Constantinople, its cultural and educational life centred around Bucharest and Jassy.

This proposition leads us first to examine the provenance and the educational background of the men who introduced into the Greek world the Enlightenment ideas which led to the Greek national revival; and secondly to look at the pan-Balkan nature of the so-called 'Greek Enlightenment', concentrating both on the 'non-Greeks' who contributed to this movement and the 'non-Greeks' who benefited from it, always bearing in mind that there were no clear national boundaries in the Balkans until the 1830s and that national feeling at the time was not as strong as was Orthodox consciousness.

First of all, then, we must examine what sort of men were these bearers of Enlightenment ideas in the Greek world, to whom I shall refer for the sake of brevity as 'enlighteners'. These were men who published books influenced by the new European science and philosophy and reflecting Enlightenment values and attitudes, or who taught such matters in Greek schools.

Schools were central to the enlightenment movement in the Balkans. The 'Enlightenment' in the Greek world had a pedagogical and popularizing character. Most of the 'enlightenment' works published in Greek were school manuals, for the most part translated or adapted from European originals. There is little original philosophy in these Greek manuals, although most translators added their own prefaces and footnotes which aimed to make the text relevant to the Balkan situation.

In the period under review, a number of manuals were published in Greek on school subjects such as Arithmetic, Algebra, Geometry, Physics, Chemistry, Geography, Astronomy, Logic, Ethics, Rhetoric and Pedagogy (it is interesting to note the almost complete absence of modern history); while there were

63

also 'extra-curricular' books on foreign languages, commerce and
book-keeping, agriculture, statecraft and natural history, and
especially manuals of etiquette. In addition there were books
containing ideas on Greek language, education and culture in
general as well as the embryonic 'national' Greek literature
which begins to appear in the 1790s.[1]

The most famous Greek schools of the time, and those which
attracted pupils from all over the Orthodox world, were situated
on the Greek islands or in the north of what might be loosely
termed the Greek world of the time: Bucharest (where the Greek
school was founded about 1689),[2] Jassy /Iaşi7 (c.1707),[3]
Istanbul (the Patriarchal Academy), Jannina (two schools
functioning since the seventeenth century together with the
Maroutsaia school, 1742, and the Kaplanis school, 1802), Mt.
Athos (the Athonias school, 1753), Patmos (especially from
1769), Chios (reconstituted 1792), Izmir (the Evangelical
School, 1733, and the Philological Gymnasium, 1808), Ayvalık
(1803), Odessa (the Commercial School, 1817), and the Thessalian
schools of Ambelakia, Milies, Zagora and Larisa.

Of 36 enlighteners that I have chosen as representative of
the period, 13 were clerics and 23 laymen (see Appendix). 10
of them came from Thessaly, while most of the rest came from
Epirus, Macedonia and the Aegean and Ionian islands, together
with individuals from Izmir, Istanbul, Acarnania, Athens and
what are now Romania and Bulgaria: that is to say chiefly
from the islands and the northern part of the Greek world of
the time (none of them, for instance, came from the Peloponnese).
The pupils at the Bucharest and Jassy Academies (consistently
the most prestigious Greek schools during our period) were
mostly from Thessaly, Epirus, Macedonia, the Aegean Islands and
Asia Minor as well as present-day Romania, Bulgaria and Albania;
very few were from the Peloponnese or even from Rumeli.[4]

The social origins of the Greek enlighteners cover a whole
range of strata from the Phanariot nobility to the peasantry.
Katartzis was a Phanariot aristocrat, perhaps of Moldavian
origin though born in Istanbul; Theotokis' family were Corfiot
noblemen; Solomos was a Zantiot count; Kairis came from a
noble Andriot family; Oikonomos was one of a line of notable
clerics and men of letters; Korais and Psalidas came from
merchant families; Christopoulos, who became an 'adopted
Phanariot',[5] came from humble origins, his father being a
simple priest; Gazis, Konstandas and Philippidis had equally

humble origins in the Pelion village of Milies; Doukas came
from a poor family in an Epirot village; Benjamin's parents
were peasants on Lesbos; and Pharmakidis' were peasants in
Thessaly.[6]

Of the 36 men I have referred to above, 21 were teachers.
Some of these were clerics, others laymen, but the education
dispensed at the Greek schools was secular, and most of the
teacher-clerics were at some time during their careers accused
of atheism, or were at least censured by the spiritual or
temporal authorities for their rationalist views: Voulgaris,
Theotokis, Moisiodax, Doukas, Vamvas, Benjamin and Kairis.
These accusations were all false, except possibly in the case
of Kairis, and were based on the fact that these men were
spreading Western (i.e. by definition atheistic) ideas.

Apart from teachers, there were doctors (Vilaras,
Sakellarios), jurists (Katartzis, Christopoulos), clerks
(Kodrikas, Zalikoglou), a merchant (Zaviras) and simply men of
letters (such as Solomos and Korais). One must also include
printers and publishers such as Vendotis and Lampanitziotis;
and I have included three poets (Christopoulos, Vilaras and
Solomos), who made important contributions to the Greek
Enlightenment on the language question. Some of the men I have
termed clerics were in fact unordained deacons; some were monks,
and one (Doungas) even became an abbot; others belonged to the
higher clergy, two of them (Voulgaris and Theotokis) becoming
bishops.

Among the Greek enlighteners there was not such a great
conflict between clerics and laymen as between the supporters
of ancient learning and those who taught the superiority of
modern science. This conflict, which was a reflection of the
famous 'débat des anciens et des modernes' in western Europe
during the Enlightenment, was central to Greek (and consequently
Balkan) cultural life at the time. It was also closely
connected with the language question, which at that time was
basically the struggle between the proponents of ancient Greek
and the supporters of the vernacular, whether the latter be
Greek, Romanian, Bulgarian or anything else. As Ariadna
Camariano-Cioran has pointed out,[7] some of those Greeks who were
opposed to the use of Romanian and Bulgarian in schools (e.g.,
Govdelas) were equally opposed to the use of modern Greek; and,
as Dimaras reminds us,[8] the archaists such as Doukas were
described by the demoticist A. Matesis about 1824 as neoglossitai

or 'newlanguagists': that is, they were criticized for being too innovative. We know that Doukas, despite his emphasis on the need for the Greeks to replace their supposedly debased vernacular by ancient Greek even in everyday conversation, was far from reactionary in his social ideas. Indeed his very desire to improve the lot of his people by leading them to the benefits of ancient culture should not be interpreted as retrogressive but rather as progressive, even if, as we see it today, totally misguided.[9] Just as Latin had been in previous centuries the language of education and culture in the West, so we should perhaps see it as natural that in the Orthodox East the language of culture was Greek.[10]

To sum up these conflicts, the picture is in fact quite complex. There are perhaps three conflicts: between priests and laymen (not very intense); between the supporters of the 'ancients' and the proponents of the 'moderns' (in ideas); and between the archaists and the vernacularists (in language). The supporters of the 'ancients' do not always coincide with the archaizers, nor do the proponents of the 'moderns' with the vernacularists. Govdelas, for instance, produced manuals translated from or based on the latest theories in mathematics, but he wrote them in archaic Greek, while Korais championed ancient culture while writing in modern Greek.[11]

Before we conclude this section we must stress that in this paper we are ignoring the 'counter-enlightenment' movement which, often inspired by the Patriarchate, should not be underestimated; and we must not forget the hold which spurious 'prophetic' books had over the common people.

In the fifty years before the Greek War of Independence, a member of one of the Balkan peoples who wanted an education had to study at a Greek school: secondary education in Romania did not begin until 1818,[12] and in Bulgaria even later. It was usually necessary to travel around the Balkans in search of the best or most renowned teachers. It was felt to be essential to hear the teacher personally rather than simply study his books. Thus we find that many men of letters studied in more than one Greek centre. Konstantas studied at Milies, Zagora, Athos, Chios and Istanbul; Benjamin at Lesbos, Athos, Ayvalık, Patmos and Chios; Vamvas at Chios, Sifnos and Patmos; and Kairis at Andros, Ayvalık, Patmos and Chios. For those who were fortunate enough to begin their schooling at Bucharest or Jassy, one Greek school might see them through their studies, but this was the exception rather than the rule.

Because of the desire to find the right teacher, and also (I believe) because of the difficulty of learning to read, write and speak ancient Greek in cases where the teacher was an archaist, schooling used to take a long time. The full course of study at the Bucharest Academy, for example, used to last 15 years,[13] and it is doubtful whether any of this would be counted today as 'higher education'. Doukas, who never studied abroad nor apparently learned any foreign language, seems to have spent his life till the age of 43 studying, and his first publications date from the age of 45. He did not take up his first regular teaching appointment until he was 55, although he had undoubtedly made a living for himself for several decades as a private tutor.

Most enlighteners went on to foreign universities, either as fully enrolled students or as 'auditors'. The most popular university, as in previous centuries, was Padua, followed closely by Vienna. Others studied at Paris, Pisa, Halle and other universities in Italy, France, Germany and Austria-Hungary. It is worth noting that while the language par excellence of the Enlightenment was French (and, secondarily, English), many of the Greek enlighteners had access to the works of the Enlightenment only by way of Italian or German.

A number of these men were still studying at university at a relatively advanced age: Korais till 40, Benjamin till 37 or 40 (depending on which date one chooses for his birth).[14] The length of time spent studying can perhaps be partly explained by the cultural gap between the Greek world and western Europe; in other words, it took the Greek enlighteners a long time to 'catch up' with their European contemporaries. Considering that almost half of the Greek enlighteners that I have chosen as representative died by the age of 65, their active teaching and publishing life was short in comparison with the time they spent acquiring their education.[15] It is worth pointing out that one of the reasons why the enlightenment movement in Greece came to an end, as Dimaras says,[16] around 1830 is that the majority of the enlighteners of the pre-Independence period died by, or soon after, this date: the majority had died by 1838, half of these during the decade 1821-1830; and there were some whose deaths were doubtless hastened by the circumstances of the War of Independence (exile, poverty, etc.).

Leaving statistics aside now, another reason for the Greek enlighteners to travel abroad, apart from their formal education, was to supervise the publication of their books. Although there were obliging Greeks in Venice and Vienna who proof-read other people's books, there were instances (quite understandable, given the circumstances of the times) of manuscripts being lost en route to the printers,[17] and it seemed expedient to certain authors to be on the spot while their books were being printed. Thus, for example, Moisiodax went to Vienna in 1780, and Govdelas in 1816, expressly to see their books printed, and Philippidis stayed in Leipzig between 1815 and 1818 for the same purpose. While abroad, these men also had the opportunity of meeting the local Greek community and bringing their knowledge up to date by talking with local luminaries and reading the latest books and journals. Similarly, those Greeks who lived abroad for a certain period published far more **then than** they did while they were living within the boundaries of the Greek world. Thus Voulgaris, who had spent the period 1742 to 1763 in Greece without publishing anything, began to publish his books, many of which had been written some time before, soon after his arrival in Leipzig;[18] and all Psalidas' published work dates from his stay in Vienna between 1787 and 1796.

Most Greek books in the eighteenth century were published in Venice, where there had been at least two Greek printing shops since the seventeenth century, but in the last decades of that century Vienna begins to take precedence, with Leipzig and other centres outside the Balkans also being used. Some Greek books were published at Bucharest and Jassy (From the seventeenth century), while in the last years before the War of Independence others were printed at Istanbul (from 1797), although these books were often of a 'counter-enlightenment' nature, Corfu (from 1798) and Chios and Ayvalık (from 1819). But the vast majority of Greek books were produced outside the Balkans, many of them sold by subscription; and it is noteworthy that of the subscribers whose names Philippos Iliou has collected from lists published in Greek books between 1749 and 1821, only 7 per cent lived in regions which in the 1820s became part of the Greek state. Many of these subscribers we know to be 'non-Greeks' - Romanians, Bulgarians, Albanians and Serbs, for instance.[19]

It is clear from the foregoing that we have in the decades preceding 1821 a thriving Greek 'culture in exile', which reaches a peak in the decade before 1821, during which a more nationalistic activity begins, reflected in the cultural sphere by the Greek patriotic theatrical performances at Bucharest (from 1817) and Odessa (from 1814).[20]

It is however equally clear that the Greek enlightenment had a profound influence on other Balkan peoples, particularly the Romanians and the Bulgarians. Before the Greek War of Independence many 'non-Greeks' became Hellenized and either contributed actively to the Greek Enlightenment or at least wrote in Greek; many of the bearers of enlightenment ideas among the other Balkan peoples were graduates of Greek schools; and the first school manuals in Romanian and Bulgarian were translated from Greek books, whether these last were original Greek works or (as they were more often) Greek translations or adaptations of European manuals. Some of these Romanian and Bulgarian translations also include the Greek translator's preface and notes.

As has been already mentioned, there was not such a strong feeling of nationality among the Balkan peoples during the period in question as there was a century or so later, and one must beware of transferring present-day national boundaries to the map of the Balkans in 1800. The vast majority of the inhabitants of the Balkan peninsula were Orthodox Christians under the spiritual aegis of the Patriarch of Constantinople, and when Rigas Velestinlis in his New Political Administration (1797) proposed to include the whole of the European part of the Ottoman Empire together with Asia Minor in a single administrative unit once the Turkish yoke should be shrugged off, he was perhaps not so much expressing an ideology of Greek imperialism as responding to what he took to be the consciousness of the Sultan's Christian subjects.

Not only educated people but merchants and ordinary folk, too, were often able to speak two or more languages. Many Bulgarians and Romanians used Greek in their writings, and some became completely Hellenized. It is often impossible for us (and perhaps it was sometimes impossible for the individual concerned!) to determine which ethnic group someone belonged to. An individual's language, like his surname, could be changed according to the group to which he wished to belong.

The dominant language and culture of the time were of course Greek, and the influences that we can observe from one culture to another are generally from Greek to other cultures.

But these cross-currents do not begin with the Phanariot period. There are many similarities to be observed in the folk cultures of the different Balkan peoples, and the well-known common Balkan syntactical characteristics seem to be due not to the influence of any one of the Balkan languages but to a similar kind of thought process prevailing throughout the Balkans.[21] Also, apart from the common stock of loan-words passing between the Balkan languages, the influence of the Greek language on its Balkan neighbours is as old as the spread of Christianity in the area.

The princes and many boyars of Wallachia and Moldavia knew and read Greek by the sixteenth century.[22] In literature, however, both popular and learned, Greek influence was paramount during the second half of the eighteenth century and the first decades of the nineteenth. At this time we see many works appearing in both Greek and Romanian (and some in Bulgarian too): chapbooks such as Aesop's Fables, Sindipa, Halima, Erotokritos, Bertoldo, the Christoithia, and the Alexander romance, together with the works of European authors (Fénelon, Montesquieu, Klopstock, Florian, Gessner, Marmontel). In almost all cases, the Romanian and Bulgarian versions are translated from Greek.[23]

There are only a few instances where Greek culture is explicitly set against another Balkan culture in Greek texts of the period; elsewhere the enlighteners, whether of Greek or non-Greek origin, take it for granted that everyone in the Balkans who has any educational and cultural aspirations is content to use Greek. One of the exceptions is the Eisagogiki Didaskalia (Introductory Teaching) of the Vlach Daniel of Moskhopolis (1802),[24] who actively encourages Albanians, Vlachs and Bulgarians to abandon their barbarous language and culture and become Greeks, pointing out to his readers that by learning the Romaic tongue ('the Mother of Wisdom') their minds will gain new ideas, their prestige among their fellow-countrymen and among foreigners will be enhanced, and their trade will improve. He encourages his readers to found schools teaching 'Romaic letters', and promises them that his book will help them 'to find both great material profit, and eternal bounty in the life to come'. In the list that Daniel gives of words and phrases in Greek, Romanian, Bulgarian and Albanian, all the non-Greek vocabulary is printed in Greek characters, which were in fact quite commonly used for Bulgarian and Albanian at the time:

70

some Bulgarian <u>damaskins</u> were written in Greek letters, and the first Albanian New Testament (published at Corfu in 1827) was printed in Greek characters.

A second example of a Vlach actively propagandizing for the use of Greek was Dimitrios Darvaris, from Klisura in Macedonia, who was one of the most prolific popularizers of Enlightenment ideas in the Greek world. He spent his career in Vienna, where he produced between 1785 and his death in 1823 grammars of ancient and modern Greek and German, and books on arithmetic, physics and history as well as etiquette. Darvaris published a 'Simple Greek Grammar for the use of the young <u>omogeneis</u>' (literally, 'members of the same race').[25] But it is only in passing that the author mentions that he is a Vlach. For example, he gives some equivalents in 'our' language of certain Greek verbs in order to point to some similarities in the use of reflexives, and while he does not state which 'our' language is, it is clear from the examples that it is Vlach (printed in Roman characters). Not until half-way through the book does he talk of 'our Vlach language'. It is nonetheless clear that Darvaris was writing his grammar (one of the first extensive grammars of standard spoken Greek) for the benefit of all users of Greek, whether Greeks, Vlachs, Slavs, or whatever else. It is also significant that Darvaris translated Greek books into Serbian (the 'Sloveno-Serbian' recension).[26] He was thus at least trilingual.

By contrast, a prime example of a Hellenized non-Greek enlightener is Iosipos Moisiodax, born at Cernavoda in the Dobrudja about 1725, who, while proudly indicating his geographical origins in his surname, seems to have had no regrets that he was in the main-stream of Greek culture; when he writes of 'our forefathers' and 'our race' there is no doubt that he sees himself as a Greek. But it is not only later Romanian and Bulgarian scholars who consider him as a Romanian or Bulgarian,[27] for some of his contemporaries were also conscious of his 'non-Greek' origins. Explaining what to him were lapses in Moisiodax's Greek style, Panayotis Kodrikas described him as 'by birth alien to the Greek race and consequently deprived of the milk of Greek upbringing'.[28] Nevertheless, Moisiodax studied at Greek schools and spent some time in Italy and Austria acquainting himself with the science and philosophy of the Enlightenment. He was one of the first followers of the 'moderns' in the Balkans: when he taught at the Greek Academies

at Bucharest (1765-66 and 1776) and Jassy (1797) he used his
own translations of mathematical books by Tacquet and La Caille
as well as publishing books on geography and pedagogy (the
latter based on the ideas of Locke). Unlike his teacher,
Evgenios Voulgaris, he used modern Greek in both his teaching
and his published work, and it is to Moisiodax's comparative
lack of knowledge of ancient Greek that Kodrikas probably
refers. Despite his Greek consciousness, however, Moisiodax
was also in a sense an 'internationalist', teaching that all
men are brothers. Even his attitude to the Turks is one not of
hatred but of mild rebuke: he believes that once the Turks
become educated in 'sound philosophy' (which for him is founded
on mathematics) they will learn to respect their subjects.[29]
Moisiodax had a profound influence on the Greek enlightenment
movement in general, and in particular on Rigas Velestinlis
and Daniel Philippidis.

In belles-lettres too there were many Moldavians and
Wallachians who abandoned their own language for the more
prestigious Greek. A man who wrote verses in both Romanian
and Greek was the boyar Alecu Văcărescu (d.1800),[30] who studied
at the Bucharest Academy and whose light love-poems in the
typical Phanariot manner appear in the miscellaneous manuscript
collections of verse known as mismayés,[31] and two of his poems
appear in Photinos' Neos Erotokritos (1818) and one in the
first printed anthology of modern Greek verse, compiled by
Daoutis (also 1818).[32] A versifier in the same tradition was
Iordache Hagi Toma Peşacov (1785-1854), who wrote verse in
Greek, Romanian and Bulgarian as well as producing a manuscript
translation into Romanian (c.1812) of Rigas' Skholeion ton
delikaton eraston (School of Delicate Lovers).[33]

Another writer who used Greek and Romanian was the vornic
Iordache Slătineanu, a friend of Rigas and later a leading
member of the 'Graeco-Dacian Literary Society', who in 1797
published a Romanian translation of Metastasio's Achille in
Sciro from a Greek version of the play by Lampanitziotis and
later, in 1817, printed a translation of the same author's
Demetrio from Italian into Greek.[34] Scarlat Ghica was another
Romanian versifier in Greek,[35] while Zinovios Pop, who
published a book of Metrics in Greek in 1803, was also of
Romanian origin.[36] Another Romanian, the mare ban Gregore
Brâncoveanu, a noted Hellenist and another leading member of
the 'Graeco-Dacian Literary Society', was responsible for a

72

translation from Latin into Greek of Heineccius' Logic.[37]

Some of the first Romanian historiographers wrote their work in Greek. Naum Rîmnîceanu and Mihai Cantacuzino wrote histories of Wallachia in Greek, although they both wrote in Romanian too.[38] Also, two histories of the Romanian lands were published by Greeks: Dionysios Photinos wrote a history of Dacia (1807-1817) and Daniel Philippidis published in 1816 a History of "Rumunia" - one of the earliest appearances of this name in print.[39] The mare vornic Iordache Golescu, one of the earliest Romanian lexicographers, was a friend of Rigas and author of a long encomium in archaic Greek verse on Rigas' map of Greece (these verses were published in the Ephimeris in 1797).[40] Apart from compiling a Romanian grammar, a Romanian dictionary, a modern Greek-Romanian dictionary and an ancient Greek-Romanian dictionary, he translated several Greek works into Romanian, including part of the Iliad. But his upbringing was such that he preferred to translate into Greek: his translations include Les Lettres Persanes and several stories by Montesquieu, and Paul et Virginie by Bernardin de St. Pierre.[41] Golescu's brother Dinicu began writing his Travels in Greek, but then switched to Romanian. Nevertheless, he expressed his difficulty in describing certain things in Romanian and came to the conclusion that his mother tongue was in fact Greek.[42]

In 1810 the Greek Academy at Bucharest was reconstituted by Metropolitan Ignatios of Hungro-Wallachia. It is worth noting that the school at this time counted more 'Dacians' (i.e., Romanians) among its pupils than any other nationality. In a speech which he delivered on the occasion of the school's re-opening and the foundation of a learned society (the 'Graeco-Dacian Literary Society'),[43] Ignatios expressed the view that the Greeks and the Dacians, already united by religion and government, were now united in philosophy too. The Dacians, he said, were now in the process of handing back to Greece the enlightenment which they had taken from her.[44] This statement, I believe, suggests Ignatios' gratitude to the Romanians (or to be more precise to the Romanian boyars, for the common people had no say in the matter) for having given hospitality to the Greeks for the last hundred years. Later, in 1818, we find the director of the Greek printing shop at Jassy, Manuel Vernardos, writing about how the Greeks have been helping the Moldavians and Wallachians to become educated, and have banished the use of Slavonic from the Principalities, replacing it with

'genuine Moldavian'.[45] Although this attitude is indeed highly
arrogant, there is some justification for it.

One of the most important manifestations of Greek culture
immediately before the outbreak of the War of Independence, and
one that was to have a great influence on the Romanian cultural
rebirth, was the building of a public theatre in Bucharest in
1818.[46] The first play to be performed there was Voltaire's
Brutus in a Greek translation by Michael Khristaris, and by the
time this theatre ceased to be a Greek institution in 1821
performances had been given of original plays by I. Zambelios,
I. R. Rangavis, Ath. Christopoulos and I. R. Neroulos. The
first performance there in Romanian was of a translation of
Molière's L'Avare in 1818,[47] although Romanian performances were
probably discouraged by the theatre's director, I. R. Rangavis.

The leading light in this Bucharest theatre was the
Greco-Romanian Constantine Aristias (Costache Aristia),[48] who by
1820 was its chief actor and producer; he also translated some
of Molière's plays into Greek for the repertory. During the
Greek War of Independence Aristia left the stage for more
practical heroic activities. He arrived back in Bucharest in
1827 and founded, with Ion Heliade Rădulescu, Dinicu Golescu
and others, the 'Romanian Literary Society' aimed at the
founding of a Romanian national literature and culture. In
1834 he and Heliade began running a school of acting and
declamation whose teachers and students put on plays as an
embryonic Romanian national theatre. Aristia's first production
there was a Romanian translation of Voltaire's Mahomet, well-
known from the pre-Revolutionary Greek repertory. The first
Romanian play he performed was Heliade's Sărbătoarea cîmpeneasca
(Country Fair, 1837). Later, however, official censorship
encouraged him to leave Bucharest and try his luck in his other
spiritual home, Athens, where he moved in 1840 with plans to
start a theatre. Despite the success of his production of
Monti's Aristodemo in his own translation, there was much ill-
feeling against him, and, not finding fertile enough ground
there, he returned to Bucharest. Greece's loss was Romania's
gain; but the fact remains that the Romanian theatre in its
infancy followed in the footsteps of the pre-Revolutionary
Greeks.

As for Ion Heliade Rădulescu, his schooling was exclusively Greek, and it seems that he did not learn to read Romanian
until the age of nine.[49] When he set about working on his

74

Romanian grammar (published in 1828), he studied the theories of Philippidis and Konstantas, Christopoulos and Vilaras and learned from their examples.[50] Finally, Costache Negruzzi[51] began his literary career in Romanian by translating Voltaire's Memnon by way of Voulgaris' translation, and Theophrastus' Characters from the modern Greek translation by Darvaris.[52]

The Romanians were not the only Balkan people to feel Greek influences. There were of course Albanians who wrote in Greek. Konstantinos Hadji-Georgiou Tzechanis of Moskhopolis published an arithmetic textbook (Halle 1769) as well as several epigrams in ancient Greek in books published in 1773 and 1777.[53] Another Moskhopolitan Albanian, Theodoros Kavalliotis, published in 1770 a book similar to that of his fellow-citizen Daniel, a book intended to help non-Greeks to learn Greek and including among other things a Vlach-Albanian-modern Greek vocabulary.[54] There were even Moslem Albanians who wrote in Greek: for example, when Hacı Sehreti set about singing the praises of his master Alı Paşa of Jannina, he wrote his Alipasias ('Alipashiad') in the language which would lend his subject most prestige.[55]

As for Bulgaria, a seminal work for the emergence of Bulgarian national literature is the Thisavros by Damaskinos Stouditis, first published at Venice in 1558,[56] which, translated into Bulgarian from about 1600, constituted the prototype for the collections of miscellaneous writings in vernacular Bulgarian known as damaskins. Again, Father Paissi's Istorija slovenobolgarska (1762), considered at the beginning of the Bulgarian cultural revival, was heavily influenced by the Khronographos (1631) of Dorotheos of Monemvasia, and the Kiriakodromion of Archbishop Sofrony (1806), the first printed book in modern Bulgarian, was a translation of Theotokis' book of the same title (1796). Later, Petar Beron's primer Bukvar (Braşov 1824) was partially based on the Eklogarion Graikikon of Darvaris (Vienna 1804), and the first Bulgarian grammar, published at Kragujevać in 1835 by Neofit Rilski, was written under the influence of Greek grammarians.

The Greek language question had a profound influence on Bulgarian writers, who tended to divide themselves into two camps, the one supporting Old Church Slavonic and the other modern Bulgarian, just as the Greeks supported ancient or vernacular Greek. Konstantin Fotinov, the founder of the first Bulgarian periodical, Ljuboslovie (the title itself is a calque

on the Greek word philologia), published at Izmir from 1842-
1846, was an archaist, and he modelled his journal on the early
Greek literary periodicals such as Logios Ermis.

The Bulgarian language controversy, however, had a
different outcome from the Greek one. V. E. Aprilov, the
founder of the first Bulgarian school at Gabrovo in 1835, shows
in his Thoughts on Present Bulgarian Education (Odessa 1847)[57]
that he has learned much from the Greek experience. He is most
concerned that the Bulgarian written language should not develop
along the archaistic lines of Greek katharevousa and commends
the efforts of Christopoulos, Vilaras and Vardalachos to
persuade the Greeks to write in the vernacular, an effort which,
he notes sadly, has proved vain in Greece. At the same time as
Aprilov was writing (1846), Petko Slavejkov was beginning to
write his first verses in vernacular Bulgarian, influenced by
the Lyrika of Christopoulos, which he translated and imitated.[58]

By contrast with those Bulgarians who were influenced by
the Greek experience in developing their own national
consciousness, there were others who became completely Hellenized, such as Nikolaos Pikkolos and Athanasios Vogoridis.
Pikkolos, who was born at Trnovo in 1792, studied at Bucharest
and Paris. His play O thanatos tou Dimosthenous (The Death of
Demosthenes) and his translation into modern Greek of Sophocles'
Philoctetes were performed at Odessa in 1818. In 1824 he
published Greek translations of Descartes' Discourse on Method
and Bernadin de St. Pierre's Paul et Virginie. He taught
philosophy at the Ionian Academy at Corfu and subsequently
practised medicine in Bucharest and Paris, at the same time
publishing critical editions of ancient texts. But in certain
poems which he published in 1838 and 1839, he appears to have
had some pangs about deserting his native Bulgaria, and his
later life seems to have been a sad one.[59]

Athanasios Vogoridis (also known as Athanasios Ioannou),
though by birth a Bulgarian, was proud to have worked for the
propagation of Greek language and culture and for the liberation of Greece. He taught literature at the Bucharest Academy,
and died prematurely in 1826 without ever having seen the Greece
whose culture he had espoused. At one point he quarrelled
bitterly with his friend Pikkolos, who in a letter to Asopios
in 1825 mocks Athanasios' grandiose surname, pointing out that
he used to be plain Načko Stojanov until he had himself
'adopted' by Tsar Boris![60]

Apart from the Hellenized Romanians and Bulgarians, and those who simply wrote in Greek, many of the leading figures in the Romanian and Bulgarian national revival had studied at the Bucharest or Jassy Academies or at other Greek schools. We have mentioned Heliade, Negruzzi and Iordache and Dinicu Golescu; similarly, Konstantin Fotinov, Ivan Seliminski, Marko Balabanov and Neofit Rilski all studied at Greek schools, as well as Petar Beron and Petko Slavejkov.[61] The same is true of some leading Serbs: Dositej Obradović, for instance, studied at the Greek school in Smyrna among other places. Thus many[62] of the leaders of the national revivals in the Balkans had been educated at Greek schools, in which the language of instruction was Greek and in which they studied ancient Greek literature.

European books were not generally available in the Balkans except in Greek translation, and Romanians and Bulgarians continued subscribing to Greek publications well after 1821; on the other hand, before 1821 Greek books circulated more freely in the Principalities than in Greece proper, since there they were less prone to suppression by the clergy or the Porte.[63] The Greek education which Balkan intellectuals received and the books which they read in Greek had a profound influence on the national movements in Romania and Bulgaria, despite the fact that these movements consisted to some extent in the struggle to liberate the people from Greek cultural and ecclesiastical domination. One can conclude that in the second half of the eighteenth and the first decades of the nineteenth century, there was a unified written culture in Greek throughout the Balkans, with racial origins playing little part. Until 1821, there seems to have been little overt anti-Greek feeling in Romania, and the same is true of Bulgaria until 1840; after this, these peoples used the Greek experience in order to free them-selves from both Ottoman and Greek political, social, cultural and linguistic influence.[64]

*   *   *   *   *

The most ironical aspect of this study is that although in 1821 the Romanians and Bulgarians were culturally far behind the Greeks and looked to the Greeks as guides in their efforts to develop their natural cultures, by the middle of the second half of the nineteenth century they had managed to establish their spoken languages in literature and had produced grammars and dictionaries of these spoken languages, while Greek literature and culture remained in the thrall of

<u>katharevousa</u> until well after 1880. While Romanian and
Bulgarian children were learning their own languages at school,
Greek children were being taught ancient Greek to the exclusion
of the modern language; and while Romanians were writing
contemporary social dramas and the Bulgarians were producing
realistic stories about everyday life, Greek writers were
generally writing about death or vainly attempting epic master-
pieces on patriotic subjects. The result was that Greece's
literature and culture were retarded for about fifty years,
their life frozen and incapable of development, while her
northern neighbours were overtaking her in their efforts to
create a national culture. While the Romanians and Bulgarians
made an effort to create something new, the Greeks refused to
be weaned away from the ancient past. Thus the period of
enlightenment in Greece was succeeded around 1830 by a period
of obscurantism whose influence can still be felt deeply today.

Appendix. Names of Greek men of letters classed as 'enlighteners' in this paper.

Christopoulos, Athanasios (Macedonia 1772-1847). Jurist.

Darvaris, Dimitrios (Macedonia 1757-1823). Publicist.

Doukas, Neophytos (Epirus 1760-1845). Priest and teacher.

Doungas, Stephanos (Thessaly ?-c.1830). Priest and teacher.

Gazis, Anthimos (Thessaly 1764-1828. Priest and publicist.

Gennadios, Georgios (Epirus/Thrace 1786-1854). Teacher.

Govdelas, Dimitrios (Thessaly 1780-c.1830). Teacher.

Kairis, Theophilos (Andros 1784-1853). Monk and teacher.

Katartzis, Dimitrios (Istanbul c.1720-1807). Jurist.

Kodrikas, Panayotis (Athens 1762-1827). Clerk.

Kommitas, Stephanos (Thessaly c.1770-c.1833). Teacher.

Konstantas, Grigorios (Thessaly 1758-1844). Monk and teacher.

Korais, Adamantios (Izmir 1748-1833). Litterateur.

Koumas, Konstantinos (Thessaly 1777-1836). Teacher.

Lampanitziotis, Polyzois (Epirus ?-?). Publisher.

Lesbos, Benjamin of (Lesbos 1762-1824). Monk and teacher.

Moisiodax, Iosipos (Dobrudja c.1725-1800). Deacon and teacher.

Oikonomos, Konstantinos (Thessaly 1780-1857). Priest and teacher.

Pamplekis, Khristodoulos (Acarnania 1733-1793). Teacher.

Pharmakidis, Theoklitos (Thessaly 1784-1860). Priest and journalist.

Philippidis, Daniel (Thessaly c.1755-1832). Monk and teacher.

Photiadis, Lambros (Epirus 1752-1805). Teacher.

Pikkolos, Nikolaos (Trnovo 1792-1866). Doctor and teacher.

Psalidas, Athanasios (Epirus 1764-1829). Teacher.

Sakellarios, Georgios (Macedonia 1767-1838). Doctor.

Solomos, Dionysios (Zante 1798-1857). Poet.

Theotokis, Nikiphoros (Corfu 1731-1800). Priest and teacher.

Vamvas, Neophytos (Chios 1770-1855). Deacon and teacher.

Vardalachos, Konstantinos (Cythera 1755-1830). Teacher.

Velestinlis, Rigas (Thessaly c.1757-1798). Publicist, litterateur, revolutionary.

Vendotis, Georgios (Zante 1757-1795). Publisher.

Vilaras, Ioannis (Epirus 1771-1823). Doctor.

Vlantis, Spyridon (Venice 1765-1830). Teacher.

Voulgaris, Evgenios (Corfu 1716-1806). Priest and teacher.

Zalikoglou, Grigorios (Macedonia 1785-1827). Clerk.

Zaviras, Georgios (Macedonia 1744-1804). Merchant.

1. C. Th. Dimaras (<u>La Grèce au temps des Lumières</u> /Geneva 1969/ 104-5) gives figures of Greek books published in each decade of the eighteenth century, dividing them into 'religious', 'grammars' and 'miscellaneous'. His aim is to illustrate the increasing secularization of Greek culture through the century, and he points to the increase in the number of grammars and miscellaneous books as evidence of this. Nevertheless, A. Angelou (in his introduction to Moisiodax, <u>Apologia</u> /Athens 1976/xxxiii) warns us against seeing the proliferation necessarily as a sign of enlightenment: on the contrary, it might just as easily be interpreted as obscurantism, since the grammars were mostly of ancient Greek.

2. A. Camariano-Cioran, <u>Les Académies Princières de Bucharest et de Jassy et leurs professeurs</u> (Thessaloniki 1974) 33.

3. Ibid., 85.

4. According to <u>Logios Ermis</u> (1819) 581-582, the Peloponnese possessed none but the most elementary schools at the time.

5. By 'adopted Phanariot' I mean someone who was born outside the Phanariot circle but subsequently became part of it.

6. Similarly, Ariadna Camariano-Cioran, in her valuable study of the Bucharest and Jassy Academies (op. cit., 277 ff.) has shown that by no means all the Romanian and Bulgarian pupils of these schools were of noble origin.

7. Ibid., 640.

8. Dimaras, op. cit., 15.

9. Camariano-Cioran, op. cit., 127-128 and 138.

10. Ibid., 10.

11. It must be stressed that although we say that Korais wrote in modern Greek, he was not a vernacularist in the true sense. There were roughly three varieties of Greek in written use in the first decade of the nineteenth century: most writers adopted the 'middle way' of Korais, which was neither true ancient Greek nor true modern Greek, though closer to the latter than to the former; Voulgaris and Doukas wrote (more or less accurately) in ancient Greek; while the real vernacular was written and supported only by a few, such as Katartzis and the poets Christopoulos, Vilaras and Solomos. Unfortunately it was not until 1974 that these poets and their successors were officially 'acknowledged' as the 'legislators' of the Greek nation in the matter of language.

12. The first high school whose classes were conducted exclusively in Romanian was founded in Bucharest by G. Lazăr in 1818. See Camariano-Cioran, op. cit., 78.

13. Ibid., 47-48.

14. Such a phenomenon was traditional: in the sixteenth and seventeenth centuries Korydallefs completed his studies at the age of 41 or 52

depending on where one fixes his date of birth. See _Istoria tou ellinikou ethnous_ x (Athens 1974) 380.

15. The average age of the enlighteners in the appendix at the time of their first school apointment or first publication was 33. Their average age of death was 67.

16. Dimaras, op. cit., ix.

17. One example is Philippidis' translation of Gasparis' _Astronomy_: see _Megali Elliniki Engyklopaidia_, s.v. Philippidis, Daniel.

18. A. Angelou, in his introduction to Iosipos Moisiodax, _Apologia_ xxviii.

19. Philippe Iliou, 'Pour une étude quantitative du public des lecteurs grecs à l'époque des Lumières et de la Révolution (1749-1832)', _Association internationale d'études du Sud-Est européen_ iv (Sofia 1969) 475-480.

20. M. Valsa, _Le Théâtre grec moderne de 1453 à 1900_ (Berlin 1960), 189 and 193. N. Laskaris, _Istoria tou neoellinikou theatrou_, vol. 1 (Athens 1938) 185-188. _Logios Ermis_ (1817) 606.

21. W. J. Entwhistle and W. A. Morison, _Russian and the Slavonic Languages_ (London 1949) 377.

22. Camariano-Cioran, op. cit., 4.

23. For details of popular literature in Greek and Romanian see Academia Republicii Socialiste România, _Istoria literaturii române_ i (Bucharest 1970) 446-471 and 663-684; for details of both popular and learned literature see A. Duțu, 'Les livres de délectation dans la culture roumaine', _Revue des études sud-est européennes_ xi (1973) 307-325.

24. Daniel the Moskhopolite, _Eisagogiki Didaskalia_ (n.p., /?Istanbul/ 1802), preface. Daniel calls himself a 'Moesiodacian', and writes for the benefit of the children of his fellow-countrymen.

25. _Grammatiki aploelliniki skhediastheisa ypo Dimitriou Nikolaou tou Darvareos tou ek Klisouras tis Makedonias eis khrisin ton omogenon neon_ (Vienna 1806).

26. E. Legrand, _Bibliographie hellénique . . . Dix-huitième siècle_ ii (Paris 1928) 450.

27. A. Camariano-Cioran, 'Un Directeur eclairé à l'Académie de Jassy il y a deux siecles: Iosip Moisiodax', _Balkan Studies_ vii (1966) 297.

28. Kodrikas continues, 'For him the Greek language was learned by study and not by habit and natural use from childhood. His sight and mind were trained in the reading of the ancient authors; but his ear was not accustomed to the harmony of the dialect of the modern Greeks. It was therefore not easy for him either to imitate the elaborate phrases of the authors, or to express himself genuinely in the simple demotic dialect. Thus he too sought shelter in the usual refuge of half-lettered pedagogues, saying that the common language of the modern Greeks is corrupt and in need of correction.' P. Kodrikas, _Meleti peri tis koinis ellinikis dialektou_ i (Paris

1818) xxiv-xxvi.

29. Moisiodax, op. cit., 36-40.

30. Acad. Rep. Soc. Rom., op. cit., ii (Bucharest 1968) 173-175, and
A. Kamarianou, 'Laika tragoudia kai phanariotika stikhourgimata', Laographia
xviii (1959) 94-112.

31. For information on the mismayés see L. I. Vranousis, Rigas /Vasiki
Vivliothiki x/ (Athens 1953) 203-211.

32. A. Kamarianou, op. cit., 100-106.

33. Acad. Rep. Soc. Rom., op. cit., ii 139-141.

34. L. I. Vranousis, I prodromi /Vasiki Vivliothiki xi/ (Athens 1955) 59.

35. Ibid., 58.

36. A. Camariano-Cioran, Académies 627.

37. Ibid., 201.

38. Acad. Rep. Soc. Rom., op. cit., ii 126 ff.

39. The word Romounos appears in a Greek book first published in 1791: one
of its authors was the same Philippidis, who was perhaps of Vlach origin.
Here the word is described as being a term which the Vlachs do not like
being applied to them. G. Konstantas and D. Philippidis, Geographia
neoteriki. Peri tis Ellados (Athens 1970) 98.

40. L. I. Vranousis, Rigas 72.

41. Acad. Rep. Soc. Rom., op. cit., ii 153.

42. For D. Golescu's Însemnare a călătoriei mele (Buda 1826) see Acad. Rep.
Soc. Rom., op. cit., ii 146.

43. An additional Balkan element is provided by the Slovene Jernej Kopitař,
who was a corresponding member of this 'Philologiki Etairia' or 'Graiko-
Dakiki Etairia'.

44. Logios Ermis (1811) 60.

45. Ibid. (1818) 565-566.

46. M. Valsa, op. cit., 186-189. N. I. Laskaris, op. cit., i 189-191.

47. G. I. Zoidis, To theatro tis Philikis Etairias (/Bucharest/ 1964) 37.

48. Ibid., 56-59, and Acad. Rep. Soc. Rom.; op. cit., ii 247.

49. Ibid., ii 262.

50. A. Camariano-Cioran, op. cit., 80.

51. Acad. Rep. Soc. Rom., op. cit., ii 381.

52. Greek influence in Romania did not stop in 1821. Dinicu Golescu
continued writing in Greek as well as Romanian, and Anton Pann published a
Romanian translation of Photinos' Neos Erotokritos in 1837; the Erotokritos
itself had already been translated in manuscript at least three times since
1780, and an imitation of it, Filerot și Antuza (published at Brăila in
1857 but existing in manuscript since the early nineteenth century) continued
to be printed until this century. See D. V. Oikonomides, 'Ellinikei
epidraseis epi tin dimodi roumanikin logotekhnian', Epetiris tou Mesaionikou

Archeiou iv (1951-1952) 50-57, and Acad. Rep. Soc. Rom., op. cit., i 676-680.

53. M. Domi, 'Quelques moments et aspects des contacts culturels de l'Albanie et du peuple albanais', _Actes du Colloque international des civilisations balkaniques_ (Sinaïa 1962) 163; E. Legrand, _Bibliographie hellénique . . . Dix-huitième siècle_ ii 184, 219, 251, and G. Ladas and A. Hatzidimou, _Elliniki vivliographia, symvoli sto dekaton ogdoo aiona_ (Athens 1964) 116.

54. E. Legrand, op. cit., ii 126-128.

55. A large portion of this verse chronicle is published in K. Sathas, _Istorikai diatrivai_ (Athens 1870). The rest is still unpublished.

56. The date of the first edition of this book is usually given wrongly as 1528 in works dealing with Greek literature.

57. V. E. Aprilov, _Săčinenija_ (Sofia 1968) 190-192. I am deeply indebted to Dr. Vivian Pinto of the School of Slavonic and East European Studies, University of London, for information on Aprilov and other Bulgarians mentioned in this paper.

58. For this section of P. R. Slavejkov's autobiography see M. Arnaudov (ed.), _Bulgarski memoari (zapiski, dnevnitsi, avtobiografi)_ (Sofia 1938) 55-56.

59. See E. G. Protopsaltis, 'O Nikolaos Pikkolos kai to ergo tou', _Athina_ lxviii (1965) 92 ff., and V. Beševliev, 'Eine wenig bekannte neugriechische Gedichtsammlung', _Serta Neograeca_ (Amsterdam 1975) 1-11.

60. S. Kougeas, 'O Korais eis tin allilographian tou Asopiou', _Ellinika_ vi (1933) 70-1. V. Beševliev, loc. cit., tacitly identifies, no doubt rightly, the 'Andipas Vogoridis' of the letter with Athanasios Vogoridis. A. Camariano-Cioran, op. cit., 56, misleadingly talks about 'Athanasios Ioannou' (for whom she has a separate entry in the index) without making it clear that he is the same person as Vogoridis, by which name he is known elsewhere in her book. He appears to be no relation of Stefanaki Bey Vogoridis, 'Prince of Samos' from 1834 to 1850, who was another Hellenized Bulgarian.

61. For other notable Bulgarian graduates of Greek schools see V. Beševliev, 'Der Widerhall des neugriechischen Sprachkampfes und der neugriechischen Literatur im Bulgarien des vorigen Jahrhunderts', in J. Irmscher ed., _Probleme der neugriechischen Literatur_ ii (Berlin 1960) 50.

62. The Greek influence on the Serbs was far smaller than on the Romanians and Bulgarians, since literacy was low and because the Serbian intellectual leaders tended to look rather northwards to Austro-Hungarian Croatia and eastwards to Russia than to Greece.

63. A. Camariano-Cioran, op. cit., 80.

64. Greek influence continued longer among the Bulgarians than among the

Romanians: Grigor Prličev (Grigorios Stavridis), who won the Greek national poetry competition in 1860, was one of many Bulgarian students and graduates resident in Athens at the time.

5

THE GREEK MERCANTILE BOURGEOISIE: 'PROGRESSIVE' OR 'REACTIONARY'?

RICHARD CLOGG

Εἴθε οἱ Πραγματευταί νά μιμηθῶσι τάς καλάς εὐεργεσίας τῶν
αὐταδέλφων ΖΩΣΙΜΑΔΩΝ! καί ΊΩΑΝΝΟΥ τοῦ ΠΡΙΓΚΟΥ! Εἴθε οἱ
Προεστῶτες
τῶν πόλεων καί χωρίων νά μιμηθῶσι τό παράδειγμα τῶν
ΚΥΔΩΝΙΑΤΩΝ!
Οἱ Μοναστηριακοί το παράδειγμα τῶν ΒΑΤΟΠΕΔΙΝΩΝ! καί οἱ
Τεχνῖται
τό τοῦ ἐν Κωνσταντινουπόλει Συλλόγου τῶν ΓΟΥΝΑΡΑΔΩΝ!
(Λόγιος ὁ Ἑρμῆς, March 1811)

Viron Karidis in Chapter VI provides a revealing insight
into the nature of Greek society in Southern Russia and more
particularly Odessa, one of the most flourishing of the paroikies
of the Greek mercantile diaspora in the years before 1821.   It is
perhaps worth recalling the Russian poet Pushkin's attitude to
the Greeks of Odessa.   Pushkin, who had earlier dallied with one
of Byron's mistresses in Kishinev, was, at the outbreak of
hostilities in 1821, a passionate champion of the cause of Greek
freedom.   He penned an ode to 'Eleferia' and expressed the firm
conviction that 'Greece will come out victorious and that the
twenty-five millions of Turks will leave Hellada which is the
legal heir of Homer and Themistocles.'   At this stage he had not
actually met many Greeks.   When he did, he became thoroughly
disillusioned with what he termed 'a nasty people made up of
bandits and shopkeepers'.   As he wrote to Davydov, in 1823 or
1824, 'we have seen the new Leonidases in the streets of Odessa
and Kishinev.   We are personally acquainted with a number of
them; we attest of their complete worthlessness; they have not
the slightest idea of military art, no concept of honour, no
enthusiasm; they will endure anything, even blows of a cane, with
a composure worthy of Themistocles'.[1]   Pushkin's sour reaction to
the Greeks of Odessa no doubt reflects the bitter disappointment
of a disillusioned philhellene, and he was by no means the first

or the last foreigner to swing from one emotional extreme to the other in his attitudes towards the Greeks.

But, more seriously, Pushkin's remarks do, I think, go some way towards confirming my increasing scepticism as to the validity of the thesis frequently advanced by historians that a radicalised Greek mercantile bourgeoisie acted as the catalyst of the Greek national movement. One of the clearest formulations of this thesis is that of L.S. Stavrianos in his important article 'Antecedents to the Balkan Revolutions of the Nineteenth Century'. The new middle class elements that began to appear in the Balkans during the course of the eighteenth century were, he has written, 'by their very nature dissatisfied with the Ottoman status quo. They had little use for a government that was unable to maintain roads, curb brigands, or prevent the open and never ending extortions on the part of its own officials'. These new middle class groups, he continues, 'tended to be radical-minded because of their contacts with the West. Merchants and seamen who had journeyed to foreign lands could not help contrasting the security and enlightenment they had witnessed abroad with the deplorable conditions at home. Very naturally they would conclude that their own future and that of their fellow country-men depended upon the earliest possible removal of the Turkish incubus.' He does allow some deviations from this norm, among them the wealthy shipping magnates of Ydra whose opposition to the war in its early stages is well known, but these were, he maintains, exceptions to the general rule.[2] Elsewhere Stavrianos had written that 'it was the middle class which was the moving spirit in the revolutionary movement and which founded the secret, revolutionary society, Philike Hetairia, and comprised the greater part of its membership. Moreover it was the wealth of the merchants and ship-owners which made it economically possible for the Greeks to strike for independence and to finance the revolution with practically no outside aid during the first three years'[3] and that 'the merchants who subsidized the translation of Locke or Newton or Voltaire were likely to support also movements for political liberation'.[4]

Variations on this general thesis are met with in many writers on the pre-independence period. It can be expressed in simplistic terms, as by Apostolos Vakalopoulos, who has written that once the merchants had won their economic independence, it was natural that they should seek their national freedom.[5] Bourgeois Greeks of the diaspora, he has written, were, like all

bourgeois, liberals.[6] A more sophisticated formulation is that
of Vasilis Kremmydas. 'The Greek merchants indeed became the
bearers, not only of a cultural renaissance, but of a
revolutionary ideology (to the degree allowed by the objective
reality). This was finally not only to call into question, but
also to shake, the basic structure of feudal society'.[7] Nikos
Mouzelis has written in similar vein that 'the Greek merchants,
especially those established in the Danubian principalities and
in the major European capitals, transmitted French revolutionary
ideas and provided leadership and considerable material
resources to the insurrectionary movement. Through their
commercial activities, their numerous contacts with the West and
their financing of schools in which students were initiated into
the rationalism and anti-clericalism of western enlightenment,
they contributed significantly to the early 'modernization'
(i.e. Westernization) of Greek culture and society . . the
bourgeoisie became the value-originators and standard-setters of
Greek society, quite early shaping its major institutions along
liberal bourgeois lines.'[8]

Stavrianos takes as typical of the attitudes and
aspirations of the Greek mercantile bourgeoisie, Ioannis Pringos
(?1725-1789), a Greek from Zagora in Thessaly who made a fortune
trading in Amsterdam, where from 1730 onwards the mercantile
privileges of the native inhabitants had been conceded to
Greeks, Jews and Armenians. Pringos, a leading light in the
Greek community of the city in the mid-eighteenth century, kept
a fascinating diary which throws much light on community affairs,
also contains news and comments on the wider world. In this
interesting document, only fragments of which have so far been
published,[9] Pringos frequently expressed his admiration for
Amsterdam, 'a great place for trade'. He was particularly
enamoured of the bourse where every day some four to five
thousand merchants congregated, gathered around the forty-six
columns according either to nationality or to the nature of
their merchandise. The Greeks and all those who traded with
Greece, Istanbul, Izmir, Thessaloniki, Alexandria, Egypt and
other such regions collected round one particular column.

Stavrianos cites Pringos' famous lament for the absence
within the Ottoman Empire of the order and justice, the
essential pre-conditions of a flourishing commerce, that he so
admired in the Netherlands:

'But all this cannot exist under the Turk. He has

87

neither order nor justice. And if the capital is one thousand he multiplies it tenfold so that he may loot and impoverish others, not realizing that the wealth of his subjects is the wealth of his kingdom . . he is altogether unjust, and he is not one for creating anything but only for destroying. May the Almighty ruin him so that Greece may become Christian, and justice may prevail, and governments may be created as in Europe where everyone has his own without fear of any injustice.'[10]

Stavrianos' citation of this key passage is from Yannis Kordatos' Rigas Pheraios kai i Valkaniki Omospondia. Kordatos, the father of Greek marxist historiography, regarded Pringos, as does Stavrianos, as being fully representative of what he termed the 'romeiki bourzouazia' or 'Romaic bourgeoisie'. The passage quoted by Stavrianos he regarded as being 'the mirror of the psychology of those Greek merchants who lived in Europe'.[11]

Yet a closer study of Pringos' writings suggests that he was anything but 'radical-minded', as Stavrianos would have us believe. There is no need to question the genuineness of Pringos' admiration for the social and economic system of the Netherlands that gave full rein to commercial enterprise or the depth of his resentment against an Ottoman social and economic system that was the very antithesis of the Dutch model. But this is not to say that Pringos was the kind of man to give practical expression to his frustrations by underwriting any kind of dynamic action to overthrow Ottoman rule. Far from being radicalised by his experience in the West, his thought world essentially reflected the neo-Byzantine Orthodoxy of the overwhelming majority of his compatriots. There is no evidence whatsoever that he placed any hope in direct action by the Greeks themselves to bring about the overthrow of their Ottoman oppressors. Rather he trusted that God would implant in the hearts of the 'Christian Kings', and more particularly the Russians, a desire to rid Greece of the 'impious Hagarene', this 'bloodthirsty wolf, this insatiable animal' who, with his impositions and taxes, was destroying Greece. Moreover, and this is a point which Kordatos appears to have missed, Pringos had a deeply rooted belief in the prophecies and oracles which formed the staple intellectual diet of the Greek masses throughout the Tourkokratia.

Probably the most widely disseminated of these prophetic books were the prophecies of Agathangelos. These were purportedly

written in Sicily in 1279 but in fact were forgeries compiled by
an Orthodox priest, Theoklitos Polyeidis of Edirne (Adrianople)
in the mid-eighteenth century. Polyeidis had for a time been
the priest of the Greek Church in Tokay in Hungary and had later
founded the Orthodox church established in Leipzig for the Greek
merchant community in the city. This contact with the West
enabled him to spice his obscure prophecies with garbled
references to events in Western Europe. Another very widely
disseminated belief was that the Greeks would receive their
emancipation at the hands of a 'fair-headed race' (xanthon genos),
assumed to be their Orthodox co-religionists, the Russians.[12]
But during the Russo-Turkish war of 1768-1774 the prophecies of
Leo the Wise held a special attraction.[13] For on one reading of
these, the Turks would be driven from Istanbul three hundred and
twenty years after the Turkish conquest of the city, i.e. in
1773. Such an occurrence must have seemed highly plausible to
contemporary observers. Certainly Pringos himself thought so,
and such an expectation is manifest in several entries in his
diary. One such, for 22 July 1771 reads:

> 'Now should the prophecies of Leo the Wise be
> fulfilled, where he says "Two eagles shall devour
> the snake". These are the two insignia, or flags
> of the Russian Empire - the double-headed eagle,
> the insignia of the Roman /Byzantine7 and the
> snake is the Turk, who has wrapped himself around
> a corpse, that is to say the Empire of the Romans
> /Byzantines7. Here Leo says, as they have
> interpreted, that the Turk shall remain for 320
> years in the City /Constantinople7. And now it is
> 317 years from 1454 /sic7 when they took the City
> until now, 1771. The Lord during these three years
> has made it possible for them /Russians7 to throw
> the Turk out of Greece and out of Europe.'[14]

Pringos, then, took the prophecies with deadly seriousness and,
with his deep concern for the ecclesiastical affairs of the
Amsterdam Greek community, cannot reasonably be described as
being 'radical-minded'.

To argue that Pringos properly belongs to the world of
neo-Byzantine Orthodox obscurantism is not to deny that during
this period traditional and modern modes of thought could co-
exist within the same person. A case in point is Nicolae Cercel,
or Nikolaos Zerzoulis, a Vlach from Metsovo, who after seven

years of study in Western Europe, where he had acquired a sound knowledge of Latin, French and Italian, was appointed successor to Evgenios Voulgaris at the Athoniada Skholi on Mount Athos. From here he moved to Jassy in Moldavia, where he directed the Princely Academy until his death in 1772. There he translated works by Christian Wolff on arithmetic, geography and trigonometry and the experimental physics of Pieter van Musschenbrock, a Dutch doctor and a follower of Newton, and also part of Newton's Elements. Yet this paragon of Enlightenment was also the author in 1768 of a 'Brief Interpretation of the Oracles of Leo the Wise concerning the Resurrection of Constantinople'. That Cercel took the whole question of the prophecies seriously is suggested by Kaisarios Dapontes' report that he did not sign this manuscript for fear of Ottoman reprisals.[15] According to Cercel's calculations the liberation of Constantinople by the Russians would take place in 1774, the year of the Treaty of Küçük Kaynarca, which, however, was seen by most Greeks as a betrayal by the Russians of their Orthodox co-religionists. The manifest disappointment occasioned by the terms of the Treaty of Küçük Kaynarca caused many Greeks to cease to place their hopes in the prophecies, not, significantly, because their hopes had proved in vain, but because it was assumed that God, on account of the sins of the Orthodox pliroma, had abrogated them.[16]

Another, if more ambiguous, example of what one might call cultural schizophrenia is afforded by Rigas Velestinlis (Pheraios), the proto-martyr of Greek independence. In the 1790's Rigas, directly influenced by the French Revolution, composed a New Political Constitution of the Inhabitants of Rumeli, Asia Minor, the Archipelago and the Danubian Principalities, which explicitly reflected the influence of the French constitutions of 1793 and 1795. This he had printed in Vienna in 1796, together with a revolutionary proclamation, a declaration of the Rights of Man, and a thourios or war song. With these he vainly hoped to revolutionise the Balkan peninsula. Yet on an earlier visit (probably in 1790-91) to Vienna, Rigas, one of the Greeks most profoundly and directly influenced by the French Revolution, may well have been responsible, as has recently been demonstrated, for the publication of the first printed edition of the prophecies of Agathangelos, the most widely disseminated prophecies of the eighteenth century.[17] Rigas' case is ambiguous for, unlike that

of Cercel, we do not know that he himself necessarily subscribed
to the prophecies. It could be that he personally did not but
that, conscious of the attachment of the Greek masses to
Agathangelos, he nonetheless published them, hoping thereby to
encourage in them the belief that eventually 'the Barbarians
would tremble', and   thus   make them more receptive to his
consciously revolutionary propaganda.

Having, I hope, demonstrated that Pringos, who is
frequently portrayed as the very epitome of the 'progressive'
bourgeois merchant, was profoundly attached to the neo-Byzantine
world of the prophecies and oracles I do not mean to suggest that
his strictures against the arbitrariness and uncertainty of life
within the Ottoman Empire, and its deleterious effects on trade,
were anything less than heartfelt or accurate. Far from it,
Pringos' protestations are echoed in many other writings of the
period. Daniil Philippidis and Grigorios Konstantas, for
instance, in their Geographia Neoteriki, first published in
Vienna in 1791, shared Pringos' admiration for Dutch commerce and
wrote that Greeks engaged in trade within the Ottoman Empire
'experience a thousand vexations from the Turks. . it is not
uncommon to see a wretched Turk ill treat a useful merchant.
so, therefore, many rich merchants who have experience of other
states and are resolved to live by commerce, exile themselves and
go and establish themselves in other countries, and a great
damage ensues for the country. Others again become subjects in
some foreign court to be protected by it in their trade.' The
Turks of Larissa, they held, were particularly biased against the
Christians. 'What commerce. .', they wrote, 'do you seek from a
place where a Turk at noon can take out his pistol and kill a
non-Turk who dared to say nay to him about something'. In the
Habsburg monarchy alone, 'where the rights of life and property
are sovereign', Phillippidis and Konstantas estimated that there
were some eighty thousand Greek families.[18] Rigas Velestinlis in
a footnote to his translation of the travels of the Young
Anacharsis wrote of his home town of Velestino that 'the frequent
unjust murders of Christians which now take place here would have
entirely desolated the town if its physical beauties had not
obliged them to endure all so as to leave their bones in the
place where their forefathers were buried.'[19]

Profits, and often substantial ones, could still be made
within the confines of the Ottoman Empire but there was no
certainty as to whether these could be retained. Apart from the

routine impositions of an increasingly unchecked Ottoman
bureaucracy there were other hazards to contend with. These
ranged from fires to violent urban riots. A Corfiot lawyer
Markos Antoniou Katsaitis witnessed a great fire that swept
through Izmir in 1742 and was appalled to see as a result the
wealthy reduced to begging for bread, a citizen could be 'la sera
ricco, e potente, e la mattina. . povero, e mendico.'[20] To these
hazards were added periodic outbursts of anti-Christian violence.
A notorious incident of this kind was the so-called 'Smyrna
rebellion' of March 1797. This developed from a minor brawl at
an exhibition in the city by some Austrian-protected rope dancers
and tumblers into a fully fledged urban riot, in which
janissaries, at this stage degenerated into an ill-disciplined,
hereditary militia, ran amok in an orgy of violence and
destruction. Eye witness acounts put the number of Greeks
slaughtered at some one thousand five hundred, with some ten
thousand houses and thirty one <u>hans</u> destroyed in the ensuing fire.
A despatch in the Greek <u>Ephimeris</u>, published in Vienna by the
brothers Markides-Poulios, dramatically reported that an entire
century would not suffice to restore Izmir to its pristine
state.[21]

It was arbitrariness and oppression of this kind which
prompted many of the more energetic merchants to trade in more
settled societies abroad and which inhibited the development of
local manufactures. The one major exception to the general rule
that Greek entrepreneurial skills and capital were primarily
invested outside the Greek lands rather than within were the
manufactories of spun red cotton in the small Thessalian town of
Ambelakia. This, in the words of the French consul in Thessaloniki
towards the end of the eighteenth century, Felix de Beaujour, 'by
the activity of its inhabitants' resembled 'rather a city of
Holland than a Turkish village'.[22] So close were the contacts of
the Ambelakiots with Central Europe that a German traveller,
J.L.S. Bartholdy, came across a small amateur theatre in the town
in which Kotzebue's <u>Menschenhass und Reue</u> was performed in the
original language.[23] Although Ambelakia was more or less a
unique example of a manufacturing enterprise within the Greek
lands, it was for a time highly profitable, yielding profits of
'from sixty to eighty, and even a hundred per cent'. Indeed,
according to Beaujour, the very profitability of the enterprise
was to bring about its ruin. 'This immense influx of wealth,' he
wrote, 'threw all. . into disorder and confusion. The directors,

become opulent, made pressing demands; the poor being enriched in their turn, refused to obey; the workmen quitted the shuttle to take the pen, instead of dyeing and spinning: everyone wished to command. The meetings became tumultuous; the workmen, who were the most numerous ruled there. .' These difficulties Beaujour attributed to 'the jealousy, the spirit of envy, the desire of injuring each other, all those petty shuffling passions, which enter into the composition of the Greek character. .'[24]

The example of Ambelakia, which attracted the eye of foreign travellers, was very much an isolated one. By far the main thrust of Greek entrepreneurial activity was directed towards trade in Central Europe and the Mediterranean. In much of the Balkans and in parts of Central Europe Greeks fulfilled the role of a mercantile middle class, and much of the carrying trade of these regions was in their hands. Traian Stoianovich has issued a salutary warning against accepting Habsburg statistics at their face value, for the Habsburg customs authorities tended indiscriminately to lump together as 'Greeks', Serbs, Macedonians, Bulgarians, Albanians and Hellenised Vlachs.[25] A contemporary observer, G.C. Rosa, noted that 'in Hungary, Saxony and the whole of Germany there is no trading city, where they /the Vlachs/ do not stand in the first rank of the merchants.'[26] But whatever qualifications are made, Greeks proper did play a major part in stimulating commercial activity in these regions, taking full advantage of the preferential customs duty conferred on Ottoman subjects by the Treaty of Passarovitz (1718) and confirmed by the Treaty of Belgrade (1739). By the mid-eighteenth century trade in the towns of Hungary and Transylvania was largely in the hands of Greeks, and their tightly knit merchant companies were established in a number of them.[27]

A striking indication of the commercial penetration by Greek merchants of the Hungarian lands is afforded by a decision of the Council of Lieutenancies of Buda (Budai Helytartótanács) in 1795 to create the position, to be financed by the Greek community itself, of overseer of the Greek Orthodox schools in the following seventeen cities of Hungary: Békés, Belényes, Eger, Gyöngyös, Györ, Gyula, Hódmezóvásárhely, Kecskemét, Komárom, Miskolc, Nagyvárad, Oravica, Pest, Tokaj, Újvidék, Ungvár and Vác.[28] Substantial Greek communities were to be found elsewhere in Central Europe, and particularly in Vienna and Leipzig. In this last city the young Goethe was particularly struck by the handsome figures and dignified clothes of the Greeks.[29]

Substantial Greek communities were also to be found in Italy, in particular in Venice, Trieste and Livorno, and in other ports of the Mediterranean.

A substantial boost to Greek seaborne commerce was given by the opening up of the Black Sea trade to the Russians by the Treaty of Küçük Kaynarca of 1774, and in particular by the convention of Aynalı Kavak of 1779 and by the Russo-Turkish commercial treaty of 1783. Much of Russia's sea borne Black Sea commerce was henceforth carried by Greeks sailing under the Russian flag. After Küçük Kaynarca, Catherine the Great encouraged Greek migration to help populate her newly acquired territories on the Black Sea and Sea of Azov. Greeks developed a dominant position in the commerce of towns such as Odessa, Taganrog and Mariupol. A further boost to Greek sea borne commerce, which was largely conducted by the fleets of the three 'nautical' islands of Hydra, Spetses and Psara, was given by the opportunities for running contraband cargoes during the French revolutionary wars and the Continental Blockade. By the end of the Napoleonic wars the Greek merchant marine is estimated to have numbered some one thousand ships.[30] During the Continental Blockade profits of between seventy to one hundred per cent were considered on the low side by Greek shipowners.[31] After 1815 average profits fell to fifteen per cent and the aggregate profits of Hydriot merchants, for instance, fell from 7,749,510 piastres in 1816 to 1,375,039 piastres in 1820. This massive decline in income was undoubtedly a precipitating factor in inclining the wealthy shipowners and sea captains of the islands to align themselves, if reluctantly to begin with, with the insurgents.

Moreover, during the course of the eighteenth century Greek merchants began to establish themselves even further afield than the Central European/Mediterranean area. As we have seen there was a flourishing Greek merchant community in Amsterdam, while a short lived attempt was made to found a Greek colony at New Smyrna in Florida.[32] Much more successful was the small but prosperous community established in Calcutta and Dacca, which was mainly composed of Greeks from Philippopolis and which produced, in Dimitrios Galanos, one of the leading indologists of his day.[33]

We have established, then, that during the eighteenth and early nineteenth centuries a substantial Greek mercantile bourgeoisie came into existence and that, because of a climate

94

within the Ottoman Empire that was generally inimical to entrepreneurial enterprise and the accumulation of capital, much of
this entrepreneurial skill was to be found outside the confines
of the Empire. But what was the significance of all this
activity for the nascent Greek national movement? Did the
merchants play the crucial role in the emergence of a dynamic
national movement that is often attributed to them? Can they, in
fact, be described as a progressive force in the context of Greek
society in the crucial decades before 1821?

One important function which the Greek mercantile
bourgeoisie undoubtedly did fulfil in this period was to underwrite the Greek intellectual revival that was to produce an
intelligentsia capable of articulating the demands of Greek
nationalists. In 1811 Adamantios Korais, the prime mentor of the
'Neo-Hellenic Enlightenment', wrote that either it was true that
a renaissance was under way in Greece or nothing in the world was
true, and this was undeniably the case. It was Korais in his
remarkable Mémoire sur l'état actuel de la civilisation dans la
Grèce,[34] read to the Parisian Société des Observateurs de l'Homme
in 1803, who correctly saw the link between the Greek commercial
revival and the Greek intellectual revival. Adverting to the
appearance for the first time of millionaires among a people who
were accustomed to regard the small number of those who possessed
a capital of a hundred purses as being filled to overflowing with
the favours of fortune, he wrote that these merchants, anxious to
conserve their wealth, had previously relied on Europeans for the
conduct of their affairs. Now, however, they were increasingly
turning to the youth of their own nation, which had been
encouraged to educate itself by the lure of substantial salaries.
The study of the languages of the countries with which they had
commercial links gave these young merchants a 'tincture of
erudition and belles-lettres'. They followed, wrote Korais,
without knowing it a course of logic in learning arithmetic and
the fine art of keeping books. 'The desire to educate themselves
and to go abroad took a hold in the soul of youth, and it was
seconded by the desire that great riches inspire in their
possessors, to increase on the one hand their commerce by
establishments in foreign countries, and, on the other, to
multiply among them the means of instruction, if only for their
own children'.[35]

The growing prosperity of this commercial bourgeoisie
provided the essential material base for what Iosipos Moisiodax

in 1761 referred to as the struggle 'to bring back the muses to their ancestral home.'[36] This manifested itself in a number of ways; in the subsidising of the printing and distribution of books reflecting the enlightened philosophies and practical knowledge of the West; in enabling increasing numbers of young Greeks to study in the universities of Western Europe; in the founding of libraries and their stocking with books in both Greek and European languages and in the foundation or re-invigoration of schools and colleges in various parts of the Greek world.

When looking at the relative precocity of the Greek national movement in the Balkan context it is instructive to recall that the first book to be printed in Bulgarian was not published until 1806. Yet Greek printing for a Greek readership had undergone a marked upsurge during the course of the eight-eenth century and it has been estimated that, during the first two decades of the nineteenth century, some one thousand three hundred different Greek titles appeared. Many of these, of course, were religious or liturgical works or popular romances, either indigenous or translated from Western languages. It was this side of Greek book production that prompted Byron's companion in Greece, John Cam Hobhouse, to comment that 'the purely literary part of /Greek book production/ seems more like 'that of a young ladies' school than of a whole nation'.[37] But, amid the translations of Metastasio, Marmontel, Gessner and Goldoni, there were a number of weighty tomes reflecting the enlightened learning of the West. There was no commercial market for such books, for the nascent Greek intelligentsia was never more than a minuscule percentage of the Greek population, and the only way such books could be published was by subscription, where the author or translator published when he had secured enough advance subscriptions to defray his expenses, or by securing the patronage of some wealthy merchant who would underwrite the cost of the whole enterprise. Much of Korais' Elliniki Vivliothiki, his multi-volume edition of some of the ancient Greek classics, prefaced by improving exhortations to the Greeks to better their lot through education, was published at the expense of the brothers Zosimas, wealthy merchants from Ioannina. Ioannis Pringos was a major benefactor of the library in his native Zagora and indeed in the Greek literary journal of the time, Ermis o Logios, the 'Scholarly Hermes', the Zosimades and Pringos, were singled out for particular praise, and other merchants were urged to follow their example.[38] And indeed many of the Greek books printed during this period bear fulsome dedications to such mercantile benefactors.

One significant category of books published during this period are the books published for a specifically merchant readership. These included Nikolaos Papadopoulos' four-volume commercial encyclopaedia <u>Ermis o Kerdoos</u>, or 'Hermes the Profit-maker'. This book, published in Venice in 1815, 'at the expense of the honourable and patriotic mercantile guild of Greek whole-sale merchants of Constantinople', gives a detailed breakdown of the commercial prospects afforded by most of the countries in the world and the kind of commodities they traded in. Interestingly, Papadopoulos in the preface to this book specifically attributed Greece's intellectual renaissance to the growth of commerce. In the preface to his German grammar published in Vienna in 1785, the Hellenised Vlach, Dimitrios Darvaris wrote that the German language is not only useful and beneficial but almost necessary for the majority of those 'who are known under the name of Greeks in the rest of Europe'. He appended to this grammar an exhortatory epistle from a certain friend to a novice merchant. This is worth looking at in some detail as it throws interesting light on the professional ethos of the Greek merchant during this period.

'Learn exactly', Darvaris exhorts his readers, 'the uncertain finality of external affairs and remain steadfast in the faith and hope of eternal life. For merchants are subject to many anomalies, changes and dangers, and suffer much damage. .' The merchant in any undertaking should be useful and just to all. He should not import anything secretly or deceive the customs authorities. 'For frequently an obol acquired in such a way ends up costing ten'. The merchant should not trade with false, useless or bare merchandise and should use accurate weights and measures. Accounts should be strictly and regularly rendered for 'in these adheres all the confidence of the merchant.' He should not venture more than he might hope to regain should a particular venture fail, nor should he ever deploy more than his capital (<u>to kapitali</u>). He should not hastily become a guarantor for someone else, for much damage could result from this. Nor should he lightly seek another to become guarantor for him. The good merchant should attend regularly at the bourse and at the assemblies of the merchants, for absence can give rise to suspicion. If he engaged in trade on account of others, then he should trade as if for himself. In this fashion he would acquire both friends and honour. He should consider friends as treasures. If he gave or received advice, he should take care that it was good. He should settle his accounts quickly and in this way guarantee long-lasting friendships. As well as maintaining a high level of commercial ethics he should also conduct his private life according to high moral principles. He should not manifest excess in dressing according to the latest fashion, but he should dress in keeping with his calling. He should appreciate that his honour was more important than wealth. 'Avoid', Darvaris counselled, 'as far as you can, bad companions and ruinous games. Shun, moreover, horses, wine and women, for these things have ruined many young merchants.'[39]

Besides subventing the publication of improving books, merchants also played a leading role in financing schools and colleges in their native towns and islands. It is no accident that two of the leading centres of higher education within the Greek world in the years immediately before 1821 were in the important commercial centres of Chios and Ayvalık (Kydonies), an almost exclusively Greek town in the gulf of Edremit, to the north of Izmir . An American missionary visiting the Academy of Chios on the eve of the War of Independence found that instruction was given in theology, rhetoric, ancient and modern Greek, Latin, French and Turkish, geometry, mathematics and chemistry. There was a good library and chemical laboratory, and a Greek from Russia had recently given twenty to thirty thousand dollars to the Academy.[40] The Academy also had a small printing press, much to the somewhat childish chagrin of Korais, who, although he had never set foot on the island, was a fanatical Chiot patriot. He was most anxious that the Chiots should secure a printing press before their great rivals the Ayvaliots. In fact, however, the Ayvaliots beat them to it, for a small press was set up in 1820 by Konstantinos Tombras, who had been sent to study the art of printing with the philhellene Ambroise Firmin Didot in Paris in 1817 at the expense of the wealthy Ayvaliot Emmanouil Saltelis.[41] Some of these schools had a specifically commercial orientation. One such was the Ellinikon Emborikon Gymnasion or Ellino-Emboriki Skholi established in Odessa in 1814. The object of this school was to teach the young 'the Greek language and culture, trade and the sciences necessary to it'. Russian and Italian was taught, as well as Greek, and by 1818 the school contained some two hundred and fifty students, from all over the

Greek world and including Russians. The various Greek insurance
companies in the city made generous subventions to the school out
of their yearly profits. That of the 'United Greeks' gave thirty
per cent, which in 1817 amounted to 32,428 roubles and 21 kopecks.
The 'New Greek' gave twenty per cent, which amounted to 17,917
roubles, the 'Greek' seven per cent, which amounted to 2,047
roubles and 45 kopecks and the 'Greco-Russian' five per cent,
which amounted to 1,500 roubles.[42]

Merchants also contributed significantly to this
intellectual revival by sponsoring the education abroad of
promising young Greeks, either directly or through the agency of
societies such as the Etairia ton Philomouson, the 'Society of
Friends of the Muses', branches of which were founded in Athens
in 1813 and in Vienna in 1815. In 1819, von Schladen, the
Prussian ambassador to the Ottoman Porte, reported that more than
fifty young Greeks /this was a very considerable underestimate/
were travelling in Italy, France and Germany at public expense.
To this end Alexander Mauro, a merchant in Constantinople, had
contributed 15,000 and N. Babazy, a merchant of Taganrog, had
contributed 50,000 piastres.[43]

Stoianovich has referred, tantalisingly briefly, to the
role of the Balkan Orthodox merchants as channels of non-material
culture into the Balkans[44] but it would appear that little of
all this cultural ferment rubbed off on the merchants themselves,
whose over-riding concern was with the maximisation of profit.
The merchants of Ioannina and Albania, described in 1793 by the
French consul in Bucharest, as being almost all sans-culottes,
who had translated the Rights of Man, which they knew by heart,
seem to have been very much an exception.[45] It was not the
merchants themselves but their protégés who became ideologues.
Once again Korais saw this at the time. The wealthy merchants,
he wrote, 'are seen endowing colleges, encouraging talents,
helping with their purse, and honouring with their friendship, I
had almost said with their respect, a young generation whose
money-making abilities do not equal the passion to learn with
which it is devoured.' Many of these young men, he wrote,
'destined for commerce, have been seen to desert the countinghouse and take refuge in some university'.[46] Foremost among
these refugees from the countinghouse was, of course, Adamantios
Korais himself, the principal figure of the Greek intellectual
revival. Korais' working life began when, at the age of twenty-
three, he was sent to Amsterdam from his native Izmir as the

99

representative of Stathis Thomas, a leading member of a merchant company in Izmir which had branches in Chios and Istanbul. Korais was accompanied as his _paragios_ or apprentice by Stamatis Petrou. Between 1772 and 1774 Petrou sent a series of letters to their common employer Thomas. These have recently been re-edited by Philippos Iliou[47] and they throw a fascinating light on the process of acculturation by which Korais, on his first contact with the West, shed the traditional, Orthodox, neo-Byzantine mores and attitudes of the Smyrniot Greek community into which he had been born, and acquired the ethos of an educated European bourgeois. A bitter personal antipathy soon developed between Korais and Petrou and, although they shared the same house, they did not talk to each other. Given their mutual loathing one should perhaps treat Petrou's remarks about Korais with a certain amount of caution but there is no reason to question the basic accuracy of Petrou's observations.

For all Korais' later reputation as an anti-clerical, it was he, paradoxically, who, soon after their arrival in Europe, insisted on the strict observance of the fast of the Dormition of the Virgin, while it was Petrou, exhausted by a day atop a post coach, who suggested that they eat meat to avoid falling ill. However, within a short time of their arrival in Amsterdam, it was Petrou, a 'sinner but not an unbeliever' and deeply attached to his Orthodox heritage, who recorded with scandalized relish´ Korais' rapid assimilation of Frankish ways. Korais took to returning home long after midnight. His attendance at the Greek church in Amsterdam soon became perfunctory and he stopped taking communion. Although initially he had been reluctant to remove his Turkish _kalpak_ or to trim his moustache, he took to dressing _alafranga_. He developed a foppish concern with his appearance, changing his clothes two or three times a day and girding himself with a sword. Like any Dutch _juffrouw_, he was seldom parted from his looking glass, hairpins and scissors, while visits to bourse or church were preceded by hour long sessions with his wigmakers.

He took to going to the opera, to reading 'diabolical French books, becoming like the prodigal son', to consorting alone with women all hours of the day and night. In short he was given over to 'pleasures and vanities'. For one appalling moment Petrou was convinced that Korais, to secure the hand of a Dutch girl, was about to apostasize and become a Calvinist. Petrou scarcely troubled to mask his relief when she died before Korais could commit the ultimate betrayal of his Orthodox inheritance.

100

Korais' sins were compounded in Petrou's view by his failure to acquire any of the commercial skills of his Dutch confrères. Petrou soon concluded that Korais was not cut out for 'negotsio or commerce, which he persisted in regarding as a hobby rather than an overriding passion.[48] He was essentially a çelebi, a gentleman much more interested in his lessons in Dutch, Hebrew, Spanish and geometry than in the rough and tumble of the market. Korais' brief and disastrous flirtation with the world of commerce lasted only six years, and after an unsuccessful attempt to set up a manufactory of woollen stuffs, he abandoned the mercantile life for good. Although it is sometimes said that Korais went bankrupt in Amsterdam this was not the case.[49]

In 1778 he briefly went back to Smyrna and then returned to France to study medicine at the University of Montpellier, never to return again to his patrida. He never practised medicine, however, and, following unsuccessful efforts by one of his French mentors to secure a post for him in Oxford, he settled in Paris in 1788. Here he remained until his death in 1833 and poured out an unending stream of exhortations to his fellow countrymen to strive for education, as a result of which he imagined that independence would be vouchsafed to the Greeks as some kind of automatic reward for virtue. Other defectors, such as he, from the countinghouses and in particular the children of merchants and those whose education in the West had been subsidised by merchants were to form the backbone of the nascent but influential intelligentsia that was to articulate the national aspirations of the Greeks.

Although the merchants provided the material base for the development of an articulated Greek nationalism their public image was, for the most part, distinctly unflattering. They are frequently depicted in contemporary literature as grasping profiteers, unconcerned with the plight of Greece. Availing themselves of the institutionalised bribery that was an endemic feature of Ottoman life, merchants engaged in the contraband export of grain from the Ottoman Empire, although such exports were in theory forbidden. Such contraband trade continued even in times of famine, and, in times of good or bad harvests, the merchants ruthlessly manipulated the market. At one such time of famine in 1774-5 an anonymous cleric, after describing how the Lord had punished Rumeli for her sins by inflicting on her a devastating famine, bitterly denounced the Hydriotes and Psariotes for exploiting the misery of both Greeks and Turks:

> 'Wheat was brought down the coast by Hydriote
> Caïques, and those who heard rushed there to buy.
> But without mercy the Hydriotes were haggling
> And would not keep their word . . .
> The Hydriotes and Psariotes working in collusion,
> Half of their caïques kept hidden at Mytika,
> Refused to sell their wheat,
> And without mercy wished to profit much,
> Amassing Rumeli's soldi and florins,
> The poor's blood they sucked like wild beasts . . .
> Both Turks and Greeks Allah beseeched
> This fortune to reverse . . .'[50]

Moreover, the merchants were attacked not only for their
exploitation of human misery but for their indifference to the
cause of Greek freedom. In the satirical poem, the
Rossanglogallos, which circulated during the first decade of the
nineteenth century, the merchant is quoted as saying that:

> 'I have given no thought to Greece
> For all that it suffers a tyrannical yoke; $/\bar{.}$. $\underline{.}7$
> I weep because my nation is under the yoke.
> But for freedom I don't give a penny. $/\bar{.}$. $\underline{.}7$
> We, the greatest part of the merchants,
> Always want money, even if we have the yoke.
> Wealth delights and consoles us,
> And the burdens of the Turks never bother us.'[51]

The anonymous author of that masterpiece of nationalist polemic,
the Elliniki Nomarkhia, published in 1806, developed the theme of
the political indifference of the merchants on a more sophisticated level. He held the two principal reasons why Greece
remained 'bound by the chains of tyranny' to be 'the ignorant
priesthood and the absence of the best fellow citizens', by whom
he meant the mercantile bourgeoisie of the diaspora.

He held this latter group to be the most dynamic in Greek
society, and the only one capable of both leading the struggle
against the Turks and of standing up to the Greeks' own domestic
oligarchy of clerics and primates. While he conceded that up
until the time he was writing emigration was both justified and
even beneficial to the national interest, the merchants of the
diaspora should now return home and place their talents and
wealth at the service of the motherland. But this they showed no
signs of doing. Instead they manifested a crass indifference to
the plight of their fellow countrymen. Obsessed with making money

and aping foreign ways they were supremely indifferent to Greece and her heritage. So ignorant were they that they considered Plutarch and Xenophon to be Americans. Instead of devoting so much as an hour to the study of their country's history they delighted in watching depraved spectacles at the theatre. They estranged themselves for ever from Greece by taking foreign wives. The conversion of these merchants began with cotton and ended with beans, that of their young began with the theatre and ended with women. The anonymous author was particularly scornful of those who studied, at the expense of their unfortunate parents, at the academies of Italy and France. Instead of studying politics, law and military tactics, 'the necessary sciences for our nation', they frittered away their time in the study of medicine or the reading of mythological poems 'of which there are more volumes in France and Italy than pumpkins in the Peloponnese'.[52]

Examples of this kind of polemic, indicating that the contemporary image of the merchant in the Greek world was unflattering, abound. Most Greeks in the early nineteenth century clearly did not expect much in the way of patriotism from the merchants. But nonetheless it is a commonplace of the text books that it was the members of this mercantile bourgeoisie who took the lead in preparing the Greeks for armed insurrection against their Ottoman rulers. In support of such a contention it has frequently been noted that merchants preponderated in the membership of the Philiki Etairia, the secret revolutionary society founded in Odessa in 1814 which laid the organisational groundwork for the revolt.[53] The precise figure is 53.7 per cent of the known membership of the Philiki Etairia; the next largest group, that of the 'professionals', i.e. teachers, doctors, clerks etc., comprised a mere 13.1 per cent.

The statement that over half of the known membership of the Philiki Etairia were merchants is certainly formally correct. The key question, however, is what kind of merchants made up the bulk of the Society's membership. Thanks to some important studies by George Frangos[54] we now have a much more precise knowledge of the composition of the membership of the Philiki Etairia and Frangos has stressed how careful we must be in using the term merchant or mercantile bourgeoisie in the context of the early nineteenth century Greek world. Historians such as Kordatos and Stavrianos have failed to make clear the social gradations within the merchant class as a whole. Included within the general term merchant were established, extremely prosperous

merchants of the diaspora, such as Pringos or the Zosimas
brothers, and the petty merchants, merchants' clerks or bankrupts
who founded the Philiki Etairia and who provided the bulk of its
membership and financial support. The mercantile membership of
the Philiki Etairia consisted very largely of these petty
merchants, frequently little more than pedlars, men who had
failed to make the grade in the harshly competitive world of the
Greek commercial diaspora. Characteristically the Society's
three founder members, Emmanuel Xanthos, Nikolaos Skouphas and
Athanasios Tsakaloff, were, respectively, a clerk in a merchant
company that had ceased to trade, an artisan and a clerk in a
shipping company. The established, prosperous merchants of the
main Greek communities of the diaspora for the most part wanted
nothing to do with the society. Wealthy merchants such as
Panayiotis Sekeris, who donated very generously to the Society's
coffers, were very much the exception. For the most part firmly
wedded to an unquestioned acceptance of the Ottoman status quo,
the established merchants wanted no part of the seemingly madcap
schemes of the Philiki Etairia. It is findings of this kind that
should oblige historians in future to be more precise about the
use of the term 'bourgeoisie' in the Greek context and to be more
circumspect in talking of the mercantile bourgeoisie as
constituting a 'progressive' force in the context of Greek
society in the decades before 1821.

1. Demetrios J. Farsolas, 'Alexander Pushkin: his attitude toward the Greek Revolution 1821-1829', Balkan Studies xii (1971) 64, 74.

2. Journal of Modern History xxix (1957) 342.

3. Balkan Federation. A History of the Movement toward Balkan Unity in Modern Times (reprinted Hamden, Conn. 1964) 33.

4. 'The influence of the West on the Balkans' in C. and B. Jelavich, eds. The Balkans in Transition. Essays on the Development of Balkan Life and Politics since the Eighteenth Century (Berkeley/Los Angeles 1963) 194.

5. Istoria tou Neou Ellinismou, iv, Tourkokratia 1669-1812 (Thessaloniki 1973) 4.

6. 'Les villes grecques dans le cadre de l'Empire Ottoman (xvie-xixe siècles) in Istanbul à la jonction des cultures balkaniques, méditerranéenes, slaves et orientales, au xvie-xixe siècles (Bucharest 1977) 79.

7. Eisagogi stin Istoria tis Neoellinikis Koinonias (1700-1821) (Athens 1976) 190-1. Cf. also Carole Rogel, 'The Wandering Monk and the Balkan National Awakening' in William W. Haddad and William Ochsenwald, eds., Nationalism in a Non-National State. The Dissolution of the Ottoman Empire (Columbus, Ohio 1977) 81.

8. Nicos P. Mouzelis, Modern Greece. Facets of Underdevelopment (London 1978) 94-5. See also 12-13.

9. By N. Andriotis, 'To khroniko tou Amsterdam', Nea Estia x (1931) 846-853, 914-920. Vangelis Skouvaras has written a useful study of Pringos, Ioannis Pringos (1725-1789). I Elliniki Paroikia tou Amsterdam. I Skholi kai i Vivliothiki Zagoras (Athens 1964). See also S. Antoniadis, 'Het dagboek van een te Amsterdam gevestigde Griekse koopman', Tijdschrift voor Geschiedenis, lxix (1956) 57-66.

10. Stavrianos, 'Antecedents', 343; Andriotis, op.cit. 851. A fuller English version of this and other passages from the Pringos diary may be found in Richard Clogg, The Movement for Greek Independence 1770-1821. A Collection of Documents (London 1976) 42-45.

11. (reprinted Athens 1974) 28.

12. F.W. Hasluck, Christianity and Islam under the Sultans (Oxford 1929) ii 471-2. It is interesting to note that a traveller among the Orthodox peasantry of southern Syria during the first decade of the nineteenth century found a belief that the hour approached when a 'yellow king' (al-malik-al-asfar) would deliver them and Syria from the Muslim yoke, J.L. Burckhardt, Travels in Syria and the Holy Land (London 1822) 40, cited in Robert M. Haddad, Syrian Christians in Muslim Society. An Interpretation (Princeton 1970) 84. On millenarian ideas among the South Slavs see Traian Stoianovich, 'Les structures millénaristes sud-slaves aux xviie et xviiie siècles', Actes du Premier Congrès International des Etudes Balkaniques et Sud-Est européennes

iii (Sofia 1969) 809-819.

13. On the prophecies of Leo the Wise, see C.A. Mango, 'The Legend of Leo the Wise', _Zbornik Radova Vizantoloshkog Instituta_ vi (1960) 59-93, see also his 'Byzantinism and Romantic Hellenism', _Journal of the Warburg and Courtauld Institutes_ xviii (1965) 34-36. A fascinating account of the various prophecies, and in particular that of the 'Emperor turned into marble', is contained in N.A. Veis, 'Peri tou istorimenou khrismologiou tis Kratikis Vivliothikis tou Verolinou (Codex Graecus fol. 62-297) kai tou thrylou tou "marmaromenou vasilia"', _Byzantinisch-Neugriechische Jahrbücher_ xiii (1937) 203-44 1st.

14. Andriotis, op.cit., 914.

15. On Cercel, see Kh. S. Tsogas, 'Nikolaos Zarzoulis o ek Metsovou', in I.E. Anastasiou and A.G. Geromikhalou, eds., _Mnimi 1821_ (Thessaloniki 1971) 129-42 and Ariadna Camariano-Cioran, _Les Academies Princières de Bucharest et de Jassy et leurs professeurs_ (Thessaloniki 1974) 599-604.

16. See for instance, Kaisarios Dapontes, _Istorikos katalogos andron episimon (1700-1784)_ in K.N. Sathas, ed. _Mesaioniki Vivliothiki_ iii (Venice 1872) 119-20 and Athanasios Komninos Ypsilantis, _Ekklisiastikon kai politikon ton eis dodeka vivlion . . itoi ta Meta tin Alosin (1453-1780)_, ed. G. Aphthonidis, (Constantinople 1870) 534.

17. A. Politis, 'I prosgraphomeni ston Riga proti ekdosi tou Agathangelou. To mono gnosto antitypo', _O Eranistis_ vii (1969) 173-92.

18. Ed. A Koumarianou (Athens 1970) 48,65,99,109. Philippidis and Konstantas noted that among the inhabitants of Zagora there were almost none to be found who had not sojourned, some more, others less, in foreign parts.

19. _To taxidion tou neou Anakharsidos eis tin Ellada_ iv (Vienna 1797) 133, cited in N.I. Pantazopoulos, _Rigas Velestinlis. I politiki ideologia tou Ellinismou. Proangelos tis Epanastaseos_ (Thessaloniki 1964) 10.

20. Philippos K. Phalbos, _Markou Antoniou Katsaiti, Dyo Taxidia sti Smyrni 1740 kai 1742_ (Athens 1972) 79.

21. See the dispatch of Francis Werry, Consul of the Levant Company's factory in Smyrna of 2 April 1797, Public Record Office State Papers 105/126 and the _Ephimeris_ of 17 April 1797 quoted in M.I. Gedeon, 'Eikosin eton ethniki istoria katopin thyellis (1791-1811)', _Theologia_ v (1927), reprinted in Alkis Angelou and Philippos Iliou, eds., _I pnevmatiki kinisis tou Genous kata ton 18 kai 19 aiona_ (Athens 1976) 66-7. On the Izmir rebellion see, for instance, N.K.Kh. Kostis, 'Smyrnaika Analekta. To en Smyrni rebellion tou 1797 kata neas anekdotous pigas', _Deltion tis Istorikis kai Ethnologikis Etaireias_, vi (1901-5) 358-72 and N.A. Veis, 'To "Megalo Rebelio" tis Smyrnis (Martios tou 1797) kata neotatas erevnas', _Mikrasiatika Khronika_ iv (1948) 411-22. For a selection of some of the more important British documents on the rebellion,

which together constitute the single most important source for this remarkable event, see my 'The Smyrna "Rebellion" of 1797. Some Documents from the British Archives', in a forthcoming issue of <u>Mnimosyni</u>. Some fifteen hundred Greeks had also been murdered in 1770 within the space of some four hours when the news of the destruction of the Ottoman fleet at Çeşme reached Izmir, C.C. de Peysonnel, <u>An Appendix to the Memoirs of Baron de Tott; being a letter from Mr. de Peysonnel, late Consul General at Smyrna.</u> . (London 1786) 96-6.

22. <u>A view of the Commerce of Greece formed after an annual average from 1787 to 1797</u>. ., (London 1800) 187. For an up to date account of Ambelakia, making use of an extensive corpus of Greek writing, see Spyros Asdrachas, 'Traditionalismes et ouvertures: le cas d'Ambelakia en Thessalie', Association Internationale d'Etudes du Sud-Est Européen, <u>Structure sociale et développement culturel des villes sud-est européennes et adriatiques aux xviie-xviiie siècles</u> (Bucharest 1975) 215-223. For an account of other attempts to set up small scale manufactories in the Greek lands see V. Kremmydas, 'Mia prospatheia gia tin idrysi sapounopoiias stin Koroni sto 18 aiona', <u>Messiniaka</u> (1968) 137-141 and <u>Oi sapounopoiies tis Kritis sto 18o aiona</u> (Athens 1974). Two important studies of Greek commerce within the Ottoman Empire are N. Svoronos, <u>Le Commerce de Salonique au XVIIIe siècle</u> (Paris 1956) and V. Kremmydas, <u>To emporio tis Peloponnisou sto 18 aiona (1715-1792)</u> (Thessaloniki 1972).

23. <u>Bruchstücke zur nähern kenntniss des heutigen Griechenlands</u>. . (Berlin 1805) 169.

24. op.cit., 193-4.

25. Traian Stoianovich, 'The Conquering Balkan Orthodox Merchant', <u>Journal of Economic History</u>, xx (1960) 289. One such list of Ottoman merchants in Vienna has been edited, without this necessary qualification, by P.K. Enepekides, <u>Griechische Handelsgesellschaften und Kaufleute in Wien auf dem Jahre 1766</u> (Thessaloniki 1959). This important distinction was, however, made by a contemporary Viennese writer, Johann Pezzl who noted in the 1780's that of the Greeks in the city, which he estimated at some 600 strong, 'Es sind theils wirkliche Griechen, theils Raizen oder Serbier', <u>Skizze von Wien</u>, iii (Vienna/ Leipzig 1787) 395-6.

26. <u>Untersuchungen über die Roumanier oder sogenannten Wlachen</u> . . <u>Exetaseis peri ton Romaion i ton onomazomenon Vlakhon</u> . . (Pest 1808) 146.

27. See, for instance, Odon Füves, <u>Oi Ellines tis Oungarias</u>, (Thessaloniki 1965); Spyridon Lambros, 'Selides ek tis istorias tou en ti Oungaria kai Austria Makedonikou Ellinismou', <u>Neos Ellinomnimon</u> viii (1911) 257-300, xviii (1923) 376-386, x (1925) 225-32, and S. Loukatos, 'O politikos vios ton Ellinon tis Viennis kata tin Tourkokratian kai ta aftokratorika pros aftous pronomia', <u>Deltion tis Istorikis kai Ethnologikis Etaireias</u> xv (1961) 287-350.

On the important Greek merchant companies of Sibiu (Hermannstadt) and Braşov (Kronstadt) in Habsburg Transylvania see N. Camariano, 'L'organisation et l'activité culturelle de la compagnie des marchands grecs de Sibiu', Balcania vi (1943) 201-41 and Cornelia Papacostea-Danielopolu, 'L'organisation de la Compagnie Grecque de Braşov (1777-1850)', Balkan Studies xiv (1973) 313-323.

28. A. Horvath, I zoi kai ta erga tou Georgiou Zavira (Budapest 1937) 5-6.

29. Goethes Werke ix (Hamburg 1955). Aus meinem Leben Dichtung und Wahrheit, 244-5.

30. On the development of the Greek mercantile marine during this period see the excellent study by G.B. Leon, 'The Greek Merchant Marine (1453-1850)', in S.A. Papadopoulos, ed., The Greek Merchant Marine, (Athens 1972) 32-43.

31. Spyros Asdrachas, 'Oikonomia' in Istoria tou Ellinikou Ethnous xi (Athens 1975) 182.

32. For the fascinating story of this effort see E.P. Panagopoulos, New Smyrna: an eighteenth century Greek Odyssey (Gainesville, Florida 1966).

33. On this community see Anon., Historical and Ecclesiastical Sketches of Bengal . . (Calcutta 1827) 221-4, I. Tantalidis, Indiki Allilographia . . (Constantinople 1852) and S. Loukatos, Ellines kai Philellines ton Indion kata tin Ellinikin Epapanastasin (Athens 1965).

34. This has been translated into English by E. Kedourie in Nationalism in Asia and Africa (London 1971) 153-88.

35. Korais, op.cit., 17-19.

36. Ithiki Philosophia (Venice 1761) preface.

37. Travels in Albania and other provinces of Turkey in 1809 and 1810 (London 1855) ii, 483.

38. Logios o Ermis, 15 March 1811, 91, quoted in Skouvaras, Ioannis Pringos, 14.

39. Grammatiki Germaniki akrivestati ek diaphoron palaion te kai neoteron syngrapheon epimelos syllekhtheisa, kai eis tin koinoteran ton nun Ellinon Dialekton dia koinin opheleian evmethodous ektetheisa . . (Vienna 1785) 471-8. In an letter writing manual of the same period the author declared that 'material ignorance is the complete destruction of commerce, and a very great damage to the merchant is when he has in his work such ignorant collaborators', Epistolarion i Epistolikos Kharaktir. Di' ou didaskontai oi philomatheis, pos na graphoun me kalin taxin Epistolas pros opoiondipote prosopon, me tous titlous exasto, kai ton kanonikon tropon, os tin simeron synithizetai i (Venice 1773) 198.

40. Missionary Herald, 1821, 103.

41. A very rare copy, which once belonged to the eccentric English philhellene, Lord Guildford, of the specimen publication produced by Tombras

108

in Paris survives in the British Library, Epistoli pros ton Khatzi Emmanouil
Salteli syntetheisa men para G. Kozaki Typaldou . . typotheisa de para
Konstantinou Tombra Kydonieos (Epitomi ek tou ekphonithentos eis to Dimotikon
Voulefteirion logou tou K.Hume peri ton evktaion apotelesmaton tis anatrophis
eis tas katoteras klaseis tis koinonias (Paris 1818).

42. Letter of Petros Ipitis, dated Odessa 28 August 1818, to Bartholomaeus
Kopitar, Ermis o Logios (1818) 583-8.

43. W.H. Heffening, 'Über Buch- und Druckwesen in der alten Türkei. Ein
Bericht des Preussischen Gesandten zu Konstantinopel aus dem Jahre 1819',
Zeitschrift der Deutschen Morgenländischen Gesellschaft ns XXV (1950) 597.

44. op.cit., 401.

45. Despatch by Hortolan to the French Ambassador in Istanbul of 15 October
1773, in E. de Hurmuzaki, Documente privitóre la Istoria Românilor, suppl. I,
vol.ii, 1781-1814, Documente culese din Archivele Ministeriului Afacerilor
Străine din Paris, ed. A.I. Odobescu, (Bucharest 1885) 94 quoted in A. Elian,
'Conspiratori greci in Principate și un favorit mavroghenesc: Turnavitu',
Revista Istorică xxi (1935) 362.

46. Mémoire, trans. Kedourie, 182-3, 162.

47. Stamatis Petrou Grammata apo to Amsterdam (Athens 1976). Useful
information on Korais' experiences in Amsterdam is also contained in B.J. Slot,
Skheseis metaxy Ollandias kai Ellados apo ton 17 aiona mekhri ton Kapodistria
(Athens 1977) 17-22.

48. Korais did, however, retain a theoretical interest in economics. He was
familiar with the French translations of Adam Smith's The Wealth of Nations
and Malthus' An Essay on the Principle of Population and despatched copies of
The Wealth of Nations to his Greek friends. Ph. Iliou in his introduction to
Stamatis Petrou Grammata, op.cit., 60.

49. Slot, op.cit., 20.

50. Spyridon Lambros, 'Vrakheia Khronika', Mnimeia tis Ellinikis Istorias i
(Athens 1933) 92-3, quoted in Leon, 'The Greek Merchant Marine', 30.

51. K. Th. Dimaras, 'To keimeno tou Rossanglogallou', Ellinika, xvii (1962)
194-5.

52. Anonymou ton Ellinos, Elliniki Nomarkhia itoi logos peri eleftherias
('Italy' 1806) reprinted, ed. G. Valetas (Athens 1957) 150ff.

53. Cf., for instance, C.W. Crawley 'John Capodistrias and the Greeks before
1821' Cambridge Historical Journal xiii (1957) 179. More recently Dennis
Skiotis in his admirable 'Mountain warriors and the Greek Revolution' has
described the Philiki Etairia as 'an initially elitist secret patriotic
society made up of middle-class Greeks, mostly merchants and intellectuals',
in V.J. Parry and M.E. Yapp eds. War, Technology and Society in the Middle
East (London 1975) 308. Cf. Mouzelis, op.cit. 161.

54. The Philike Etaireia, 1814-1821: A Social and Historical Analysis
(unpublished doctoral dissertation, Columbia University, 1971); 'The
Philiki Etairia: A Premature National Coalition' in Richard Clogg ed. The
Struggle for Greek Independence (London 1973) 87-103.

6

A GREEK MERCANTILE PAROIKIA:
ODESSA 1774–1829

VIRON KARIDIS

The commanding importance of the Greek communities in
Southern Russia in the movement for Greek independence has always
been recognised by historians, who have amassed a rich literature
on the Philiki Etairia, a revolutionary society established in
1814 by three Greek immigrants in Odessa.[1] However the story of
emigration, settlement and adaptation has not received the
attention it merits.[2] This is partly due to the inaccessibility
to Greek scholars of primary sources relating to this subject in
the Soviet Archives, a problem which should improve with the
recent establishment of cultural relations between Greece and the
USSR. In the meantime however, I should like to undertake the
task and say something about the Greek immigrants who settled in
Odessa between 1794 and 1829, both as individuals and as members
of an immigrant community. I firmly believe that there is much
that can be dealt with and that one can made progress not merely
with spade-work but with actual construction.[3]

−I−

In September 1789, during Catherine II's second Turkish war
(1787–92), Russian forces led by General de Ribas captured the
small Tatar village of Hacıbey located on a large bay of the
Black Sea between the mouths of the Bug and the Dniester rivers.[4]
Immediately after the war the harbour attracted the attention of
Prince Platon Zubov, Governor-General of Novorossiia (New Russia)
and Catherine's favourite at the time, as a most suitable
situation for a naval, as well as commercial, centre in the
south west corner of Russia.[5] On 27 May 1794, de Ribas was
formally commissioned together with the Dutch engineer de
Voland to construct a city where a small Turkish fortress
(Yeni Dunai) and a few miserable huts had once stood.[6] A
year later, in 1795, in the classical spirit then fashionable,
the new settlement was called Odessa, after an ancient city
which had supposedly stood there and whose name could be
conveniently confused with that of Ulysses of the Odyssey.[7]

111

The principal consideration which induced the Russian government to select Hacıbey as a commercial depot appears to have been its healthy conditions and its situation near the open sea, advantages which could never be enjoyed by the delta city of Kherson, which would otherwise have answered all the purposes of an important maritime station.[8] Furthermore, in contrast to Kherson and Taganrog, it was much easier to reach by sea, was ice-free nearly all seasons of the year and could accommodate large ships from the Mediterranean.[9] It was also easier to reach by land from Ukraine, and by its western position could considerably facilitate the export of grain from the recently incorporated Polish provinces.[10] Its main disadvantages were that being placed in a barren steppe, it had neither wood nor water, the former brought from Kherson and the latter from the nearby springs; it had no inland communications by water; and was not a very safe port in heavy weather.[11]

In 1794 Odessa, by all accounts, was a thinly-inhabited town consisting of a military and a residential quarter. While 498 of the 560 lots were occupied in the former area, only 415 of the 720 were occupied in the latter.[12] Realizing that more decisive measures needed to be taken to attract population to the area, Catherine, on 19 April 1795, confirmed proposals by de Ribas concerning foreign settlers to be attracted from the Aegean Archipelago and elsewhere to Odessa.[13] Immediately, the relevant ukaz (decree) was translated into modern Greek and sent to the Russian ambassador at Istanbul, Count Victor Kochubey, with the purpose of disseminating it amongst the Greeks of the Ottoman Empire.[14] It comprised two parts: one provided for permanent quarters on the outskirts of Odessa for those Greeks and Albanians who had taken refuge in South Russia following their service with the Russian forces during the recent war with Turkey;[15] the other related to the invitation from the Aegean Islands and other foreign areas of persons who might wish to settle in the town itself.[16]

For the military colonists, who were to form a 300-man Greek Division the decree authorized the setting aside of 15,000 desiatinas (1 desiatina = 2.7 acres) of suitable land in the neighbourhood of Odessa. Staff officers were given 120 desiatinas, officers 50, and lower ranks received 25 desiatinas each. It allotted as well 10,000 roubles for the erection of a small church. In addition to these funds, which were not subject to repayment, a loan of 20,000 roubles was extended, to

112

be repaid after ten years in three annual payments, for use in developing economic enterprises.[17]

The civilian colonists were free from all taxes and military service for ten years, while stone houses were to be built for them at a cost of 22,000 roubles. Poor immigrants were granted 100-150 roubles, repayable after ten years in three equal annual parts. Freedom of worship went without saying and a church was to be constructed free of charge at a cost of up to 2,000 roubles. To encourage trade, the government allowed settlers to bring in goods for sale duty free to the value of 300 roubles. Finally, a special office was established, that of the Popechitel (Guardian) whose duties consisted of protecting the newcomers from any oppression and to see that peace would reign in their settlement.[18] Colonel A. Kesoglou, being a Greek immigrant himself, was appointed to this post 'as a sign of respect and trust in the Greek nation.'[19]

A census conducted on 21 July 1795 by de Ribas showed that there were 2,349 persons living in Odessa at the time, not including members of the nobility, civil servants, military personnel and the Greek Division. Greeks of various professions amounted to 223 persons (129 males - 94 females) excluding those who were registered with the merchant guilds of the town.[20] By November of the same year, Zubov could report that the Greek Division had been formed to full strength and that 62 settler families, 5 second guild merchants, 22 third guild merchants and 14 people of various status had already arrived in Odessa. According to the same report, 32 of the proposed houses had been constructed and were given to the needy immigrants.[21]

On 14 November 1795, the Gorodovoi Magistrat (Town Council) was founded in accordance with the 1785 Charter of the Cities.[22] In this newly-created institution a considerable number of Greeks, elected by the merchants and artisans, were responsible for the collection of taxes, the adjudication of local disputes and the administration of the funds for the Greek civilian settlement in the town.[23] This magistracy enjoyed a short lifetime however; by an ukaz of 20 May 1797, Emperor Paul I ordered the establishment of a Russkii Magistrat for the affairs of the Russian population and of a so-called Inostrannyi Magistrat for the benefit of the foreign settlers.[24] This sort of dual administration very soon proved of no use and served only to set the native and foreign elements against one another.[25] Therefore, on 26 January 1798, the Russian body was dissolved and all the inhabitants of Odessa regardless of their country of origin were subordinated to the Magistrat dlia Inostrantsev, in which the Greek population predominated.[26]

During Paul's reign the Greek civilian project in the town fared rather well, but this was not the case with the military settlement. On 18 April 1797, N. M. Berdiaev, the newly-appointed Governor-General of New Russia, presented to the Emperor an economic survey of Odessa. In it he stated that out of the 238 men then serving the Greek Division, only 83 had actually actively participated in the Russo-Turkish War of 1787-92. He pointed out also, that a great number of its men were not Greeks but Ukrainians and Poles who were not entitled to the privileges granted to them.[27] On receiving this report, Paul ordered, by his decree of 14 July 1797, the disbanding of the Greek Division.[28] In fact, after the dismantlement of this military unit, its men were left without any means of support. Some of them had no other choice but to go abroad; others departed to various towns in South Russia; and many remained in Odessa starting up different commercial enterprises.

At that time the male population of Odessa was 3,455 including 269 Greeks, Albanians and Moldavians, 33 Bulgarians and 404 Black Sea Cossacks. There were also 677 merchants, 434 small traders and craftsmen, 78 farmers and 1,223 people of various professions.[29] In the years 1797-1800 there were numerous attempts by the mercantile community, which included many second and third guild Greek merchants,[30] to obtain from the central government certain commercial privileges. In November 1797, A. Kesoglou was sent in St. Petersburg and requested, at one and the same time, a grant of armorial bearings, for immunities such as Riga and Reval enjoyed, and for the freedom of the port. Of all these favours, he managed to obtain only the Gerb Goroda Odessy - the city emblem of Odessa.[31] Soon after the magistrates, like true traders, even thought of seducing the Tsar with a present, which was apparently rare at that time. In February 1800, Roxamatis, a Greek officer of the dissolved Greek Division, was dispatched to the capital carrying with him, as a present of homage towards the court, 3,000 of the finest oranges that could be found. Paul graciously expressed his acknowledgements, upon which importunate demands for monopoly and freedom were again immediately urged. Unfortunately, Odessa received these petitions back, torn

114

up, with no answer other than that such a request was absurd.[32]

Nevertheless, the day at last came when the persevering
efforts of the Greek merchants were crowned with success.
Prince G. P. Gagarin, President of the College of Trade
(Ministry of Commerce), as the Minister of that Department, was
called and interceded with the Emperor in favour of his subjects
of New Russia.[33] Thus, towards the end of his reign, on 1
March 1800, Paul bestowed the most signal privileges upon
Odessa. He conceded to its inhabitants the farming of spirits
and approved a loan of 250,000 roubles without interest to be
repaid in 14 years stating that the construction of the port
and the necessary establishments (i.e. a lazaretto) to be
completed in four years. He also made a gift of all those
building materials that had been collected for port construction and subsequently placed in storage in Odessa. Finally,
the local population was exempted from all taxes and from
providing soldiers for another 14 years, an extension of the
special privileges that Catherine had granted to the town in
1795.[34]

Following the accession of Alexander I to the throne in
March 1801, the Greek population of New Russia was increased by
new settlers mainly derived from Rumelia (Southern Bulgaria).
In September, 148 Greeks and Bulgarians from the village of
Küçük Busliki in the district of Adrianople (Edirne), who
suffered most from the Turkish brigand Kara-Feci, sought refuge
in Odessa. According to their own accounts several thousands
of their fellow countrymen wanted to emigrate to Southern
Russia.[35] The refugees met with a friendly welcome from the
Russian government and on 5 January 1802 special privileges
were issued according to their situation.[36] Later in the year
the immigrants dispersed from Odessa to different towns,
settled mainly in the region of Kerch, and were very soon joined
by newcomers from Rumelia.[37]

At that time the Odessa Greek Division was also due to be
reformed. During the first decade of the nineteenth century,
the Russian policy on the Greek question became more active as
a result of the Russo-French competition for influence in the
Balkans.[38] Alexander, in his endeavour to give a new proof of
his patronage and care for co-religionist Greeks, ordered by
his decree of 22 October 1803, addressed to the Ministry of War,
the restoration of the Greek Division.[39] The division began to
take shape in January 1804, largely on the initiative of

Konstantinos Ypsilantis, hospodar of Moldavia, who wanted to take advantage of the anti-Turkish revolutionary movement in Serbia.[40] At the beginning it was planned that the division should consist of three infantry companies with 46 officers (commissioned and non-commissioned), 423 privates, 9 non-combatants and 6 drummers. The men who joined its ranks were mainly Greeks brought from the Principalities, mainland Greece and the Aegean Islands. In 1807, a year after the outbreak of a new Russo-Turkish conflict, the Odessa Greek Division was sent to the front in the Danube under the command of Major Paterakis and participated in the Russian military operations against the Turks.[41]

By the mid 1810s the population of Odessa numbered, according to some accounts, about 35,000 inhabitants.[42] In view of the absence of exact statistical data it is difficult to say how many were Greek. We may assume, however, that the proportion of Ionian Greeks was quite considerable. In December 1814, Henry Yeames complained to Lord Castlereagh that:

> Applications are frequently made to me for passports, by His Majesty's Hanoverian subjects, as also, by the natives of the Ionian islands, trading here: I intreat Your Lordship to instruct me whether I be authorized to grant them.[43]

According to the Foreign Office's reply of February 1815:

> nor is there any /ōbjection7 to your granting passports to such of his Majesty's Hanoverian Subjects and others who may apply to you for them provided that by so doing, you shall not break the laws and regulations of the country where you reside.[44]

In May 1815, Yeames, presumably having not yet received the Foreign Office reply of February, wrote to Lord Castlereagh:

> I now take the liberty again, of intreating, your lord-ship, to be instructed, whether I be authorised to grant passports to His Majesty's Hanoverian subjects, and particularly to the natives of the Ionian islands, numbers of whom are arriving here, either in mercantile concerns, or seeking employment on board the merchant ships. The Russian Government, absolutely requiring, from all strangers a passport, from the Consul, or other legal authority, of the country they are subject to: and the Ionian islands, being now, under the protection

116

of Great Britain, these people are referred to me. No
foreigner is permitted to reside here, without a document
of this kind, or unless he become a subject. The passports, I have hitherto been obliged to issue, were founded
on the authority of those granted by His Majesty's
Ambassador at Constantinople (serving only for the voyage
of this place) or other legal documents. [45]

About a year later, in March 1816, the British Consul in Odessa
repeated his request to the Foreign Office 'for instructions on
this subject'; [46] and by November 1819, he was definitely
authorized 'to protect Ionians'. [47]

From the above correspondence, it is obvious that regular
trade routes enabled Ionian Greeks to obtain jobs as skippers
and sailors on board the Russian ships navigating the
Mediterranean and the Black Sea. It is evident also that in a
great many cases they preferred to settle in South Russia. [48]
The need for Ionians to obtain British passports arose from a
change in the Russian colonization policy. We know that at that
time the Russian Government decided to make the legal grounds on
which overseas settlers could emigrate to Russia much clearer.
It is likely that the acceptance of Russian citizenship was the
most important criterion. [49] Therefore, the Greek immigrants
could no longer enjoy the benefits of dual nationality and
consequently they had to apply for naturalization. On the other
hand, at the end of the eighteenth and beginning of the nineteenth centuries, the Greek people witnessed a period of resurg-
ence and a growth of patriotic feelings which influenced the
Greeks in Russia as well. Presumably a great number of them
did not like the idea of applying for Russian citizenship
because, apart from the fact that the formalities connected with
naturalization were cumbersome, the idea of becoming Russian
citizens more or less meant for Greeks the renunciation of any
hope of returning to a homeland which was still under Ottoman
rule.

In spite of this policy, the revolt in the Principalities
(1821), the commencement of the Greek War of Independence (1821-
7) and the Russo-Turkish War (1828-9) brought further growth to
the Greek population of Odessa. The chief impetus behind the
move was Turkish persecution. Life was becoming increasingly
uncomfortable for Greeks, both in Moldavia and Wallachia and
more particularly in mainland Greece and the Aegean Islands,
where, as the local inhabitants joined the fight for Greek

independence, massacre was followed by counter-massacre. In
May 1821, James Yeames was reporting to Lord Castlereagh of the
Foreign Office:

> A greater degree of circumspection has succeeded the
> warmth with which the Grecian Cause was at first received
> in this part of the Country. The passages over the Pruth
> are now strictly guarded, and impediments are placed in
> the way of the Greek Agents, who at the commencement, were
> openly allowed to recruit adventurers, and procure arms
> and money.
>
> It has long been known, that the Pasha of Braila
> was receiving reinforcements from Varna and other places,
> but the Greeks indulged the idea, that the fear of giving
> offence would prevent actual hostilities on these front-
> iers; the accounts now received from the Danube have
> however dissolved the illusion, and Galatz stormed,
> utterly destroyed and its inhabitants put to the sword,
> offers a dreadful example of the vengeance intended to be
> drawn from the previous cruelties of the insurgent
> patriots . . .
>
> Numbers of fugitives continue to flock to this City,
> by sea from the Bosphorus, and by land from the neighbour-
> ing provinces; and among the latter are some discouraged
> and discontented followers of Prince Ypselandi. The
> family of the Hospodar of Moldavia has been here since
> some time.[50]

From the consular reports of the time, it is obvious that
during the 1820s another source of constant occupation for the
British representatives in the Black Sea ports had arisen from
the various affairs of the natives of the Ionian Islands who,
in great numbers, at the critical concurrence of events in the
Ottoman Empire, had taken refuge in South Russia, under circumstances of peculiar distress.[51] It seems that those who were
already settled in Odessa tried very often unsuccessfully to
get their families to join them through the aid of British
diplomats. In September 1822, for instance, Derrick Hamilton,
secretary of the British Embassy at Istanbul, wrote about such
activities to James Yeames:

> With respect to the petition of Stavro Papadopulo I have
> only to say, that his wife is a subject of the Porte, and
> as such not permitted to quit the country, it being a
> principle long established by this Government never to

118

allow a marriage with a foreigner to affect in any way its
rights over its Rayahs. Could I expect that any represent-
ations on my part be attended with any effect, I should
be happy to meet your wishes. I will endeavour to do so,
but fear there is no reason to anticipate success
particularly as the woman has been so long here and from
the late circumstances became an object of notoriety.[52]

For all this, by the end of the third decade of the nineteenth
century, and in spite of all the difficulties, a great many
Greeks, mainly from Rumelia and the Principalities, afraid of
the vengeance of the Turks after the signing of the Treaty of
Adrianople (September 1829) were prepared to follow the retreat
of the Russian army and give up all hopes of ever being able to
settle again in the south of the Balkans. Still it appears that
they disliked the idea of moving from the areas colonized by
their ancestors centuries ago and where their descendants had
engaged in a profitable trade.[53] Nevertheless, the chaotic
situation reigning in the Ottoman Empire at the time and the
absence of any effective system of control on the frontiers,
created very favourable conditions for this illegal and, in a
sense, forced emigration movement in Russia's new territories.

The Treaty of Adrianople can be considered a terminus post
quem for the Greek paroikia in Odessa. It ended a period of
nearly forty years during which Greeks, mostly coming from the
Ottoman dominions of Europe, had established themselves as
merchants, commercial agents and petty-dealers in the southwest
corner of Russia. Their immigration which was part of the last
Greek exodus that accompanied the upsurge of commercial activity
in the Balkans during the wars of the French Revolution was
related not merely to the successive Russo-Turkish wars but also
to the well-disposed policy of the Russian governments towards
the foreign colonists in South Russia. Undoubtedly a common
religion, freedom from military service and from taxation, great
demand for labour, the chance to acquire land and the momentum
to the growth of trade, together created possibilities of free
life, quick enrichment and development that attracted Greeks
who came to seek their fortunes in Odessa. In the remaining
part of this article we shall try to explore, as far as the
available sources permit, the Greek share in Odessa's economic
growth, and to see the factors which enabled the Greek community
to become an important trading centre in the Black Sea.

By the late eighteenth century the trade of Odessa, though in its infancy and labouring under many disadvantages, was apparently increasing. In 1795 Odessa's imports were valued at 43,065 roubles and its exports 24,824 roubles. By 1797 imports had grown to 79,091 roubles and exports to 124,492 roubles. In three years the worth of imports increased roughly two times and that of exports was growing five times. By now Odessa was the second most important port of the Black Sea after Taganrog.[54] The chief imports were wines, dried fruits, olive oil, cotton and silks from the Levant; exports in order of importance were grain, corn, caviar, butter, fur, tufts and cordage.[55] In 1802 with the renewal of peace in Europe (Treaty of Amiens) and the opening of the Black Sea to the subjects of Great Britain and France by the Ottoman Turks, Odessa became the centre of great speculations.[56] The commerce of that year was exceptional; 256 ships left port and above 300,000 chetverts (1 chetvert = 5.77 bushels) of grain were exported, wheat representing 95 per cent of the total.[57]

For all that, Odessa was still a poor town provided with every inconvenience for active and profitable trade. According to some accounts in the early nineteenth century although the population amounted to about 8,000 to 9,000 there were only a few badly built stone houses; no mercantile institutions; scarcely any efficient warehouses; a very incomplete quarantine; and a single mole which afforded vessels poor protection from the southeast winds.[58] The environs were uncultivated and deserted to such extent that commercial connexions suffered by this isolated situation. In addition the want of transport was no less felt, the lighters going to and from Kherson and the Crimea being few, ineffectively manned and poorly constructed. Under those conditions it was not strange that the exportation of many commodities abroad was problematic.[59]

The government, aware of Odessa's wants, eagerly consulted its interests. In March 1803, a French émigré, the Duc de Richelieu, a man of talents and ability, was named governor of Odessa.[60] A general confidence was immediately diffused by this appointment as the Duc set about developing the economy of the town. To the duties upon spirits were also added a tenth of the whole products of the customs house, and new funds to cover necessary expenses. A considerable amount of money was also put at the disposal of a town committee to lend to the inhabitants who wished to build houses at the rate of 6 per cent per year. A part of this fund was disposed of in the construction of a more commodious and more secure port and of an extensive new quarantine. Finally, the administration, in an attempt to fill and exploit uninhabited territory, established many colonies of Bulgarians and Germans, who deliberately abandoned their country, in the vicinity of the town.[61]

Besides these very encouraging measures, on 5 March 1804, Odessa was declared for a period of five years an entrepôt for the merchandise arriving by sea. Also the merchants were allowed to store their goods in the warehouses without paying any duties until their commodities were sold or reshipped in the interior of the Empire.[62] This was considered a very important privilege at the time because, as the import duties were considerable, the merchants would have been obliged to draw heavily on their capital, had they been compelled to defray them at once.[63] By another decree issued on the same date the government allowed transit, free of duty, to all foreign goods which were not prohibited in Odessa, or which arrived there from other towns of Russia. Such goods, if destined for Moldavia or Wallachia, were to pass through the custom houses of Mogilev and Dubossary; for Austria through those of Radzivilov; and for Prussia through those of Krinsky. Foreign goods sent through these four establishments to Odessa were allowed free transit there by sea.[64] These liberal and very enlightened arrangements vastly augmented the prosperity of the port and it is not surprising that the years 1804 and 1805 were ones of feverish commercial activity.[65]

In the following years however, the high level of trading was not maintained. In 1806 political circumstances, through the outbreak of the Russo-Turkish war (1806-12), became unfavourable to the navigation of neutral vessels and had a great effect upon the commercial relations of Southern Russian ports with Europe.[66] Nevertheless, the suspension of commerce between the two empires had produced reciprocal wants. Turkey, deprived of its grain and butter which was formerly furnished to it by Moldavia and Wallachia, now occupied by the Russian troops, was in total want of these commodities. In addition, the grain of the Morea (Peloponnese) could no longer reach Istanbul through the Dardanelles, while Egypt had scarcely any connexion with the capital and Anatolia was in a state of anarchy.[67] These causes had reduced Istanbul, Izmir and other cities of the

121

Levant to their only resource: the coast of Russia on the Euxine, and thus gave rise to the remarkably increased commerce of Odessa during the years 1811-13.[68]

The economy of Odessa was further stimulated by the Imperial decree of 16 April 1817, which provided for the free importation of all kind of merchandise without any restriction for a term of thirty years.[69] Two years later, on 4 July 1819, the conditions of the 1817 ukaz concerning the free port status were put into effect.[70] In addition to this favourable commercial policy, the following years saw the favourable circumstances which had worked so powerfully to increase exports in the early 1800s repeated almost exactly. After the end of the Napoleonic wars the agriculture of Western Europe was in a very depressed condition, and it was necessary to have recourse to South Russia for grain which other countries could not raise in sufficient quantity for their own subsistence.[71] Thus from 1815 onwards, Odessa became gradually a vast granary to which the European markets turned in time of scarcity. An annual average of 97,189 chetverts of wheat were exported from 1816-26, while the total shipping which was cleared from Odessa during the same period averaged 122,456 tons per year; grain tonnage representing roughly 93 per cent of the total.[72]

It should be noted, however, that after 1821 the unstable political situation in the Ottoman Empire contributed to a temporary diminution of Odessa's trading importance. In 1822 for example, a year after the commencement of the Greek War of Independence, less than 60,700 chetverts of wheat were exported compared to over 107,000 in 1819.[73] During the Russo-Turkish war of 1828-9 foreign trade was almost entirely suspended in Odessa. Only 43 commercial vessels totalling 11,542 tons arrived at the port during the first six months of 1828, while just 16 vessels totalling 3,323 tons left in the first half of 1829.[74] But after the signature of the peace, trade was quickly resumed. For the second half of 1829 official figures showed the arrival of 271 ships and the departure of 239, an astonishing increase, if we bear in mind that for the first half of the same year the corresponding numbers were 12 and 16.[75] With the Treaty of Adrianople, then, which guaranteed freedom of navigation for merchant vessels on the Black Sea not only for Russia but also for most of the mercantile nations, it seemed that Odessa had at last succeeded in securing its economic development and the ability to move ahead to the full realization of its great promise.

To what degree did the Greek merchants participate in the overseas trade of Odessa? At the moment, the non-availability of a substantial amount of sources (i.e. private commercial papers, custom registry books etc.) which exist presumably in the provincial archives of Odessa makes it difficult, if not impossible, to give a definite answer to that question. Fortunately however, we have the aid of many contemporary observations, and even of statistics, to help us with this problem. For the importance of the Greek contribution in the Russian Black Sea commerce was an issue which attracted the attention of both natives and non-Russians alike.[76]

The orientation of the Black Sea exports and imports might be revealed by reviewing the amount of Greek shipping which was cleared from Odessa during the period under consideration. In the first five years of the nineteenth century the ships which left its port bore the following flags:

TABLE 1

Ships which Sailed from Odessa in 1801-5

	1801	1802	1803	1804	1805
Russian	28	79	112	117	135
Ottoman	43	42	24	37	74
Austrian	24	128	274	170	255
French	4	5	27	13	12
English	–	–	5	17	32
TOTAL	99	254	442	354	508

Source: 'Tableau de Navires sortis d'Odessa depuis 1801' in PRO FO 359/1

The above table is perhaps more valuable in illustrating the scale and vigour of Odessa's commerce than in reliably informing as to the extent of Greek participation in it. Nevertheless, it is interesting to note that the flag under which a ship sailed or the country from which it originated could easily be shifted and it is not a good clue of the ship's nationality. 'Ottoman' meant primarily ships from the Aegean Archipelago, Alexandria, Thessaloniki, Izmir, Istanbul, the chief Levantine ports of the Ottoman Empire and many were really Greek and Italian ships. There is something especially suspicious in the large number of Russian ships, as Russia could not then or for many years after boast a large merchant marine. Undoubtedly many 'Russian' ships were Greek flying the Russian flag in order to facilitate their passage through the Straits, as the Ottomans were treaty-bound to admit all Russian ships.[77] Moreover, a great number of the vessels that belonged to Russia were navigated by Greeks residing in the Black Sea ports.[78]

In some periods, as the tables below indicate, the number of Greek ships which left Odessa laden with grain for Istanbul was astonishing, while the amount of the Ionian tonnage which was cleared from the port was quite considerable.

TABLE 2

Ships which Sailed from Odessa in 1810-13

	1809	1810	1811	1812	1813
Russian	2	2	23	22	134
Ottoman	73	35	5	2	51
Austrian	28	6	13	2	2
French	43	21	6	3	-
English	-	-	1	-	9
Greek	6	121	444	483	102
TOTAL	152	185	492	512	298

Source: 'Tableau de Navires sortis d'Odessa depuis 1801' in PRO FO 359/1

TABLE 3

Ionian ships which Sailed from Odessa in 1821-6

Year	Number of Vessels	Tonnage	Crews	Value of Cargo in £ Sterling
1821	22	2680	374	26950
1822	15	2360	241	18700
1824	40	6950	673	34450
1825	46	8912	825	48030
1826	42	6054	750	36830
TOTAL	165	26956	2863	164960

Source: Trade papers in PRO FO 359/1

In analysing these tables it should be understood that they represent multiple clearances. From Odessa sailing ships required 5 or 6 days to reach Istanbul; 20 to 25 days to Messina; 25 to 30 days to Naples; 35 to 40 days to Trieste; 40 to 50 days to Marseilles; and 60 to 70 days to England.[79] I presume that by 'Greek' is meant the obviously Greek name of the skippers, who had at that time no national flag to fly. The Greek flag appears in the British consular reports from the

Black Sea ports in the last six months of 1829.[80] From Table
3 it is obvious that the average capacity of an Ionian vessel
was 163 tons and its crew was about 17 persons. Finally, it
must be noted that very few of the ships were constructed in
South Russia (i.e. Kherson) and the great majority had their
proprietors in the ports of the Adriatic and the Levant.[81]

What percentage did the Greek merchants constitute of the
commercial classes of Odessa? Before giving an answer to this
question we have to notice that in a technical sense membership
in the commercial classes of the Southern Russian port cities
involved membership in one of the three mercantile guilds. By
law Russian merchants since the eighteenth century had been
divided for tax purposes into three guilds (gil'dia). Those in
the first and second guilds were allowed to engage in both
interior and foreign trade, and only those in the first guild
were permitted to own merchant ships, banks, insurance companies
and large commercial and industrial enterprises. The third
guild included the small merchants who were restricted to
regional and urban trade within the empire.[82] Foreigners until
the early years of the nineteenth century were enjoying the same
privileges as the Russian subjects. However, in 1807, following
petitions from the Russian merchants a check was put to the
foreign business activities. It was now that an inostrannyi
gost (foreign merchant) had to pay full first guild fees in
order to be allowed to trade in Russia.[83]

On this basis the relative importance of the Greek
merchants in Odessa, at least for the year 1800, might be
disclosed more accurately from the following table:

TABLE 4
Greek Merchants Trading in Odessa on 31 January 1800

Guild	Name of Merchant	Number of Partners	Capital in Roubles
First	Andreas Vandaras	1	11,000
	Nikolaos Doundas	1	16,000
	Aggelos Linaris	1	18,000
	Anastasios Papadopoulos	1	16,500
Second	Anastasios Karapanos	1	10,000
	Dimitrios Kalafatis	1	6,000
	Lorenzis Mavrokordatos	1	10.000
	Anastasios Raftopoulos	1	8,500

Guild	Name of Merchant	Number of Partners	Capital in Roubles
Second	Khristoforos Vandaras	1	8,600
	Khristodoulos Maraboutas	1	5,010
	Nikolaos Panagos	1	8,000
	Mikhail Doullouas	1	8,200
	Ioannis Khavanis	1	5,050
	Konstantinos Saliagas	2	5,050
	Petros Kalogerakis	1	5,010
	Stamatis Lambros	1	5,010
	Iosif Panagos	1	5,010
	Ioannis Amvrosiou	1	5,010
	Antonios Theognostis	1	5,010
	Konstantinos Khaletzis	1	5,010
	Simeon Digopoulos	3	5,010
	Ioannis Palaiologos	1	5,010
	Vasileios Kouskoulis	2	5,010
Third	Dimitrios Karavias	1	2,100
	Stratis Papazoglou	1	2,000
	Antonios Kyriazis	1	2,010
	Igor Paterakis	1	2,100
	Kostis Dimos	1	1,010
	Georgios Tzanis	1	1,010
	Vasileios Tzouras	1	1,010
	Giannis Diamantis	1	1,010
	Damianis Triantafyllos	1	2,010
	Georgios Khatzis	4	2,010
	Georgios Theodoropoulos	1	2,010
	TOTAL	41	199,280

Source: A. Orlov, Istoricheskii Ocherk Odessy s 1794 po 1803 god (Odessa 1885) 123-7

The above table, which does not include a very small number of merchants whose names can be disputed as not being Greek, represent only 15 per cent - 41 out of 273 - of the wholesale traders of Odessa. Nevertheless, 54 per cent of the total capital of 113,720 roubles which was declared at the time by the ten first guild merchants was in Greek hands. The proportion was even greater in the second guild where 23 Greek merchants out of 37 possessed 61 per cent of the capital. Another conclusion we can draw is that by the turn of the

126

eighteenth century very few Greeks were members of the third merchant guild - 14 out of 226 - and that a considerable number who had the _inostrannyi gost_ legal position in the previous years had moved to the first or second guilds.[84] This does not imply that they turned into Russian subjects because we know that the Russian government, in its anxiety to promote the export trade in the Black Sea, had allowed foreigners to settle and trade in the towns and cities of Southern Russia without sometimes becoming guild members or naturalized citizens. Those advantages which were associated with the Imperial decrees of 1793 and 1802 in the case of Odessa were extended with the free-port status after 1817.[85]

In the course of the first two decades of the nineteenth century the Greek merchants had greatly figured in the economic transformation of Odessa. Exploiting to the full the advantageous conditions created for the Greek merchant marine by Napoleon's Continental System (1806) and the war between the Russian and the Ottoman empires they became principal carriers of the Southern Russian produce to Western Europe and Turkey and they managed to amass large fortunes.[86] At the same time they played a prominent role in the creation of the local commercial institutions. In Odessa, for example, they founded together with other European merchants the first commercial insurance company (_Camera Imperiale della assicurazioni_). In 1808 probably because of mistreatment by their Italian, French and English rivals they established their own commercial association (_Graikorossiki Syntrofia ton Asfaleion_); and by 1817 they had their own bank (_Emporikon Daneion Kivotion_) and they owned another insurance firm (_Etaireia ton Inomenon Asfaliston Graikon_).[87]

Basically of course the Greeks were successful because they were familiar with the localities and used methods of conducting their business which were well adapted to local conditions. In comparison with the Western Europeans, they were at an advantage because colonies of their own race were established in all the important ports of the area and were even in some cases, as that of the Mariupol Greeks, agriculturalists.[88] They also had multiple family contacts among the prosperous Greek merchants of Western and Central Europe and, therefore, excellent access to commercial information.[89] To judge from the conduct of their business in Odessa, ethnic kinship with local agents enabled them to purchase the grain on

127

the spot, cheaper, as they seized the moment to make the deal when the producers were short of money.[90] In addition, whereas foreigners paid the full 5 per cent brokerage to their brokers, the Greeks saved that charge and at most paid 0.5 per cent. Finally, their merchandise was always accompanied by a partner, a 'supercargo', who was responsible for buying in the foreign port, and possibly for selling, if the sales were not made in the home port.[91] Such methods, which required of the merchant much hard work, were adaptable in an area where modern commercial institutions and banking facilities were generally poor, and did not in the initial stages depend on the possession of large quantities of capital.[92]

To conclude with I would like to lay emphasis on the fact that the Greek mercantile paroikia in Odessa managed, to a great extent, to preserve its national identity within the social and economic framework of Southern Russia. As a general rule the Greek immigrants lived in compact masses, near one another, in lanes adjacent to a main street known as Deribasovskaia.[93] But apart from the fact that their settlement had a group character they were helped as well because they could find jobs easily as skippers, sailors and commercial agents in all the Greek vessels navigating the Black Sea and the Mediterranean, sources of existence in trade and navigation habitual to them. In addition the Greek cultural revival of the late eighteenth and early nineteenth centuries had a great impact on the Greek settlers and enabled them not only to maintain their singularity in the surrounding environment but also to turn their community into a very important centre for the Greek national movement.[94]

1. A full bibliography on the Philiki Etairia up to 1970 will be found in G. L. Arsh, Eteristkoe dvizhenie v Rossii (Moscow 1970) 353-8. For an interesting interpretation of the role played by the Etairia in the Greek Revolution, see the important article of G. D. Frangos, 'The Philiki Etairia: A premature National Coalition', in Richard Clogg, ed. The Struggle for Greek Independence (London 1973) 87-103.

2. The article of Arsh, 'Grecheskaia emigratsiia v Rossii v Kontse XVIII-nachale XIX v.', Sovetskaia Ethnografiia iii (1963) 85-95 is the only attempt at a coherent presentation of Greek emigration in South Russia during the 1774-1812 period. By contrast the more general work of K. Palaiologos, 'O en ti Notio Rosia Ellinismos apo ton arkhaiotaton Khronon mekhri ton kath' imas', Parnassos v (1881) 143-53, 409-20, 534-50, 585-616 is decidedly superficial.

3. This paper relies heavily upon the numerous Imperial decrees which established the administration of Odessa and defined the terms of settlement in the city, both for Russians and for foreign colonists. These decrees are published in the monumental Polnoe Sobranie Zakonov Rossiiskii Imperii s 1649 goda (45 vols., St. Petersburg 1830), hereafter cited as PSZ. I have made use also of the unpublished despatches of Henry and James Yeames, British consuls in Odessa, to the Embassy in St. Petersburg and to the Foreign Office in London, now in the Public Record Office, London. References to despatches are prefixed by PRO FO and are to a file number followed by their date.

4. Gabriel de Castelnau, Essai sur l'Histoire ancienne et moderne de la Nouvelle Russie iii (Paris 1827) 5-9. Cf. A. Skal'kovskii, Pervoe tridtsatiletie istorii goroda Odessy, 1793-1823 (Odessa 1837) 4-19 (hereafter cited as Pervoe tridtsatiletie).

5. For government debates on the establishment of a trading port in the Black Sea see Skal'kovskii, Pervoe tridtsatiletie, 28-33. Cf. K. Smol'ianinov Istoriia Odessy (Odessa 1853) 16-22; V. K. Nadler, Odessa v pervye epokhi ee sushchestvovaniia (Odessa 1893) 18-19. See also Odessa, 1794-1894. Izdanie gorodskogo obshchestvennogo upravleniia K stletiiu goroda (Odessa 1894) 159-63 (hereafter quoted as Odessa, 1794-1894).

6. For a text of the decree see PSZ xxiii no. 17208 514.

7. According to legend, the ancient city was called Odessos, but Catherine during a court ball changed its gender. 'Let Hacıbey bear the ancient Hellenic name', she is reported to have commanded, 'but in the feminine gender'. On the naming of Odessa see A. Orlov, Istoricheskii Ocherk Odessy s 1794 po 1803 god (Odessa 1885) XI-XII. Cp. Nadler, op. cit., 28.

8. The port of Kherson, which was founded in 1778 on the right bank of the Dnieper, could not escape the unhealthy air of the coastal swamps. Cf. accounts of M. Guthrie, A tour performed in the years 1795-6 through the

Taurida or Crimea . . . (London 1802) 32-3; and J. E. Alexander, Travels to the Seat of the War ii (London 1830) 242.

9. For the inconveniences in navigation of Taganrog and Kherson see E. D. Clarke, Travels in Various Countries . . . Part 1: Russia, Tartary and Turkey (Cambridge 1810) 328, 600. Cf. R. Lyall, Travels in Russia, the Krimea, the Caucasus and Georgia i (London 1825) 159-60. See also a copy of H. Yeame's first report on the Black Sea ports to the Embassy in St. Petersburg in the despatch of 13 January, 1803 in PRO FO 65/52.

10. Anthoine de Saint-Joseph, Essai historique sur le commerce et la navigation de la Mer-Noire . . . (Paris 1820) 52-3.

11. Cf. W. Eton, A concise account of the commerce and navigation of the Black Sea (London 1805) 13-4; and G. M. Jones, Travels in Norway, Sweden, Finland, Russia and Turkey . . ., ii (London 1827) 356-8. See also PRO FO 65/52 passim.

12. V. A. Iakovlev, K istorii zaseleniia Khadzhibeia 1789-1795 (Odessa 1889) 19; and F. W. Skinner, City Planning in Russia: The Development of Odessa, 1789-1892 (unpublished Ph.D. thesis, University of Princeton 1973) 54.

13. PSZ xxiii no. 17320, 686-8.

14. Arsh, SE iii (1963) 88. It must be noted that by this period there were small Greek communities in the Crimea (Kerch, Yenikale, Balaklava), in south west Russia (Kherson, Nikolaev), and in the ports of the Azov Sea (Taganrog, Mariupol). For all these settlements see Arsh, loc. cit., 85-7; and B. A. Karidis, The Greek communities in South Russia: Aspects of their formation and commercial enterprise, 1774-1829 (unpublished M.A. thesis, University of Birmingham 1976) 32-41.

15. For a complete coverage of the Greek involvement in the Russo-Turkish war of 1787-92 see G. J. Kolias, Oi Ellines kata ton rosotourkikon polemon, 1797-1792 (Athens 1940). Cp. E. G. Protopsaltis, 'I epanastatiki kinisis ton Ellinon kata ton defteron epi Aikaterinis B' rosotourkikon polemon (1787-1792). Loudovikos Sotiris', Deltion Istorikis Kai Ethnologikis Etairias xiv (1960) 33-155; and M. S. Anderson, 'Russia in the Mediterranean, 1788-1791: A Little-Known Chapter in the History of Naval Warfare and Privateering', Mariner's Mirror lxv (February 1959) 25-35.

16. It is worth mentioning that on 9 January 1792, the Ottoman Empire by the Treaty of Jassy (Art. IV, par. IV) promised: 'To allow families who wish to leave their country /Principalities/ and settle elsewhere to depart freely and take with them their goods . . .'; quoted in M. S. Anderson, ed. Documents in Modern History: The Great Powers and the Near East, 1774-1923 (London 1970) 17.

17. PSZ xxiii no. 17320, 688. The division was formed after the example of the Albanskoe Voisko (Albanian Army) which consisted largely of Greeks and Albanians who had served under Alexis Orlov during Catherine's first Russo-

Turkish war of 1768-74. See the decree of 28 March 1775, in PSZ xx
no. 14282, 101-4.

18. PSZ xxiii no. 17320, 686-7.

19. Cited in Orlov, op.cit., 7.

20. Skal'kovskii, _Pervoe tridtsatiletie_, 47-8. Cf. Orlov, op. cit., 38-9;
and Iakovlev, op. cit., 39-40.

21. The report is published in PSZ vviii no. 17406, 813-5. Among the Greek
immigrants who arrived at that time in Odessa were Konstantinos Saliagas
(Khiotis), Antonios Kouskoulis, Dimitrios Gorgolis, Georgios Stelalis, Pavlos
Alexinos, Georgios Andronikos, KonstantinosMavrokordatos, Stefanos Peristeriou
Petros Georgiou, Dimitrios Psarianis; see Orlov, op. cit., 10-11.

22. PSZ xxiii no. 17406, 813. For a discussion of the 1785 Charter see
I. I. Ditiatin, _Ustroistvo i upravlenie gorodov Rossii_ i (St. Petersburg
1875) 415-72; and A. A. Kizevetter, _Mestroe samoupravlenie v Rossii_ (Moscow
1910) 114-33.

23. The Greeks who held important posts in the _Magistrat_ were: Theodoros
Flogaitis, a second guild merchant, _burgomistr_ (councillor); in his absence
he was replaced by Leonardos Berdoni, a first guild merchant; Konstantinos
Mavrokordatos, a third guild merchant, Khristodoulos Maraboutas and Dimitrios
Kalafatis, second guild merchants, _ratmany_ (militiamen). Cp. Skal'kovskii,
Pervoe tridtsatiletie 47; and Orlov, op. cit., 45.

24. PSZ xxiv no. 17967, 614.

25. Smol'ianinov, op. cit., 83.

26. PSZ xxv no. 18346, 49-50; and Orlov, op. cit., 51ff.

27. Smol'ianinov, op. cit., 86-8.

28. PSZ xxiv no. 17967, 614.

29. Skal'kovskii, _Pervoe tridtsatiletie_ 61-2. Cp. Smol'ianinov, op. cit.,
78-80.

30. For this period see a very interesting list of Greek merchants in Orlov,
op. cit., 110ff.

31. Cf. Skal'kovskii, _Pervoe tridtsatiletie_ 68-73; and Smol'iainov, op. cit.,
101-5.

32. Cf. Skal'kovskii, _Pervoe tridtsatiletie_ 84-7; Smol'ianinov, op. cit.,
109-12; and Alexander de Ribas, _Staraia Odessa. Istoricheskie ocherki i_
vospominaniia (Odessa 1913) 61-6.

33. Skal'kovskii, op. cit., 91-2.

34. PSZ xxvi no. 19828, 609; see also Gagarin's order of 18 March 1800, to
M. Kir'iakov, director of the Odessa custom house in Skal'kovskii, op. cit.,
283-6. For Catherine's various concessions to Odessa, on 2 October 1795,
see PSZ xxiii no. 17392, 793-4.

35. See the report of M. P. Miklashevskii, Governor-General of New Russia,
in PSZ, xxvi no. 20035, 806-7.

36. PSZ xxvii no. 20103, 5-7.

37. PSZ xxvii no. 20343, 202; and Skal'kovskii, Bolgarskii Kolonii v Bessarabii i Novorossiiskom Kray (Odessa 1848) 9ff.

38. A. Vakalopoulos, Istoria tou Neou Ellinismou . . . iv (Thessaloniki 1973) 705-10; N. E. Saul, Russia and the Mediterranean 1797-1807 (Chicago 1970) 211-6.

39. PSZ xxvii no. 20998, 938-9.

40. Vakalopoulos, op. cit., 703.

41. Arsh, SE iii (1963) 89; Vakalopoulos, op. cit., 704.

42. Duc de Richelieu, 'Mémoire sur Odessa', SIRIO liv (1886) 369. Cp. Castelnau, op. cit., iii 26; M. Vsevoloiskii, Dictionnaire Géographique - Historique de l'Empire de Russie ii (Moscow 1833) 38.

43. Despatch of 1/13 December 1814, in PRO FO 65/93.

44. Despatch of 17 February 1815, in PRO FO 65/69.

45. Despatch of 18/30 May 1815, in PRO FO 65/99.

46. Despatch of 14/26 March 1816, in PRO FO 65/105.

47. Despatch of 26 November 1819, in PRO FO 65/118.

48. Despatches of 23 July/3 August 1819, in PRO FO 65/118 and of 23 January 1820, in PRO FO 65/123.

49. Imperial decrees of 20 February 1804, and of 5 August 1819, in PSZ xxviii no. 21163, 137-40; xxxvi no. 27912, 325. On the Russian colonization policy see the very interesting work of R. P. Bartlett, Foreign Settlement in Russia, 1762-1804: Aspects of Government Policy and Implementation (unpublished D.Phil. thesis, University of Oxford 1971).

50. Despatch of 12/24 May 1821, in PRO FO 65/130.

51. Cf. despatches of 6/18 June 1822, in PRO FO 65/137 and of 3 November 1825, in PRO FO 65/150.

52. Cited in a letter of 15 September 1822, in PRO FO 257/1.

53. See the reports of E. L. Blutte from Bucharest of 9 April and 4 June 1830, in PRO FO 97/402; and the account of J. E. Alexander, Travels to the Seat of the War in the East, through Russia and the Crimea in 1829 . . . ii (London 1830) 51.

54. J. Oddy, European Commerce . . . (London 1805) 175.

55. See Oddy, op. cit., 177-8; and H. Dearborn, A Memoir on the Commerce and Navigation of the Black Sea . . . i (Boston 1819) 241-8.

56. Anthoine, op. cit., 252-6.

57. Data in PRO FO 359/1. See also 'A Comparative View of the Trade of the whole Russian Empire in the Years 1801 and 1802 and Amounts of Duties Collected' by Stephen Shairp, in his despatch of 8 March 1804, from St. Petersburg in PRO FO 65/54.

58. Cf. Gabriel de Castelnau, op. cit., iii 10-11, 26; and Ch. Sicard, 'Notice sur onze années de la vie du Duc de Richelieu à Odessa pour servir à

l'histoire de sa vie', SIRIO liv (1886) 29-30. For population figures see also J. Reuilly, Voyage en Crimée et sur les bords de la Mer Noire pendant l'année 1803 (Paris 1806) 264, n.1.

59. See Yeame's first report on the Black Sea ports in PRO FO 65/52.

60. On the Duc's appointment see J. B. Warren's despatch of 25 March 1803, from St. Petersburg, in PRO FO 65/52.

61. Castelnau, op. cit., iii 17ff. For contemporary accounts of the Duc's administration of Odessa see also, Oddy, op. cit., 169; Dearborn, op. cit., i 235-9; and Anthoine, op. cit., 67. Richelieu's own memoirs as well as those of Charles Sicard, a contemporary French merchant, are published in SIRIO liv (1886). For general information of New Russia under Richelieu, where he became a Governor-General in 1805, see Crousaz-Cretet, Le Duc de Richelieu en Russie et en France, 1766-1822 (Paris 1897) 58ff.

62. PSZ xxviii no. 21197, 195-7; part of this decree is translated into English by Oddy, op. cit., 170.

63. Anthoine, op. cit., 56-7.

64. PSZ xxviii no. 21196, 191-4; partly translated into English by Oddy, op. cit., 170-1.

65. In 1804, 391 ships (130 Russian, 129 Austrian, 65 Turkish, 25 British, 25 Ragusans, 10 Ionians, 6 Neapolitans, 1 French) sailed from Odessa, exporting about 510,000 chetverts of grain; see Shairp's letter of 4 September 1806 from London, in PRO FO 65/66; and PRO FO 359/1. A year later, in 1805, Odessa's imports were valued at 2,156,844 roubles and exports at 3,399,291 roubles; see Shairp's report on the 'State of the Trade of the Russian Empire for the years 1804-1805' of 16 June 1807, London, in PRO FO 65/71.

66. In 1806 only 104 ships (37 Russian, 24 Ottoman, 27 Austrian, 7 French, 9 Ragusan) left the port of Odessa exporting just 80,479 chetverts of grain, while the value of exports had fallen to 813,664 roubles; see PRO FO 359/1 and Shairp's report on the 'State of the Trade of the Russian Empire for the year 1805-1806', of 11 August 1807, London, in PRO FO 65/71.

67. For the disorders in the Ottoman provinces which caused a great hindrance to trade, see S. J. Shaw, Between Old and New: The Ottoman Empire under Sultan Selim III, 1789-1807 (Harvard 1971) 283ff.

68. During the period 1811-13 an average of 157,059 chetverts of grain per year were exported, wheat representing about 80 per cent of the total, while 84,262 shipping tonnage was employed for grain; data in PRO FO 359/1. See also Crousaz-Crétet, op. cit., 64-9.

69. PSZ xxxiv no. 26792, 257-8; see the main points in the despatch of 26 May/7 June 1817, from St. Petersburg in PRO FO 65/108 and in the despatch of 5/17 June 1817, Odessa, in PRO FO 65/110. For the debates which preceded the publication of this important decree, between Count de Langeron, who

succeeded de Richelieu as Governor of Odessa in 1816, and St. Petersburg, see despatches of 14/28 January and 14/26 March 1816, in PRO FO 65/105.

70. PSZ xxxvi no. 27866, 257-8; see also despatches of 22 July/3 August 1819 from St. Petersburg and from Odessa in PRO FO 65/118.

71. On the widespread crop failures in Western Europe from 1815 to 1818 see A. Zobi, Manuale storico di economia toscana (Florence 1847) 361.

72. Data in PRO FO 359/1; see also V. J. Puryear, 'Odessa: Its rise and International Importance 1815-50', Pacific Historical Review v (1934) 196-7.

73. PRO FO 359/1; despatch of 31 January 1822, in PRO FO 65/137; and Puryear, op. cit., 198.

74. PRO FO 359/1; despatch of 18 January 1829, in PRO FO 65/182; and Puryear, op. cit., 199.

75. PRO FO 359/1.

76. See for example the accounts of Felix de Beaujour, A View of the Commerce of Greece . . . (Trans. from French, London 1800) 317; Oddy, op. cit., 179; and Castelnau, op. cit., iii 51-2, 73-4; all of them agree that a great portion of the Russian commerce in the Black Sea and in particular that of Odessa was under Greek control.

77. Tr. Stoianovich, 'The Conquering Balkan Orthodox Merchant', Journal of Economic History xx (1960) 288-9. Cf. G. B. Leon, 'The Greek Merchant Marine 1453-1850' in S. A. Papadopoulos, ed. The Greek Merchant Marine (Athens 1972).27.

78. According to J. B. Warren's despatch of 20 October 1803, from St. Petersburg, Count Vorontsov, Chancellor of Russia, 'observed that a number of the Subjects of the Empire in the Black Sea were Greeks; and the Commerce from Odessa and other Ports was chiefly carried on by vessels that belonged to Russia and were navigated by Greek-Russian subjects.' in PRO FO 65/53.

79. J. C. Kohl, Russia . . . (London 1842) 429.

80. During the half year ending on 31 December 1829, only one Greek ship arrived in Odessa; by contrast, during the half year ending on 31 December 1830, 53 ships arrived and 54 departed under the Greek colours. In the following years the Greek flag appears regularly in the commercial despatches from the Black Sea ports and steadily increases until the Crimean War.

81. G. P. Nebolsine, Statisticheskoe obozrenie vneshnei torgovli Rossii i (St. Petersburg 1835) 81-2.

82. W. L. Blackwell, The Beginnings of Russian Industrialization 1800-1860 i (Princeton 1968) 102.

83. Idem., i 247. There is a copy in French of the 1807 regulations on commerce in PRO FO 359/2.

84. Such was the case with Anastasios Papadopoulos, Anastasios Karapanos, Nikolaos Panagos, Iosif Panagos, Ioannis Amvrosiou and Ioannis Palaiologos; see the 1799 catalogue of Odessa's foreign merchants in Orlov, op. cit., 128.

85. See J. Yeames' despatch of 1 July 1825, on the foreign merchants of Odessa in PRO FO 65/150.

86. J. R. Neroulos, Histoire moderne de la Grèce depuis la chute de l'empire d'Orient (Genève 1828) 212-3. By 1816 Theodoros Serafinos, Alexandros Mavros, Dimitrios Iglezis, Alexandros Koumparis, Vasileios Giannopoulos, Grigorios Maraslis, Kyriakos Pappakhatzis, Ilias Manesis, Ioannis Amvrosiou and Dimitrios Palaiologos, had combined a fortune of about ten million paper roubles; cited in Anonymous, 'Diatrivi filogenous tinos Graikou peri tis Katastaseos ton en Odisso oikounton Graikon kata to etos 1816' Logios Ermis (Parartima) i (January 1817) 13-4.

87. Cf. Anonymous, Logios Ermis i (January 1817) 2-4; and Anonymous, 'Antirrisis eis tin en to Parartimati tou L.E. Ar. 1. ekdotheisan peri Odessis diatrivin, syggrafeisa para tinos Graikou ek Symferoupoleos tis en Tavridi', Logios Ermis (Parartima) xi (June 1817) 3, 8.

88. For the Greeks in Mariupol see the travellers' accounts of P. S. Pallas, Travels through the Southern Provinces of the Russian Empire in the Years 1793 and 1794 i (Trans. from German, London 1812) 512-4; R. Walpole, Travels in Various Countries of the East . . . ii (London 1820) 464; M. Holderness, New Russia . . . (London 1823) 142-3; and E. Henderson, Biblical Researches and Travels in Russia . . . (London 1826) 394. On the general history of their community see D. Spiridonov, 'Istorichnii interes vivcheniia govirok Mariupil's'kikh grekiv', Skhidnii Svit, Vostochnuy Mir xii (1930) 171-81; and I. I. Sokolov 'Mariupol'skie greki', Trudy Instituta Slavianovedeniia AN SSSR i (1932) 287-317.

89. Such was the case with the wealthy Ralli family. One of the five original brothers Pantias remained in London, Eustratios moved to Manchester, Augustus was in Marseilles, Thomas in Constantinople and John in Odessa. The second of the five original brothers Pantias was the head of the family and was nicknamed Zeus; see J. Gennadius, Stephen A. Ralli (privately published London 1902) 23-4; and E. W. Fletcher and T. E. Dowling, Hellenism in England (London 1915) 53.

90. Castelnau, op. cit., iii 51-2.

91. Oddy, op. cit., 179-80.

92. According to Julius de Hagemeister, the Greeks and the Italians in the Russian Black Sea ports brought connections and industriousness rather than money; see J. de Hagemeister, Report on the Commerce of the Ports of New Russia, Moldavia and Wallachia . . . (London 1835) 215.

93. That type of settlement had left evidence in the city (i.e. Greek Square, Greek Market) which remained unchanged up to the beginning of the twentieth century; see Arsh, SE iii (1963) 93.

94. In 1800, for example, a Greek school was opened by E. Vretos and 70 pupils were taught Greek, Italian and Russian, cited in Arsh SE iii (1963) 94.

Seventeen years later a commercial school (<u>Ellinoemporiki Skholi</u>), financed by the local merchants, was founded and eventually became one of the most remarkable Greek colleges of the period; on this school see the valuable work of Kh. Volodimos, <u>Proti Pentikontaetiris tis en Odisso Ellinoemporikis skholis 1817-1867</u> (Odessa 1871).

7

SOCIETY IN SERBIA, 1791-1830

STEVAN PAVLOWITCH

The Yugoslav lands, astride the Save and Danube border, extending far into the dominions of the Habsburg Emperor and of the Ottoman Sultan, were in a phase of transition at the end of the eighteenth century, and it was in this changing world that the French Revolution sowed the seeds of modern nationalism.[1]

Throughout these territories and further afield, there were people who identified themselves as Serbs: from northern Hungary to the Adriatic Sea and the mountains of Albania, from western Croatia to the Banat and into Macedonia; from the original embryonic principalities around present-day Shkodër /Scutari7 and Novi Pazar, across the spread of the mediaeval Serbian monarchy, then northwards and westwards with the migrations that had accompanied the expansion and retraction of Ottoman power. Ethnic consciousness among these people had not as yet generally progressed beyond the initial stage of cultural identification, but such identification was obvious when in contact with the ruling Ottomans and with the urban Greeks everywhere, with the Moslem Slavs of Bosnia and Herzegovina, with the Catholics of Hungary and Croatia, in other words where political, religious, linguistic and social factors combined to show the difference.

'Serbia' was but a dream, but a dream with clearer images where conditions allowed Serbs to benefit from social and cultural promotion, or where the Ottoman grip was weaker. This was specifically the case in the border region between Austria and Turkey where the division between the advanced and strong Habsburg Monarchy, on the one hand, and the backward and weak Ottoman Empire, on the other, was destined to start the process of emancipation. It was the contact between the new ideas and techniques north of the Danube, and the plight of the population driven to despair south of the river that was to spark off revolution.

abdication in 1839, epitomizes the outcome of this evolution.
Professor Georges Castellan has described it as a turning
point when the population of the Principality consciously
perceived itself as being 'Serbia'[13] It is interesting to note
that, although so much still had to be done to improve the
educational and living standards of the parish clergy, and to
build churches, it was to the monasteries that the new authorities devoted more attention, to restore monastic discipline as
well as monastic buildings.[14] Monasteries were seen as playing
a relatively important part in this national consciousness, not
only as symbols of historic continuity but also as providers of
traditional elementary schooling. Although the number of small
private schools in towns had increased from six in 1800 to
sixteen in 1826, it was not until the late 1830s that the
government of the illiterate Prince was able to find time and
money to spend on education. By 1839, however, it had set up
eighty-four primary schools, three half-gymnasiums, one full
gymnasium in Belgrade, with an embryo institution of further
education, and a seminary for the clergy. The 1830s also saw
other cultural developments, such as the first printing press
in 1832 and the first newspaper in 1834.

Once the status of Serbia in relation to the Ottoman
Empire had been settled, and with it the national problem,
at least for some years to come; once society in Serbia had
acquired a measure of self-control and an even greater one of
consciousness, Miloš's despotic authority was no longer felt to
be delegated by the collectivity. The Prince no longer acted
or thought as the notables, or even as the majority of peasants
wanted him to. His abuses of power would no longer be endured
by all sections of the population. Not only did he appear as
'Turkish', that is to say outmoded, he also appeared as an
obstacle to further political, social and economic developments.
Once new men had begun to rise socially from the peasant mass,
and other ways and ideas were filtering into the Principality,
his paternalistic rule was no longer accepted. And the peasants
too, although they did not use such words, felt the need for a
legal guarantee of the 'rights' they had acquired in the course
of the revolution.

That revolution, which had quickly come to be seen as a
'struggle for freedom', turned into a contest for power
between the oligarchy and the Prince. To combat the crystall-
ization of an autocratic monarchical prerogative, the oligarchs

Local self-rule under the Turks, 1791-1801

    Serbia the dream was to take shape in Serbia the
territorial entity, in a region affected by half a century of
dislocationand turmoil, between 1788 and 1839 - present-day
northern inner Serbia, at that time the Ottoman sancak of
Belgrade. A border province since the end of the seventeenth
century, and a particularly distant one from Istanbul,[2]
it had been under the authority of Austria between 1718 and
1739 when the territory had been officially called Serbia for
the first time since 1459. Having enjoyed the political and
economic advantages of two decades of Austrian rule, many of
the inhabitants had left with the Austrians in 1739, and
during the last Austro-Turkish war of 1788-91 the population
of Serbia rose again. This time, however, there were no
reprisals when the Turks returned. The privileges of the
border province were confirmed, so that not only were the links
with Serbs over the border kept up, but conditions in Serbia
attracted immigration from the South.

    The political and economic impact of these two periods of
Austrian rule was enormous. Of all the Slav lands under the
Sultan's government, it was in the province of Belgrade that
autonomy at local level was most apparent. Confirmed and
extended by the Austrians, then again by the Turks between
1791 and 1796, it consisted in a virtual federation of village
republics where the zadruga (extended family) heads elected
their own kmet (headman), and the village headmen in turn
elected the district knez (primate). These native headmen
assessed and collected taxes, and acted as rural magistrates.
The right to build and restore places of Christian worship, to
carry arms, and to trade with Austria completed the privileges.
As part of Selim III's general attempt to face the challenge of
defeat and anarchy in Europe, the reforms in Serbia were
intended to bolster up the Sultan's authority in a key border
province with the help of the natives, against the rebellious
janissaries, the robber barons and the war-lords who were
asserting themselves throughout Roumelia.

    The Ottoman order in Serbia was an almost exclusively
urban one. With the exception of some Moslem Slav villagers
settled in western Serbia on the border with Bosnia, from where
they had originally come, the Moslem inhabitants of Serbia (some
20,000, excluding the garrisons) were all town-dwellers, administrators and tradesmen, or sipahi holders of military 'fiefs'

139

living off the income of their tenures. Most of them were not even Anatolian Turks, but Bosnian Slavs. The drift towards the Moslem révolte nobiliaire in the Balkans, fostered by the unsettled social conditions of the time, establishing large çiftlik holdings and reducing the peasantry to factual serfdom, had hardly touched Serbia. What little of it had taken place on the fringes disappeared with the last Austrian occupation. Under their nine hundred or so sipahis, the tillers of the soil were considered as the real possessors, and except for the sipahi's nominal lordship and that of the Sultan above it, the rural world was that of the Serbian peasantry. It was a world characterized by extreme mobility and recent settlement. People had migrated into Serbia from all the surrounding regions to the West, South and East, especially during the periods of Austrian occupation, and immigration had continued after 1791, so that the population density per square kilometre had risen from 7.8 in 1735 to 10 in 1800.[3] As others had emigrated across the border with retreating Austrian troops, an important proportion of the estimated population of 300-400,000 had only recently arrived in the province.

Little is known quantitatively about the wealth of the territory or the scope of its economic activities. A satellite photograph of the sancak would have shown about ten clear, open areas under cultivation, made up of plateaux and hill-land, and separated by thick forests corresponding to the valleys. Cultivation generally stayed away from the rivers because their irregular flow turned their banks into swamp-land, and elsewhere armies marched through the valley roads. Serbia was an underpopulated and under-cultivated region of average natural wealth where the land was worked only to the extent of making it yield the basic needs of a self-sufficient society. These were essentially maize and accessorily vine. Before agriculture, however, came animal breeding, especially the breeding of pigs, fed almost without expense in the extensive oak-woods. 'The land of pigs' is how the Turks deprecatingly called Serbia, where emphasis was placed in the country-side on meat and drink held in contempt by Moslems, thus strengthening what Sir Duncan Wilson has called the virtual apartheid between urban Ottomans and rural Serbs.[4]

The deteriorating urban economy concentrated around the administrative, military and trade centres. Crafts, apart from those of the self-sustained village economy, and trade, again apart from the rural pig trade, belonged essentially to non-Serbs. Whereas those Serbs who took up town life were looked upon by their own people as having been estranged, peasants in the country-side who also traded, who profited from their fellow villagers and who maintained contacts outside their villages, were looked upon with favour. It was from this social background that the political leadership would emerge.

The decade that followed 1791 was one of peace in Serbia when compared to the almost incessant warfare of the preceding century and to the turbulence of the adjoining Ottoman territories. It favoured not only the immigration of man-power, but also the emigration of pigs, the export of which to the Habsburg dominions is estimated to have increased by two-thirds, to 200,000 heads a year by the end of the decade. 'Trade' thus came to mean the pig trade, pushing far behind the urban-based transit trade between East and West. Naturally enough, the knezes belonged to those families who tended to have more land than the average and who often engaged in the pig trade. Tax collecting, too, was not without yielding some profit. These intermediaries between the Ottoman administration and the peasant population became notables in the full sense of the word. More often than not illiterate, some of them were on the way to founding little local dynasties while others barely stood above the general level.

There was, on the whole, not much social differentiation as yet in rural Serbia, which was essentially, according to the interesting analysis of a French ethnopsychologist, Madame Yvonne Castellan, a communal rather than a patriarchal society. The Ottoman fiscal and penal systems called for group responsibility, while the zadruga was also a social form specially suited for a pioneering, 'frontier' situation. Such a society was characterized by cohesion and mobility. While people moved freely from one village to another, they usually moved in families, and social authority was vested in the group. For practical reasons, it was delegated to the headman, who was not expected to be permanent, all-powerful or wise, but to think and act precisely as all the members of the group would think and act. Leadership was conceived only as a temporary emanation of the group, which was at once social, economic and political. Beyond these immediately conceivable, delegated and revocable forms, accepted authority could only be remote, vague and mysterious. Whether that of Church, of Sultan, of Emperor or

141

of Tsar, it belonged to another world.

Such a society, which had no trading or administrative bourgeoisie, had no intelligentsia either - for not even the clergy can be claimed to have approached that status. The two episcopal sees of the province had been under the direct jurisdiction of the Patriarchate of Constantinople since 1776 and were filled by Greek or Hellenized prelates, associated with the urban, politically dominant, Ottoman world. There was not much contact between them and their rural Serbian clergy. Although contacts had developed between the latter and the richer Serbian Church organization in Austria, the standards of religious learning, living and discipline were low in the Belgrade sancak. This was due both to more general conditions prevailing in the Orthodox Church of the Ottoman Empire at that time and, in material terms, to more particular circumstances. The Church had taken an active part in the wars, on the side of the Sultan's enemies, and had suffered accordingly. Monasteries had been guerrilla centres, and many of them lay in ruins. Churches were few and far between. The priest was not really a holy man, he was hardly educated if at all, and he certainly was not privileged. He was simply a peasant whose function it was to administer the sacraments and to celebrate the liturgy, not all that regularly. Church attendance was irregular, and the head of the zadruga really acted as household celebrant for basic day-to-day worship. In fact, the Serbs cared for their monks more than for their popes (priests), as the monasteries, however decayed, represented a form of historic continuity and of cultural heritage. They were religious, cultural, social and trade centres. The peasants were sincere in their reverence for the Church, which was a link with more than one other world, but they were unlikely to take individual priests, or even monks, too seriously as persons.

More than in mysticism or spiritual curiosity, their religiosity found expression in a messianic cult of liberation that had grown throughout the eighteenth century. As Professor Traian Stoianovich rightly stresses, it was 're-volutionary' in outlook, in the old sense of a return to the golden age, but its synchronization with revolution in the modern sense made it ready to respond to the ideas of Enlightenment and Revolution.[5] The people who would respond, and be the catalysts of what Ranke first called 'Die Serbische Revolution', were precisely the rural merchants, the knezes, the wealthier peasants,

142

relatively recently settled, even the priests, not to mention the hayduks, who had completely broken with the Ottoman order. They had all emerged from that transitory phase of the late eighteenth century. Those who did business with the Habsburg dominions were in contact with their more educated kith across the rivers, and were aware of new European trends. So were those who had fought with Austria. It is more than probable that at least most notables among them were satisfied with the Ottoman order such as it prevailed in Serbia in 1791-1801 - for as long as it did prevail. But as they increased their wealth and influence, the notables provoked the envy of the insurgent Ottoman aristocracy and of the established urban guild merchants, and so contributed to destroying the thin line of defence against insecurity. Most of them were, anyhow, unfavourably disposed towards the Ottoman city. They were full of prejudice against the Greeks, and even more so against the Moslem Slavs. The latter represented the Serbian face of the Ottoman order, and its uglier face as well; the former were very much part of it, and were seen as its auxiliaries. Smaller than their opposite numbers in the Greek lands, the notables of Serbia had so much less to lose.

Karageorge's Rising and Revolution, 1804-13

As the eighteenth century drew to a close, the Porte was no longer able to contain the insurgent Ottoman nobles and janissaries of the Sultan's European provinces. Recruiting the dregs of society, the Turkish rebels infused fear into the hearts of all their potential victims. As incursions into the Belgrade sancak grew more frequent, collective fear spread and hayduk activity increased. By the end of 1801, janissary deys had begun to terrorize and oppress parts of the province into çiftliks . Their aim was to do away with old-established sipahis and new notables alike, taking away from the first their lordship of the land, from the others their local authority and their wealth. They gradually overcame the resistance put up jointly by the regular administration and the knezes until, by the beginning of 1804, the sancak had completely fallen into the hands of the rebellious janissaries.

In reaction to the massacre of seventy-two native elders in February of that year, there was a spontaneous explosion against the terror that was being felt by everyone. The frightened rural notables organized the terrified peasantry

143

with former Austrian volunteers and <u>hayduks</u>. Generally
speaking , this was not a political rising against the Sultan's
authority. <u>Knezes</u>, more particularly in western Serbia, tended
to stick to the 'legitimate' Turks and to look to Austria for
help in returning to the privileges of the 1790s. At the same
time, in the woodland core of Šumadija, Karageorge's maquis
started off, as early as January, by a <u>hayduk</u>'s gesture - setting fire to a <u>khan</u> and killing all the Turks it could lay its
hands on. Karageorge's dominant personality and his background
(that of a well-to-do peasant pig dealer, who had also been a
<u>hayduk</u> and a commander of the native auxiliaries of the
Austrian army) made him a natural leader. Within three months,
the northern part of the <u>sancak</u> had been rid of all Turks, and
by the end of the fighting season in 1804 the whole province had
been freed from the janissaries at least. Carried by its own
momentum, the insurrection did not stop there, and loyalist
<u>knezes</u> followed on. By the summer of 1805 the Christian
insurgents had defeated the Sultan's armies as well, and the
following year, as the revolt had extended beyond the borders
of the <u>sancak</u>, they were gambling on winning complete independence with the help of Russia.

In the process of ridding their province of rebellious
janissaries, the insurgents had carried out a revolution that
had destroyed the foundations of Turkish rule in Serbia. The
Ottoman administrative and military superstructure had vanished.
What <u>çiftlik</u> property had been established disappeared again in
the early days of 1804. By 1806 no more taxes were being paid
to the Sultan, or dues to the <u>sipahis</u>, so that the peasants had,
in fact, become owners of the land they tilled. The personal,
as opposed to the 'feudal', holdings of Turks had been taken
over by the new authorities, sold, rented or distributed free
to the refugees who poured in from the neighbouring provinces,
and much was acquired by the Serbian leaders. If the property
situation was often far from clear, at any rate one thing was
clear: the liberated territory had been emptied of nearly all
its Turkish population. When Belgrade had fallen to the
insurgents, many of the Turks there were killed while women and
children were forced through baptism. When Užice - a large
Turkish centre that had, furthermore, attracted many refugees
from the North - was taken, <u>sipahis</u> were systematically
massacred, merchants were made to pay for their lives and
Turkish houses were destroyed. The terrible violence quite

144

simply meant that the Turkish population fled the liberated
territory.

This liberated territory was defended by a local militia
and run by a rudimentary government. Militarily, apart from
the territorial peasantry-in-arms, called up for the greater
campaigning efforts, there was a small permanent, mobile,
nucleus of beskućnici ('homeless') refugee fighters who had
come from the neighbouring provinces. Administratively, over
the existing forms of local government, rough forms of central
government had emerged, with a general assembly of military
commanders, clergy and headmen, and a supreme governing council
of one delegate from each of the liberated districts. Over and
above them all stood the vožd (leader), Karageorge, the man who
provided the military, the organizational and the revolutionary
drive, generally supported by the peasants and the fighters,
watched jealously by most of the other leaders. All of these
clung to their power and prestige, over their portion of
territory and over their armed followers, jealous of Karageorge,
but jealous of one another too, for the knezes were losing
ground to the captains, politically, economically and socially.
The commanders had some power through their own armed men; they
were acquiring land; they were entering the live-stock trade;
they also took to representing the districts on the governing
council. All these people dressed like Ottoman worthies. The
hayduks had been the first to swagger about in forbidden
colours and materials to taunt the Turks. The insurgent leaders
now all adopted Ottoman dress - silk, embroidery, green, horse
and all - to make their victory obvious, and the notables took
to wearing turbans and pelisses.

By 1813 the population of liberated Serbia had increased
to some 450,000, with a density of 11.9 to the square kilometre,
and that in spite of the war losses and of the departure of
the Turks - both amply compensated by immigration. And so had
the pig population, to over a million, more than twice the
number of humans, in an intensified export drive, to provide
money to buy arms.[6]

With no far-reaching intellectual background or political
project, the Serbian revolution had begun at a time of general
fermentation, in an obscure territory, unknown to Europe, amidst
contrasts which were sufficiently strong to mark many of its
inhabitants. It had been a spontaneous explosion due to special
local conditions and, for a few years after 1806, it did seem as

if it might become a Balkan revolution. But it attracted little attention in Europe where the Powers were busy with Napoleon, and the Turks eventually found themselves free to crush the first Serbian revolt.

In the autumn of 1813, Serbia was devastated by the Ottoman military. Most of the leaders, with their families and many of the fighters, took refuge in Austria. Along the roads on which the troops advanced, villages were burnt down, the population that had not taken flight was massacred, men were impaled, women and children were taken away as slaves. In the wake of the armies, the Turkish population returned. The years 1813-15 were characterized, to a large extent, by the exactions and claims of the Turkish survivors of the massacres of 1804-06 who now sought justice, compensation, revenge. They were the smaller fry of the Moslem Slav settlers. And since most of the troops who had restored order were also Bosnians, it is estimated that well above two-thirds of the 'new' Turkish population of Serbia were made up of Moslem Slavs. Yet the formal restoration of the Sultan's authority, accompanied though it was by military repression and a return of part of the Turkish population, did not restore the foundations of Turkish power, which had been destroyed. Ami Boué noted in the 1830s: 'Ceux-ci /the Turks7 auraient peut-être réussi dans leur guerre contre les Serbes s'ils avaient tâché d'exterminer non les hommes, mais les cochons, c'est-à-dire s'ils avaient brûlé /not the villages, but7 les forêts où ces animaux se nourissaient sans frais pour les habitants'.[7]

Miloš's Rising and 'De Facto' Autonomy, 1815-30

The Serbs of the Belgrade sancak thus rose again in April 1815, under Miloš Obrenović, who had attained some prominence towards the last years of the first rising and who had not left Serbia in 1813. This time, by exploiting the prolonged crisis of the Ottoman state, they achieved more lasting success. The strategy was completely different. On the one hand, Russia was free to take up their cause. On the other, neither peasantry nor notables were any longer willing to risk going the whole hog. Tired and impoverished, people did not have as much energy as in 1804. This time they wished to settle for something livable. Indeed, some of them actually fought with the Turks against Miloš Obrenović, whose mentality was anyhow different from Karageorge's. He negotiated at the same time as he fought, and

fought only to be in a position to bargain. By October of that
year, he had come to a verbal, <u>de facto</u>, agreement with the
local Ottoman military commander. After that, talks between
the Serbian leadership and the Porte for a final solution were
to be long and arduous but, in the meanwhile, a double régime
had in fact been set up in Serbia.

Except for the Sultan's ultimate sovereignty, the
military presence of garrisons, and limited economic advantages,
what remained of the Ottoman order was largely formal. It was
vested in the governor of the province who had direct authority
over the Turks. After all that had happened, their number was
probably a few thousand below the 20,000 (excluding the
garrisons) estimated at the beginning of the century. The
<u>sipahis</u>, resident or not, were once again to receive their dues
according to law. The end of direct Ottoman rule had left the
administration in the hands of the Serbian headmen. The native
hierarchy was not only fully restored to its functions, but
capped by a paramount <u>knez</u>, none other than Miloš himself, who
now had supreme authority over the native population. In 1830
the political and legal situation of Serbia in relation to the
Porte was at last defined, and in 1833 its frontiers were fixed
to include all eighteen districts of Karageorge's insurgent
territory (37,540 sq.km). The settlement solemnly recognized
all that had been achieved in fact. Completing the transition
from the local acceptation of the word <u>knez</u>, through his recently
acquired position as paramount <u>knez</u>, to its wider meaning as
'prince', Miloš became hereditary prince of an autonomous,
tributary Principality of Serbia. One lump sum was fixed as an
annual tribute to the Porte, to include the revenues of the
<u>sipahis</u>' tenures, now abolished, and compensation for all Moslem
holdings. There were to be no Moslems in Serbia except for the
garrisons of six fortresses, but in spite of provisions for
Turkish property owners to sell and emigrate, the question
would still take many years to solve.[8]

On the now formally enlarged territory there lived a
population of some 700,000 with a density of 18.6 to the square
kilometre, the overwhelming majority in small villages of less
than four hundred inhabitants. At the top, the development
would thereafter accelerate in the later years of Miloš's reign,
between 1834 and 1839, of an élite as yet both too undiffer-
entiated and too heterogeneous to be called a 'class'. The
notables were now a mixed bunch: those village or district

147

headmen whose families formed real local dynasties, the merchants of relatively ancient standing, and the men who had risen
in Miloš's service. All of peasant stock and still primarily
attached to the soil, they were, however, at that time, on the
way to becoming an aristocracy. To the live-stock trade, the
notables added another means of increasing their wealth.
Holders of local authority, they took the best of the reclaimed
lands and availed themselves of the free labour services formerly owed to the Ottoman administration and fief-holders. These
services had been retained for public works as well as for work
on the lands of the Prince and of public officials - by way of
remuneration. Having appropriated to themselves landed estates
large by Serbian standards, they aspired to a restoration on
their behalf of the Turkish fiefs abolished in 1830, and longed
to model their manner of living on that of the Wallachian boyar
aristocracy. Owing to the very determined attitude taken by
Prince Miloš, this social phenomenon was to be nipped in the bud.

Miloš himself was the first of the notables who, in one
way or another, was to accumulate, by his abdication in 1839, a
capital worth 1,078,000 gold sovereigns, 53 per cent in cash
and 47 per cent in personal and real property. His only
experience of government was that of the Ottoman administration,
and he naturally looked to that model for both his own way of
life and his own administration.[9] His own feelings towards the
Turks were ambivalent. He understood their mentality; he never
used physical cruelty against them; he respected the Sultan's
authority, and cheated it as much as he could. He ruled over
'his' country with the unlimited sway of a Turkish paşa. Yet
he was also a national hero, the head of the second Serbian
insurrection, the liberator of Serbia, acknowledged as the
supreme leader against the Turks and the embodiment of Serbian
nationalism. He had begun to give shape to the dream of Serbia
by consolidating a restricted Serbian territory, not in the
centre of the historical lands of the mediaeval monarchy, but
in the fringe territory of Šumadija. As such his authority was
accepted as the delegated authority of Serbia by the population
at large against the jealous notables. It was even grudgingly
accepted by most of the notables most of the time.

The general consensus of this delegated authority was
expressed through the skupština, which had become the traditional meeting of Prince and notables. These assemblies were
not unlike the early English parliaments. They met regularly

to authorize taxes, and <u>ad hoc</u> to approve some important measure
or to transmit to the people at large instructions from above.
They had no real political duties, and yet they acted as a link
between government and governed in so far as the notables were
still part of the classless peasant society of Serbia. Otherwise the Prince ruled with a household, the members of which
were considered by Miloš as being one large family, his family,
whose marriages he authorized, the christening of whose children
he sponsored, for whose material benefit he provided. In spite
of appearances, Miloš, more than anybody else, was a new man who
realized that new times were starting. Whereas the notables in
essence wanted to transfer to themselves the prerogatives of
Ottoman power, Miloš was building something new that could no
longer be described as delegated authority, except in so far as
he believed himself to be the direct emanation of the new
'freedom'. He considered that a permanent, centralized, all-
powerful authority was necessary to maintain that freedom
recently acquired. He was making the nucleus of a restored
Serbian state by taking both from the Ottoman authority and
from the local native authority.

Although harshly ruled, with no written laws and very
little administrative machinery, by 1830 Serbia was gradually
being equipped with a rudimentary government, a military force,
basic schools and its own ecclesiastical organization. Miloš
himself was suspicious of Greeks. Generally speaking, Serbs
had mixed feelings towards Greeks - at best indifference, at
worst distrust. The latter were people of the towns; they
belonged to the Ottoman order if they were not actually in the
service of the Ottoman administration. Greek bishops had acted
as intermediaries between the Serbian leaders and the Ottoman
generals, and the insurgents had on the whole benefited from
such mediation, as well as from financial facilities offered
by the Phanar. While this was acknowledged, the new élite,
backed by popular opinion, wanted to take over the local government of the Church, along with everything else - political
power, the land, trade and the towns. In fact, no sooner had
Miloš established a measure of autonomy than negotiations were
started with the Patriarchate for the appointment of native
bishops, an autonomous status and financial compensation. By
1830 the bishops in Serbia were already natives, and two years
later the grant of autonomy for the Church in Serbia was
formalized by the Patriarch of Constantinople.

The Projection of a New Society, 1830-39

1830 was a real turning point, for that year saw not only a political transfer of power but an economic and social transfer as well. The abolition of Ottoman military land tenure made the peasants absolute owners of the land, except for the land tax to the Serbian government, but they had as yet no legal guarantee of their ownership and they still had to provide labour services. As a result of autonomy, of the loosened political ties with the Porte and of the freeing of the land, the Serbian economy entered, within the limits of its exclusively agrarian structure, a rapid phase of development, closely linked with political developments.

Miloš was a new man in more ways than one. His economic policy was a radical one, in promoting immigration, resettlement of whole villages across Serbia, land clearing, the regularization of rivers, and in emphasizing the virtues of production. As early as 1815, he began to act as though he were heir to the Sultan, distributing unoccupied lands (the Sultan's in theory) and forest lands (in principle granted for exploitation to sipahis and religious foundations). Such grants, coupled with tax exemptions of up to three years, the absence of fighting, and the disappearance from Serbia of the spectre of famine, which continued endemic all around, were all stimuli to immigration and economic activity.

Demographic growth advanced dynamically throughout the 1830s and until the early 'forties, with an estimated annual increase of 2.4 per cent from 1834 until 1842 or so when the population reached some 850,000, with a density of 22.6 per square kilometre. If well over 90 per cent was still rural in 1834, the self-contained economic structure of the countryside had largely broken apart as soon as unfettered, for about three-quarters of the peasants were by then outside the confines of the zadruga, which had anyhow lost much of its vigour. They lived in small villages that tended to be territorial communities rather than concentrations of houses. Houses were generally dispersed over the territory of the village. Villages - some of which were very recent, while others had moved from one part of Serbia to another - were legal and political entities, units of collective tax assessment, and, until 1838, subject to collective criminal responsibility. Their kmets were slowly turning from representatives of the local communities into representatives of the Prince's authority.

Extensive animal breeding still dominated rural economic
activity, although in the 1830s the trend was slowly turning to
intensive agriculture.[10] Maize was still the basic cereal,
feeding men and animals alike,[11] with wheat starting up after
1830. The potato was also introduced at that time alongside
the traditional vegetables (beans, followed by cabbages, pumpkins, onions and green peppers). Of the fruit traditionally
grown (plums, followed by cherries, apples, pears and peaches),
grape production went up with the end of Moslem landholding,
until by 1835 vineyards took up about half the area devoted to
agricultural production, meadows excluded - although wine was
still produced almost exclusively for immediate and family
consumption. Tobacco was also now grown in Serbia. The haphazard exploitation of forests went on uncontrolled throughout
Miloš's reign, so that by 1830 the woods of Serbia were somewhat thinner as a result of constant immigration accompanied
with reclamation. It is difficult to say with any degree of
precision how much deforestation had occurred by 1830, although
woodland is thought to have still covered 65 per cent of the
total area of the Principality at that time.

Some thirty-five 'towns', most of which were no more than
semi-rural townships, generally stood out from the peasant-
rural sea around them. A mixed world of some 60,000 Serbs,
Turks, Jews, Greeks, Aroumanians (Vlachs) and Gypsies, the urban
world was still different, though less so, and was gradually
becoming 'naturalized'. By far the largest town was Belgrade,
with a population estimated by contemporaries at 15-30,000 (the
largest figure being equal to half the total urban population),
including some 10,000 Serbs. 1830 is the year when the face of
Belgrade began to change. While the residential part retained
its eastern appearance, with Turkish-type ground-floor houses
surrounded by gardens, the first official buildings adopted a
European, Hungarian-type architecture. The rapid population
increase caused real-estate speculation, the proliferation of
bidonville-type makeshift huts, and a lack of balance between
the sexes.

Native Serbs (with the help of Serbs from Austria) would,
in the 1830s, evolve an urban society which mirrored both the
old Graeco-Turkish and the new Central European ways. Fashion
symbolized this evolution, with the dress of the urban élite
adapting to European models - Central European or Russian
bureaucratic uniforms, Hungarian noble attire or even the sombre

Western frock-coat. The Greeks, and with them the Hellenized
urban Aroumanians, gradually either emigrated or turned Serbian,
still providing much of the business and professional element.
The Jews, on the other hand, would take another generation or
two to integrate. Some 1,500 in number, mainly Sephardic, and
nearly all in Belgrade, they too were in business, and kept to
themselves. Serbia did not attract 'European' immigrants apart
from Habsburg Serbs, and real foreigners were still rare in the
'thirties. That the second-largest town in the mid-1830s was
Kragujevac, with no more than 2-3,000 inhabitants, is explained
by the rapid emigration of Turks, due to pressures of all sorts,
which actually caused a sharp drop in the population of middle-
range towns.[12] Thus the Serbian revolution at first provoked
a further deterioration of the long-declining urban economy.

The 1830s were a transitional phase for urban crafts and
urban trade which were no longer so sharply differentiated from
their rural counterparts as Serbs started taking them over.
Traditional urban crafts had been organized into the guilds of
Moslem law. With the departure of Turkish capital-owners and
skilled labour, their number diminished, as Serbs first set up
their own guilds on the Turkish model, then gradually took over
the old ones. At the same time, both faced the competition of
independent craftsmen immigrating from Austria, and of imported
Austrian manufactured goods. The relative wealth of the land
in proportion to the total population until about 1860, the
ample supply of food in terms of the prevailing style of life,
and the abundance of fuel wood meant that no industrial development at all would take place until well into the latter half of
the century.

All existing coins, Ottoman and European, were in circulation and their market-value simply varied according to offer and
demand. The money business provided a living for a whole section of the urban trading community. The money-dealers, who
changed and lent, were generally small jobbers, concentrated in
Belgrade - Jews, Serbs and, still, mainly Greeks. Although
natives were gradually moving into those fields of business
which had been the preserve of urban Turks, Greeks or Jews,
trade was not yet completely free in the 'thirties, because of
the many Turkish monopolies simply taken over by Miloš. Furthermore, town traders, supported by the Prince, were able to prevent the opening of village shops until the Constitution of
1838.

The zadruga, which had been almost completely self-sufficient, was breaking up, and the peasant needed the goods that he could no longer make within the smaller family unit, quite apart from the new needs being suggested to him as they appeared in the town. He had always needed some cash to buy salt, and taxes now also had to be paid in cash. All this led the peasant to sell his produce. On the other hand, towns - and especially Belgrade - had to buy more produce from the country-side. There existed a network of markets and fairs, in market towns and in monasteries. But the infra-structure of communications was primitive. There were no ballasted roads before 1830, and rivers were usually forded. Distances were long by ox-waggon or horse-cart, and even on horse-back it took the best part of twenty-four hours to get from Belgrade to Kragujevac. During Miloš's reign, and on his initiative, especially in the 'thirties, numerous hans were built, and new roads constructed, while many more roads were ballasted.

Commerce on a larger scale dealt with live-stock exports or with the transit trade. Middlemen travelled the country, buying pigs from the peasant producers and selling them again to the wholesale exporters - fifty-six of them in 1820, all more or less in partnership with Miloš. The pigs were then ferried across the Save and walked off by night, for six to eight weeks, as far as Budapest or even Vienna. Transit through Serbia, from Turkey to Austria, dealt mainly with cotton and wool. Typically, the Ottoman customs at Belgrade were taken up on lease from the Sultan by Miloš as early as 1815. Serbia was also involved in the changes that affected shipping along the lower, Ottoman, stretch of the Danube from Belgrade to the sea. Ownership passed rapidly from predominantly Turkish into Christian, essentially Greek, and Jewish hands, with quite a few Serbian owners by 1830. Belgrade and Smederevo became shipbuilding centres in the 'thirties, so that by 1834 there were already about two hundred small Serbian craft plying along the Save and Danube, although Serbian shipowners were quickly confronted with the competition of foreign steam. The first Austrian steamboat was put into operation between Belgrade and the Iron Gates in 1834, and by the middle of the century there no longer was a Serbian merchant marine.

The period of the 1830s accelerated the evolution under-gone in all fields of life since 1804, so that the constitutional crisis of the late 'thirties, ending with Miloš Obrenović's defended the Germanic principle of a <u>Rechtsstaat</u> and the Western European principle of a limited monarchy under a constitution. In essence, however, what they objected to was the institution-alization of the ruler's irrevocable personal authority, all-powerful, centralizing, immanent in, rather than emanating from, society. What they really desired at first was the transfer to themselves of the old monopolies rather than their abolition, and, when this proved impossible, the return to delegated group authority. The continuation of this mentality from the largely self-governing and self-sufficient <u>sancak</u> of Belgrade in the late eighteenth century, into the nineteenth century once the territory had been constituted as a state, goes a long way towards explaining why modern Serbia found it somewhat difficult to maintain stable government. The history of Serbia in the nineteenth century could indeed be described as a quest for stable government in terms of the political mentality set forth in this paper. Surviving even into the twentieth century when Serbia was merged into Yugoslavia, the description also goes some way to explaining how and when authoritarian régimes are accepted or rejected.

1. The historical and ethnographical works of Vuk St. Karadžić (originally published between 1827 and 1860; Serbian government edition, Skupljeni istoriski i etnografski spisi, Belgrade 1898; modern popular editions, Prvi i Drugi srpski ustanak, Belgrade: Prosveta 1947, and Vukovi zapisi, Belgrade: SKZ 1964) and Tihomir R. Djordjević (originally published between 1901 and 1932; Geca Kon editions, Iz Srbije kneza Miloša, 2 vols, Belgrade 1922-24, and Naš narodni život, 10 vols., Belgrade 1930-34) are fundamental, along with Mateja Nenadović's memoirs (originally published in 1867 and available in English tr. and ed. by L. Edwards, The Memoirs of the Prota Mateja Nenadović, Oxford 1969), Mita Petrović's archival and statistical Financije i ustanove obnovljene Srbije do 1842 (3 vols., Belgrade 1899-1901), and Ami Boué, La Turquie d'Europe (4 tomes in 2 vols., Paris 1840). Leopold Ranke, Die Serbische Revolution (originally published in 1829 and available in English tr., The History of Servia and the Servian Revolution, London 1835), written from data provided by Karadžić, is a vivid contemporary study of the transformation of Serbia during the period.

    Important works in Serbo-Croatian published during the past twenty years are: M. Ekmečić, 'Srpska revolucija i jugoslovenske zemlje u vreme napoleonskih ratova' in Istorija Jugoslavije (by I. Božić, S. Ćirković, M. Ekmečić and V. Dedijer, Belgrade: Prosveta 1972); N. Konstantinović, Beogradski pašaluk: Severna Srbija pod Turcima (Belgrade 1970); M. Djordjević, O pitanju samouprave Srbije 1791-1830 (Belgrade 1972); V. Stojančević, Miloš Obrenović i njegovo doba (Belgrade 1966); N. Vučo, Raspadanje esnafa u Srbiji (2 vols., Belgrade 1954-58); and D. Milić-Milojković, Trgovina Srbije 1815-39 (Belgrade 1959).

    Important works in English and French are: T. Stoianovich, A Study in Balkan Civilization (New York 1967) and 'The Social Foundations of Balkan Politics 1750-1941' in C. and B. Jelavich eds., The Balkans in Transition: Essays on the Development of Balkan Life and Politics since the Eighteenth Century (Berkeley and Los Angeles 1963); D. Wilson, The Life and Times of Vuk Stefanović Karadžić 1787-1864: Literacy, Literature and National Independence in Serbia (Oxford 1970); S. Pavlowitch, Anglo-Russian Rivalry in Serbia 1837-39 (Paris and The Hague 1961); J. and B. Halpern, A Serbian Village in Historical Perspective (New York 1972); M. Petrovich, A History of Modern Serbia 1804-1918, I (New York and London 1976); D. Djordjević, Révolutions nationales des peuples balkaniques 1804-1914 (Belgrade 1965); G. Castellan, La Vie quotidienne en Serbie au seuil de l'indépendance 1815-39 (Paris 1967) and 'Directions nouvelles de l'histoire des Balkans' in Revue historique CCXXXVI/I (Paris 1966); and Y. Castellan, La Culture serbe au seuil de l'indépendance 1800-40 (Paris 1967).

2. Belgrade was at a distance of 1,500 km from the Ottoman capital, i.e. five to ten days for a government messenger and two to three weeks for a

155

mounted troop. (All figures in this paper are compounded from various estimations quoted in the works listed above.)

3. Population figures, estimated on the basis of taxes paid by villages and households, are always meant to cover both the twelve districts of the <u>sancak</u> (some 25,000 sq. km) and the six additional districts, liberated by Karageorge's insurrection and incorporated again in Miloš's Principality in 1834 (some 13,000 sq. km) – a total area of 37,540 sq. km. This is in order to be able to make meaningful comparisons.

4. <u>The Life and Times of V. St. Karadžić</u>, 28.

5. <u>A Study in Balkan Civilization</u>, 147.

6. 'C'est la principale branche d'industrie des Serbes; c'est elle qui leur a fourni assez d'argent /. . ./ pour se procurer les munitions nécessaires afin de pouvoir résister aux Turcs' (Boué, t. III, 140).

7. Ibid.

8. By 1834 the Moslem population of Serbia was down to 15,000, including the garrisons of the six fortresses, and concentrated mainly in Belgrade (6,000) and in Užice (4,000). Constantly shrinking in size throughout the '30s, it was in a pitiful state, composed of soldiers, of a handful of poorly paid officials, of former landlords deprived of their land or waiting to sell out, of miserable artisans and of a crowd of parasites of all sorts.

9. Miloš who, at that time, wore a turban more often than not and kept what almost amounted to a harem, continued the Ottoman fiscal system, suitably adapted, until 1835.

10. In 1830 some 12 per cent of the total land area was under cultivation, including meadows - but only 5 per cent excluding meadows.

11. Its annual production around 1830 is estimated at 180-200 kg per inhabitant.

12. Some by as much as half or more between 1820 and 1830, the most dramatic declines being the largely Turkish Užice that fell from 13,000 to 700, Smederevo (another garrison town) from 8,000 to 4,000, and Valjevo from 2,500 to under 1,000.

13. <u>La Vie quotidienne en Serbie au seuil de l'indépendance</u>, 290.

14. There were 38 monasteries in 1840, with 123 monks.

8

BULGARIAN SOCIETY IN THE EARLY 19th CENTURY

R. J. CRAMPTON

Comparatively little academic research has been devoted to the social structure of the Bulgarians in the first half of the nineteenth century. This is in large measure due to the lack of social and political stability during this period. From the 1780s to the mid-1810s central government had all but collapsed to produce the anarchy of local banditry which the Bulgarians call the kurdzhaliistvo,[1] but even the restoration of central control did not produce stability. During the 1820s there were political tensions consequent upon the Greek revolt and that decade closed with the Russo-Turkish war of 1828-29 which, as will be seen, had profound social effects in some parts of the Bulgarian lands. The 1830s saw no invasions or major wars but the reforms which began in 1832 dismantled the existing social structure without having any concept of what was to replace it,[2] ever a sure recipe for instability and disorder, and the local-ised risings of the 1840s and 1850s were indeed largely the result of the inadequacies of the reforms.

The instability produced constant shifts and changes within Bulgarian society and the isolation of separate and distinct social groups is consequently extremely difficult. In fact little about the nature of Bulgarian society in this period can be established beyond dispute. The population can certainly not be measured accurately though the total of all racial groups was probably somewhere between four and six million.[3] The majority of these were Bulgarians, most of whom lived in small villages and were almost entirely dependent on agriculture for their livelihood, with many communities still at or only a little beyond the stage of subsistence farming; even many of the Bulgarians who had moved into the towns retained some land of their own and engaged in occupations which were closely connected with agriculture. This was a reflection of the fact that the Bulgarians were in general late-comers to the towns, which at the end of the eighteenth century were still

157

predominantly Turkish, especially the garrison towns, with sizeable minorities of Greeks, Armenians or Jews.* There were also
ethnic minorities in the countryside; Albanians were to be
found in western Macedonia, Turks and Romanians in the north
Bulgarian plain and the Dobrudja, Vlachs in Macedonia and other
mountainous areas, Greeks south and west of a line from
Istanbul to the Rhodope mountains, and some Arabs and Tatars
had settled south of the central mountain range, though the
latter did not arrive in large numbers till after the Crimean
War.[4]

The settlement of Tatars and Circassians in the Bulgarian
lands after 1856 was to precipitate important social and
political changes but in the first half of the century the
major changes - social, economic, political and cultural -
were connected with or precipitated by the collapse and abolition of the established land-holding system of the Ottoman
Empire.

This system, which had become obsolete and ineffective by
the turn of the century and which was finally yet gradually
dissolved in the reforms of the 1830s and thereafter, was complex.[5] Most peasants owned their own homes and plots of land
within the village boundary or up to about a kilometre from it;
this land, mülk property, was in complete private ownership with
the proprietor having full independence to buy, sell, lease etc..
There were also a few large estates, the gaz-i-mülk, given by
the Sultan as hereditary, private possessions, to especially
deserving generals. In addition there were vakuf estates, that
is estates whose income had been entailed in part or in its
entirety to the upkeep of a religious or charitable institution;
on these estates the peasants were exempt from state taxation,[6]**
the main item of which was the tithe in kind. On the few large
estates of the Sultan's private demesnes the peasants were
exempt from some taxation and from the forced labour, angariya,
required on all other estates. Outside the villages were the
pastures and the large fields, usually two or three divided into
strips, on which the villagers relied for their grazing and their
staple crops. These, the so-called mirii lands, belonged to the

---

* There were notable exceptions. The largest ethnic group in Thessaloniki
  was Jewish, and administrative centres were likely to have larger Greek
  settlements.

** State taxation is to be differentiated from the taxes most Christian

158

Sultan but were leased to tenants who, in return, provided services to the state. These estates were divided, according to the value of the income of the tenancy, into three basic categories, the khaş, the ziamet and the timar, the latter two being far more numerous than the first.[7] The great majority of these tenancies were spahiluks; that is the tenant of the Sultan was a spahi or one required in time of war to provide a number of fighting men for the Sultan's armies, that number varying directly with the size of the tenancy. In order to equip and maintain those men the spahi was to collect the tithe from the mirii lands included in his estate and he was also able to require a set number of labour days together with other minor taxes from the peasants who worked those lands. The spahi, however, could not interfere with the working of the land; what crops were to be grown, when they were to be harvested, etc., was entirely the business of the peasant, nor could the spahi interfere with the passing on by hereditary succession of the lands held by a peasant family. These peasant rights were firmly and clearly set out in the tapii, documents issued by the spahi and confirmed by the kadi but kept in the possession of the raya, or peasant.

The spahis also acted as a form of local government, taking responsibility for the upkeep of roads etc., maintaining law and order, and also collecting state taxes from the peasants on their estates. Here lay a hidden danger. For centuries the spahis had levied both state taxes and the rents due to them as landlords, both payments almost invariably being in kind, but the two levies were generally collected by the same people and at the same time. State taxes and the purely tenurial obligations were therefore handed over together and inevitably the distinction between them became blurred or even forgotten. Yet the distinction became vital when the spahi system collapsed and the collection of rent had to be separated from the payment of taxes.

The reasons for the collapse of the spahi system were numerous. Military technology had made the spahi-based army inadequate, the division of holdings had made many spahiluks too small to be viable, and price movements, especially at the end of the eighteenth century, disadvantaged those whose income

communities paid for the upkeep of their churches and clergy. See note 6.

was in staple crops but whose expenditure was on manufactured or imported items.[8] In contrast, those who were able to insist that their estates produced the new cash crops, primarily cotton and tobacco, could secure high profits from the rapidly expanding trade in these items; in some areas around large towns secure livings could also be made from cereals, vegetables, etc. To take full advantage of commodity production, therefore, it was necessary to establish full economic control over an estate, that is, to possess the right not only to the income off that land, but also the right to determine how the land should be used, what crops should be grown and under what conditions the raya tenants should work the land. To do this the existing landlord had to call in the current tapii and either change them drastically or suppress them completely.

This would be not only a contravention of law and custom but also a usurpation of local political power, for changes in the tenurial patterns and in the political power structure of the Ottoman empire were inextricably linked, with the latter being both cause and result of the former. The ayani, or local administrative and political bosses[*] who appeared in the eighteenth century, invariably based their authority upon full possession of a landed estate[9] and conversely, when Ottoman central government collapsed during the chaos of the 1780s and 1810s, local political power could be used to extend landed properties; later periods of instability witnessed similar though less widespread extension of the private control of the land, especially in north-west Bulgaria.

It has been customary to apply to estates under private control the term chiflik. Though chifliks had long existed political and social conditions during the kurdzhaliistvo were ideal for their rapid multiplication and they have come to be associated, particularly in the more traditional of Marxist interpretations, with the transition from feudalism to capitalism; they were according to one such interpretation:

> established on the most productive land situated near the larger centres of consumption. Chifliks were large-scale

---

[*] As is often the case German provides a more workable equivalent to a Balkan term; the German term for aġa, or aya, is Bezirksvorsteher. Another example of the superiority of the German over the English equivalent is that of Kulturheim rather than 'reading room' for the Bulgarian chitalishte.

agricultural units set up in response to commodity
production and to the use of money in commercial
exchanges. On the chifliks peasants lacked the right to
determine how the land was to be used; they were landless
and worked the land at the dictates of the landlord as
share-croppers (izpolichari) and agricultural labourers.
Alongside the feudal methods of production prevalent in
the eighteenth and nineteenth century there also began to
emerge capitalist forms of production. Thus chifliks may
be defined as a transitional form of feudal tenure in
which capitalism was born.[10]

Or, from the same author in another place,

The chifliks were commodity farms. They came into being
in the neighbourhood of the larger administrative and
military centres of the Empire, in the proximity of river
and sea ports, where farming produce could be more easily
and rapidly marketed.[11]

Such wide and unqualified definitions will not serve to
explain changes in tenurial relationships during the first half
of the nineteenth century, but before this point is developed
it may be advantageous to isolate some general characteristics
of the new private estates, admitting temporarily the unqualified use of the terms chiflik and chiflikchiya (estate owner).

In the first place the chifliks of the late eighteenth
and early nineteenth century were mainly vehicles for the
preservation in changing circumstances of existing power and
wealth for most chiflikchii were those who had enjoyed these
precious commodities in pre-Kurdzhalii times: the ayani, the
Janissaries, local officials, tax-farmers, money-lenders, the
pudari (field guards), nearly all of whom would have been
Moslem. There were some chiflik owners whose wealth and power
lay in manufacturing and trading, one such being the Christian
merchant, money-lender and entrepreneur, Khristo Rachev of
Gabrovo, who bought an extensive estate of some eight hundred
dyunyuma,[12*] but chiflikchii in this second category rarely
owned large estates.[13] Institutions such as monasteries could
also own chifliks; the great Rila foundation, for example, had
long owned land in various parts of Bulgaria and in 1821 was
able to buy near the monastery a large chiflik which for the
next thirty years at least was to be its main source of income.[14]

---

* A dyunyuma was equal to 19.9 square metres.

Chifliks included pastures and woodland as well as arable
fields, and on occasions chiflikchiya assumed control of mülk
as well as mirii lands; chifliks were also set up on the unused
land which was so extensive in the Balkans at this time.
Chifliks established on this unused land usually consisted of a
number of buildings and peasant homes clustered around a tower
which served as a look-out post to warn of approaching marauders
and as a vantage point from which work in the fields could be
supervised; in Macedonia many such chifliks were walled.[15]
Chifliks based on existing villages did not often disturb the
established settlement pattern, that of the dispersed village
with its separate maxala (wards) all of which were by origin
homesteads derived from one Ur-zadruga, if such a linguistic
Mischling may be tolerated.[16]

The form of tenure traditionally associated with chifliks
is that of share-cropping. The most common variant of this
phenomenon was izpolicharstvo or ortakchiistvo.[17] This system
prevailed in areas where most rather than all the land had been
chiflikised. Peasants owned their own homes and some land but
this was not sufficient for their upkeep. They therefore leased
extra parcels of land from the chiflikchiya; the latter usually
provided seed but the tenants, the izpolichari, used their own
implements and animals. The rent paid for the parcels of land
was a proportion of the crop, usually a half of the arable
crop and two-thirds of the hay mown, though in the Stara Zagora
area a third of the arable crop was the normal requirement, this
variant of izpolicharstvo being known as yuurdzhum. The division
of the crop took place after the tithe had been assessed, the
standard practice being to make the division after the harvest
had been gathered, though around Stara Zagora the crop was
divided whilst still on the stalk; in addition to handing over
a proportion of the crop the izpolichari were often required to
provide labour for the estate owner. The peasant was free to
leave the land to go either to another estate where conditions
might be more favourable, or to the towns, a factor of some
importance in the 1830s and thereafter when the Bulgarian towns
entered upon a period of rapid growth. The landlord could
transfer the land worked by the izpolichari to another
chiflikchiya at any time but could not deprive a tenant of his
plots until the crop sown by that peasant had been harvested.
The peasant could not leave his parcels of land to his children
though this did not often mean dispossession of a deceased

peasant's sons for the custom was to conclude new contracts.

A far more exacting form of tenure was the kesimdzhiistvo.[18] Here the rent was not a proportion of the crop but the kesim, a yearly quantity agreed when the contract was entered upon. The great danger for the tenant was in years of poor harvest for then he might well be forced to borrow produce both to keep himself and to pay the kesim. The tenant, the kesimdzhiya, also had to render labour services to his landlord, perhaps even being required to cart produce to a port or to market or even to collect the kesim from other tenants; in addition he was often obliged to provide the landlord with extra food - butter, cheese, mutton, etc. - at certain Moslem religious festivals. The kesimdzhiya usually owned his own house and implements and the kesim tenancy could be passed on by inheritance. For his part the landlord could not interfere with how the land was used, his function being to supervise its distribution. He also had a theoretical duty to ensure that all families on his estates had sufficient land and that any newcomers were provided with land, homes, implements and animals; the landlord could suspend a tenancy agreement but only when the current harvest had been taken in, though he could sell his estate to another chiflikchiya at any time, and he could also transfer to another estate - his own or that of any other chiflikchiya - the labour owed to him by his peasants. The peasant, on the other hand, had the right to leave the land whenever he pleased though there is evidence to suggest that landlords occasionally used force to prevent the exercise of this right, particularly in times of bad harvest.[19]

A feature of many of the largest chifliks was the use of agricultural labourers, the ratai or momtsi. The ratai were found more frequently on chifliks established on previously unused land than on those set up in established villages for those in the latter were reluctant to give up their plots, however small, whilst those in the new chifliks were less able to resist becoming wage earners; ratai were particularly numerous in Macedonia with its relatively high concentration on the new cash crops: cotton tobacco and maize. Agricultural labourers also formed the main part of the kekhai or gangs of migrant seasonal workers which at the beginning of the nineteenth century had been organised on a co-operative, profit-sharing basis but which quickly became gangs employed by the gang-leaders.[20] Although there were great local variations and cash payments were known even early in the nineteenth century[21] for

most _ratai_ payment was in kind, that is in cereals, cheese and
other foodstuffs, and also in hides, wool, material for making
shoes, etc.. Even though the employer was obliged to pay all
taxes for the _ratai_ and to provide him with security few _ratai_
families were able to live above subsistence level, existing on
a diet of rye-bread and vegetables and eating meat only at the
great religious festivals; in extreme cases labourers might
become indebted to their employer and thus fall into total
dependence upon him.

These categories of tenure are general ones and the divi-
sions between them were by no means so clear-cut. It is difficult to accept as _chifliks_ in the narrow sense of the term the
kesim estates or the _gospodarlutsi_ of north-western Bulgaria
which will be discussed below, for here few landlords made any
attempt to interfere with the working of the land or to sub-
stitute commodity for subsistence production. Many villages
contained a variety of tenures and could be divided among a
number of different landlords; likewise some households within a
community would remain free whilst others fell under the control
of a _chiflikchiya_. This multiplicity of tenure was due in part
to the fact that many households held land in other villages
(the so-called _parakende_ land) which had become theirs usually
as part of a dowry, and it could be that a household in a
chiflik village could maintain itself on its _parakende_ lands and
therefore had no need to rent what had been the _mirii_ land used
by its native village and what was now a _chiflik_ estate. A
further complication of the simple picture was that many of the
poorest _ratai_ or _kesimdzhii_ held some land of their own and some
of them actually rented out these small plots to other peasants,
usually on _izpolicharstvo_, whilst a number of completely landless _ratai_, despite the generally meagre level of payment in
kind, were able to establish themselves as freeholders after
working for six to ten years as agricultural labourers. There
was, in fact, something of an impulse away from the propertyless
condition. Many _ratai_ received as part of their remuneration a
small plot of land for their own use, and in some areas so large
were these plots, the _paraspor_, that the _ratai_ were spending
only two days per week wage-earning on the _chiflik_ estate, and
in the Nova Zagora area, where land holdings were generally
larger than usual, _paraspors_ could be as much as four or even
ten _uvrat_[*] in size.[22] A similar natural abhorrence of the

[*] An _uvrat_ was equal to 1,600 square metres.

propertyless state is seen in the large flocks of sheep, for
employed shepherds usually had the right to graze a score or so
of their own animals in the huge flocks of their employers.[23]

In that the chiflik, as ideologically defined, does not
help in explaining the profusion of agrarian relationships which
emerged in the early nineteenth century we would be much better
off invoking the concept of Lokalvernunft so beloved of certain
eighteenth century German philosophers, for greatly varying
local conditions and local traditions were the real determinants in the social evolution of the Balkans at this time.

The kesimdzhiistvo, for example, is explained by a
combination of geographical and political factors which was
mercifully rare, for kesim tenants were found only around
Radomir, Kiustendil and Dupnitsa, with only four kesim villages
being identified in the latter area,[24] whilst in the territory
of the present-day Macedonian Federal Republic only 1.4 per
cent of the villages were entirely dependent upon kesim tenure
during the nineteenth century.[25] For a landlord kesimdzhiistvo
was ideal for villages located on poor soil, in that a share
of crops from such soil might not be sufficient, whereas the
kesim could be set at a level which would ensure a profitable
income. Yet to impose so harsh a system the landlord would
need unfettered political power, and in the kesim areas that
was indeed his in the crucial decade and a half at the beginning
of the nineteenth century. This political power rested partly
upon the smallness and isolation and therefore the weakness,
even in normal times, of the mountain communities, but more
specifically upon the fact that during the years of the Serbian
revolt these areas, and especially Kiustendil where the main
concentration of kesim tenures was to be found, had been flooded
with Ottoman troops going to and from operations in the revolted
province. Many troop commanders, frequently in collusion with
local Moslem beys, had taken advantage of the weakness of the
local communities and of their virtual immunity from civilian
political control and had established themselves in the villages, often making their first step the seemingly innocuous
request to graze animals on village pastures, a practice to be
condemned in a later Imperial decree as 'contrary to law and to
custom'.[26] Once the right to pasture had been secured other
demands followed and many troop commanders and beys collected
taxes from the villages - there were even cases of demands
for payment in respect of the dung left by grazing animals -

the intended and usually achieved result being to force the
peasants so far into debt that they would have to surrender
their tapii and accept new ones based on the kesim, or, if a
form of kesim tenure already existed, to accept one which was
more onerous. If this crude financial pressure failed there
were yet cruder methods for, given the lack of political
control from the centre, it was easy enough to use violence or
the threat thereof to extract the tapii and perhaps mülk
property too, and there were few communities in these areas
which had not seen at least one of their number impaled pour
encourager les autres.[27] With the end of military operations
against the Serbs and the restoration of central government
after the kurdzhaliistvo Kiustendil and Dupnitsa returned to
their former status of being backwaters which meant that even
in the reform era the civilian authorities of the Ottoman
state were not strong enough in these areas to eliminate the
evils that its military arm had introduced.

Factors of a military and political nature also played
an important part in determining social evolution in the north-
western areas of the Bulgarian lands, those around Vidin, Lom,
Belogradchik, Pirot and Nish.

The eyalet of Vidin had since 1396 been administered under
somewhat different conditions from the rest of European Turkey[28]
and within this area there had been established a relatively
large number of Imperial and vizirial khas estates but by the
end of the eighteenth century the income of many villages on
these estates was, with official consent, being collected by
local money-lenders or other prominenti, a system which
inevitably meant that once central power had weakened this and
other khas land would be seized by those who collected the
income from it. Late in the eighteenth century the situation
was complicated by the frequent passage of the armies in the
Austrian war of 1787-91, the disturbances and insecurity which
the troops caused being such as to drive the peasants into
refuge in the mountains or into exile across the Danube. In the
1790s plague caused further devastation, so much so that even
the bishop of Vidin could not find enough villagers to raise a
sum sufficient for his upkeep.[29] If the peasants' land were
left untilled for three years their tapii were automatically
forfeit and any would-be chiflikchiya could issue new ones on
terms suitable to his own purpose. Yet by the 1790s there was
little need to wait for the expiry of the three-year legal limit.

The gradual decay of Ottoman central power had now reached the point where the Porte could no longer prevent the rise of local adventurers, and the efforts made to subdue the famous Pasvanoğlu of Vidin only compounded local problems; the six-month siege of the city in 1798, for example, introduced into the region 100,000 ill-disciplined Ottoman troops who succeeded only in depressing yet further the condition of the local peasantry,[30] a depression perpetuated after 1804 by the flow of troops first to Serbia and then, after 1806, to the war with Russia. Neither the peasants nor the government could gainsay the local forces, nor were there, as there were in the Belgrade Paşalık, enough local spahis to check the confiscation of land by these forces which had been quickly organised under Pasvanoğlu's leadership.[31] Pasvanoğlu's power had been based on the twenty-five chifliks owned by his father[32] but to these he added scores of others, many of which were used to reward his supporters; indeed the advent of Pasvanoğlu 'signified the removal of all obstacles and hindrances to the wholesale expropriation of the peasantry, to the unfettered transfer of demesne (khas) lands into objects for private use . . .'[33]

With the death of Pasvanoğlu in 1813 and the defeat of his successor a year later central power was sufficiently restored for the government to decide that khas lands expropriated during the recent upheavals would become state property, not the property of the peasants. This was the seed of much later trouble. Peasants who had retained their tapii, and there were some such peasants, believed that they now had full control over these lands and that the produce they handed over to the tax-farmer represented taxation not rent;* further-more, in the vicinity of Vidin the state allowed the new owners to purchase the khas lands they had taken, many of these purchases being confirmed in local courts in the 1820s and 1830s.[34]

In 1828-29 further disruptions were caused by the Russo-Turkish war. The advance of the Russian army alarmed local Moslems and when the fanatical Mustafa Paşa Bushatlı of Scutari camped near Vidin with his army Moslem frustration unleashed such a fury that once again thousands of peasants fled to the mountains, to Serbia or to Romania. After the war came

---

* See above p.159 for the origin of the difficulty in distinguishing taxation from rent.

the agrarian reforms. Beginning in 1832 the spahis were to give up their right to collect taxes and were thereafter to withdraw from the land receiving a pension in lieu of their former income. Yet only mirii land was affected by the reforms; inevitably the result was that before the process had progressed far landlords were anxious to convert as much mirii land as possible into mülk property. In this they were encouraged by Mehmet Izzet Paşa, valı of Vidin and Nicolpol from 1832 to 1833,[35] nor did the Porte much object to the consolidation of Moslem control over land in this area which was now not only a frontier zone but also both one in which Moslems were in a minority, and one in which Turks did not live in the villages,[36] so that to allow villages to fall under the authority of a local Moslem lord would not antagonise indigenous Turks. By 1842-43 the central authorities were even allowing villages which had not been under the control of a local aya to be put up for sale by auction and when the peasants themselves attempted to buy their tapii the local Moslem notables declared that for genera-tions this area, especially Belogradchik, Lom and Vidin, had been a frontier zone in which, because of their commitment to the defence of the Empire, only Moslems could own land; the Grand Vizir accepted the argument and some twenty villages were sold and therefore passed into the control of an aya[37] or, in the local Slav usage, a gospodar, becoming in the process gospodarluks, i.e. the property of a gospodar.

To summarise, by the 1840s the gospodarluk had become the dominant form of property in the north-west of Bulgaria, having emerged first on the former khas estates and then being formed on what had been the mirii lands until fear of the reforms in the 1830s drove the local notables to turn these lands into mülk property; by the mid-1840s the system had enveloped almost all of the villages in the Belogradchik, Kulsko and Vidin areas and the great majority of those around Pirot and Nish.[38] Most peasants on the gospodarluks were izpolichari but in many villages which were incorporated into a gospodarluk after 1839 the gospodar was allowed to collect his rent in the form of the kharizma, a fixed payment in kind similar in essence to but of a different origin from the kesim.[39]

The phenomenon of the gospodarluk was virtually confined to the north-west of Bulgaria and it is no coincidence that it was in this area that there occurred most of the agrarian unrest in the Bulgarian lands in the years after the reforms,

the most serious outbursts being the Nish revolt of 1841 and
the Vidin rising of 1850, though there were outbreaks in the
1830s, for example those at Berkovitsa in 1835 and 1836 and at
Pirot also in 1836. An important cause of these revolts was
the unsatisfactory nature of the reforms themselves. These had,
inter alia, abolished the spahi system, confirmed mirii lands
as state property, declared labour services illegal, and
outlawed tax-farming. This raised all sorts of expectations
which, given the nature of the Ottoman political machine, and
the confusion of the tax and land teneurial systems, could never
be fulfilled. And so it was; forced labour continued - the
peasants of Karlovo doing corvée on roads as late as 1870;[40]
the substitution of state for private tax-gatherers meant not
the end of abuses but their transference to new hands,[41] and,
most important of all, '. . . the abolition of the spahi system
created in the minds of the peasantry the idea that they were
now the real owners of the land.'[42] In many areas of Bulgaria
they did become so but the peasant on the gospodarluk was not
so fortunate. Not only were his expectations belied but his
material condition deteriorated significantly. The main
problem was double taxation. The reforms, while requiring all
state taxes to be paid to the new officials, the muhasils, did
not restrict the gospodar's right to collect rent on his private
estates. As has been noted above the same tax-farmer had
previously collected both the taxes paid via the spahi and the
rent due to the spahi in his role as landlord; after the
reforms these two payments were separated but often the muhasil
and the gospodar both exacted what had previously been handed
over in a single combined payment, that is they both exacted
what had been the sum of two different obligations. A further
complication in this and other areas was that the peasant had
to pay in addition to taxes and rent a sum to provide pensions
for the former spahis. The reforms in fact made a bad system
much worse and many taxes were collected more than once a year
for, in the absence of written records, the peasants could not
prove that payment had already been made. Not long after the
reforms some peasants were losing up to 50 per cent of their
meagre crops as tax thus allowing the money-lender endless
opportunity to ply his destructive trade. At the same time the
method of collection alone was more often than not a just cause
for complaint.[43] On the gospodarluks the peasant also had to
contend with older forms of oppression; forced labour continued;

peasants around Vidin being required to work two or three days a week on the gospodar's own holding,[44] whilst petitions from villages in the eastern Morava valley as late as 1858 and 1859 speak of gospodars threatening to evict anyone who refused to provide young girls for their enjoyment.[45]

Only after the Vidin rising of 1850 did the government begin to dismantle the gospodarluk system, nor were its early efforts in this direction successful for it had to suspend redemption payments - ironically in 1861 - when the possibility of further massive emigration to Serbia threatened to depopulate this vital border area.[46]

Another area where a relatively large proportion of the land had by the mid-nineteenth century passed into private ownership was Macedonia, and even at the beginning of the twentieth century, when the profitability of land was in decline and chiflikchii were selling out in considerable numbers, there were still between three thousand and three thousand five hundred chifliks in the area.[47] Even before the eighteenth century trading links with central and western Europe via Thessaloniki in the south and the Morava valley in the north had stimulated commodity production. In the eighteenth century came a considerable increase in the production of cash crops, especially cotton and tobacco.[48] As early as 1729 Macedonian cotton was being sold in Leipzig[49] and the trade continued to flourish throughout the century, recovering quickly even from the setbacks of the kurdzhaliistvo. Commodity production was the main economic impulse to the formation of private estates but there were also political ones. Macedonia's distance from the centre of political power together with the presence, at least in the west, of unruly Albanian notables allowed abuses which until the collapse of central authority in the 1790s would not have been tolerated elsewhere; in Macedonia, for example, there was an unusually high incidence of peasant indebtedness caused by excessive taxation and leading to the surrender of the peasant tapiis to the tax-farmers and money-lenders, a process so widespread that it received especial mention in an Imperial edict of 1795 which attempted to put a stop to the suppression of peasant rights.[50] As elsewhere the kurdzhaliistvo allowed mass expropriation of villages by local ayani etc.; Ali Paşa Tepelenli, the most famous of these, amassed between eight and nine hundred private estates, dispossessing over five thousand families in the process,[51] and

170

his practices were copied, albeit on a lesser scale, by such figures as Cjeladin Bey in Okhrid and Ismail Paşa in Serres.[52]

Some peasants sought to escape from the local chieftains by placing themselves under the protection of a derudedzhiya. The latter, usually a Moslem and a townsman, made himself responsible for handing over to government officials the taxes due from the community and he also interceded on behalf of that community with the local ayani or war lords. The community paid the taxes to the derudedzhiya and, of course, paid him extra sums for his efforts on their behalf. By the early nineteenth century hundreds of Macedonian villages had placed themselves under a derudedzhiya, and some small towns did the same, Krushevo, for example, relied for its protection upon Said Ahmed Bey of Bitola to whom each household in the town paid twenty groschen per annum. Yet this system could be a danger. Protector could all too easily turn persecutor and attempt to seize the peasants' tapii, and when, after the kurdzhaliistvo, the derudedzhiya was less necessary it was often difficult to escape from him, and many villages in the 1820s are seen to change from one protector to another in an attempt to escape a burden which seemed to increase as the need for it decreased. The system was officially banned in 1830 but persisted in some cases to 1912 as a form of covert protection racket.[53]

The number of chiflik holdings in Macedonia was large, covering in all probably a third and in some kazas as much as 70 per cent of the land worked.[54] Yet relatively little of this land was in the form of the large chiflik and by no means all were chifliks in the economic sense, that is units using share-cropping or wage-labour to produce for the market. Such estates did exist, especially in the cotton-growing areas around Serres or in the Drama area, the only one in the Balkans where by the mid-nineteenth century the value of the tobacco grown exceeded that of cereals.[55] Many private holdings, however, were chifliks only in the technical or legal sense, that is their owner enjoyed both the right to the income from the land and the right to determine how the land should be worked. Originally the word chiflik had meant that area of land which could be worked with one pair (chift) of oxen and the term had been no more than the Turkish equivalent of the Slav bashtina, the small self-sufficient holding farmed by one peasant household. In the nineteenth century many technical chifliks were still of this type; in the 1800s in the Bitola

171

region alone there were eleven hundred so-called chifliks worked
by a single family using no outside share-croppers or wage
labourers,[56] and by the late nineteenth century the average
chiflik holding was 65.5 dyunyuma with most being between
seventy and one hundred and fifty dyunyuma.[57] According to an
eminent Bulgarian agrarian historian, Strashimir Dimitrov, it
was only on holdings of over three hundred dyunyuma that labour
had to be employed all the year round, with seasonal labour
being required usually on plots of over two hundred dyunyuma and
occasional labour on some holdings of above one hundred and
fifty dyunyuma.[58] Clearly most chifliks in Macedonia were in
external appearances virtually indistinguishable from the small
peasant freeholding, and the same was true of chifliks in the
mountains to the west of Sofia.[59]

The incidence of large chifliks seems to have been greatest in the Adrianople region. Here in the 1860s there were one
hundred and forty very large estates, varying between two and
three thousand dyunyuma;[60] the total number of chifliks in this
area has been estimated at between a thousand and twelve hundred,[61] but once again most of these would have been chifliks
only in the legal sense and the full chiflik was far from
being the dominant form of tenure for only fifteen to twenty
per cent of all the worked land was chiflik land.[62] Those
larger commercial units which did exist had clearly emerged
mainly because of the proximity of two large centres of consumption, Adrianople and Istanbul, and many of these chifliks had
emerged during the kurdzhaliistvo which was particularly severe
in Thrace as no one local figure became strong enough to impose
his own peace and order.

The case of Thrace and Adrianople conforms to the notion
of chifliks emerging as a result of the development of commodity
production but in the areas so far undiscussed - the Plovdiv
region, the Black Sea coast, the central mountains, and the
fertile plains of northern and north-eastern Bulgaria, including
the Dobrudja - the ideological postulates do not become reality
despite the fact that many of the conditions which should have
precipitated commercial chifliks were present. Chifliks were
to be found in all these areas more especially in the rich
wheat lands of the Dobrudja, and there were chiflikchii who
owned very large amounts of land: Hacı Bekir in the Sofia
region, for example, had between a thousand and fifteen hundred
dyunyuma[63] and near Stara Zagora there were some estates of over

172

four thousand dyunyuma,[64] but these were exceptions. In the
regions of Plovdiv, the Black Sea coast, the central mountains,
the Sofia basin, the north and the north-east of Bulgaria,
excluding the Dobrudja, no more than 5 per cent of the land was
in chiflik ownership.[65]

Why, then, were chifliks relatively rare in areas where
conditions should have forced their growth? Figures from the
Russe district indicate an increase in the number of chifliks
early in the eighteenth century with a peak year in 1737 after
which there was a slight decline with numbers remaining stable
even during the kurdzhaliistvo.[66] This could be explained by
the fact that before the great expansion of the Danube trade in
grain Russe was too remote from a suitable market to allow anything but that accumulation of chifliks round the town itself
which took place in the early eighteenth century. But this
argument could not be applied to the area around Burgas. Here,
as an Austrian traveller of the 1840s noted, was a fertile area
with a port which had encouraged a lively trade with the great
Istanbul market and yet there were few chifliks and after the
reforms most of the land was in the hands of small peasant
freeholders, selling grain through local Greek merchants.[67]
Around Plovdiv, too, a large local market and a fertile plain
failed to produce a large number of chifliks; indeed, this area
' . . . more economically advanced, with higher returns from the
land, and with an agriculture more geared to commodity production, had in the 1860s about fifty chifliks of which twenty-
eight, more than half, were less than one hundred dyunyuma in
extent.'[68]

A partial explanation of the lack of chiflikisation in
these areas is gained from examining the great population movements which took place in the first thirty years of the nineteenth century, for large-scale commercial chifliks were
dependent upon a ready supply of cheap labour, Professor
Stoianovich noting that the chiflik marked ' . . . the transition
from a social and economic structure founded upon moderate
land rent and few labour services to one of excessive land rent
and exaggerated services.'[69] Yet many parts of the Bulgarian
lands experienced considerable emigration and significant
depopulation. In some areas, as in Thrace, this might be merely
taking temporary refuge in a town during the kurdzhaliistvo or
flight to nearby mountains until stability returned, but in
some regions the depopulation was more lasting and had profound

effects. By 1840 northern Bulgaria had seen massive emigration and scores of villages were deserted[70] but even more
dramatic were events in eastern Bulgaria, particularly south
of the Stara Planina. Emigration from the area had begun in
the late eighteenth century and by the end of the war of 1806-
12 there were an estimated 100,000 Bulgarians in Wallachia and
southern Russia.[71] More followed in the next decade and a half
but it was the war of 1828-29 which produced the most extensive
movement. In these years, and especially after the Treaty of
Adrianople had proclaimed the return of Ottoman power, eastern
Bulgaria, again especially south of the central mountains, was
virtually devoid of Christians.[72] In contrast, areas where
emigration was very difficult because the Russian army did not
occupy them or because local figures such as the ayani, the
field-guards, or the kesim landlords prevented flight from the
villages,[73] all such areas experienced some measure of
chiflikisation in its widest sense.

When, after 1830, many families returned to the depopulated areas of eastern Bulgaria a number of factors hindered
chiflikisation. In the first place not enough families returned
to guarantee the abundant labour-supply necessary for any would-
be chiflikchiya, and initially many returning families were
those from vakuf estates which were legally protected from
chiflikisation.[74] Political factors combined with social ones
to impede the formation of chifliks. In the years immediately
after 1830 the Ottoman government was anxious to persuade the
peasants to return; to this end it offered concessions including
a promise to the peasants of the Sliven area to pay compensation
for the harvests lost during their emigration,[75] and in such an
atmosphere the authorities were not likely to stand by and allow
chiflikchii to subjugate the returning peasants, nor could local
Moslems plead the case put forward by the gospodari of north-
west Bulgaria, for this was not a frontier zone where strategy
demanded a strong local Moslem land-holding element.* The

---

* This was portentous for the Moslem landlords. In the 1830s the need to
repair the deleterious effects of depopulation led the government not to
champion the Moslem land-owner - though it did not move against him - and in
the 1850s it was fear of depopulation which induced the Porte to abandon the
gospodar and grant concessions to the Christian peasantry of the north-
west.

reforms of the 1830s further restricted the possibilites of chiflikisation. The peasant was now free to leave the land when he wished and in the depopulated areas there was little to prevent him exercising this right, and there are recorded instances of peasants in centres as far apart as Plovdiv, Pleven and even Serres simply refusing to become chiflik tenants;[76] if that could happen then no doubt other peasants adopted a less resolute form of resistance and, rather than become chiflik tenants, moved into the towns which were beginning to expand significantly in the 1830s. Furthermore, the abolition of the spahis did away with the obvious potential chiflikchii for there were now no local power-holders who could assume the role played by the gospodari in the north-west or by the ayani of Macedonia and the south-west. Meanwhile the potential Christian chiflikchiya had also been removed, for many of the Bulgarians who had begun to accumulate wealth stayed in exile where more stable conditions offered a more promising base for commercial and manufacturing enterprise; many leading Bulgarian mercantile houses were for this reason established outside the Bulgarian lands, particularly in the Danubian principalities and in southern Russia.

It is impossible to establish whether chiflikisation was taking place in the affected areas before 1828 but by the time relative stability returned the political factors which had allowed chiflikisation to occur had altered and so too had the social conditions in which these factors operated.

The critical shortage of resident labour in these areas continued throughout the first half and more of the nineteenth century. In the state-owned rice fields of Plovdiv and Tatar Pazardzhik where wage labour was employed workers were often passed from one estate to another on a ration-basis and some controllers or renters of state rice fields even high-jacked labourers for work on their own estates.[77] A further proof of labour shortages in the plains was the migration of seasonal workers. Since the late eighteenth century craftsmen had sought seasonal work in the larger towns, especially Istanbul, and after the first decade of the nineteenth century hundreds of others, particularly market gardeners, did likewise;[78] at the same time, organised gangs of harvesters, threshers and hay-makers moved into areas with insufficient labour; by the middle of the century thousands were involved in these movements with the wheat fields of the Dobrudja being worked by gangs from the

Turnovo area, whilst over three thousand harvesters from Elena alone went to 'the Sultan's and other chifliks in Thrace';[79] seasonal labourers from the Macedonian highlands harvested cotton in Serres and Demirhisar and were also to be found in northern and southern Bulgaria, the Dobrudja and as far afield as Romania and Russia.[80] Yet even the migrant workers could not meet all the demands for labour, not, that is, in a free labour market. In many areas the gangs refused to work for employers who had a reputation for low or irregular pay and the state was therefore forced, later in the century, to step in and regulate to some degree the supply of labour; thus the Turnovo district was ordered to provide three thousand harvesters for the Dobrudja and there was similar direction of labour to southern Bulgaria and to parts of Macedonia.[81] State intervention was often welcomed by the gangs themselves for it could guarantee fair treatment, and groups sometimes went to Turkish officials not only to ensure payment etc. but also to ask them to find employment and to guarantee safe passages to and from the place of work.[82]

If any general conclusions can be drawn from the confused and at times apparently contradictory social changes taking place in the Bulgarian countryside in the first half of the nineteenth century they are: that, leaving aside the gospodarluks of the north-west, large and compact chifliks were rare, Todorov reckoning those outside Macedonia as ' . . . a few hundred dispersed through the country and covering no more than four hundred to five hundred dekars',[83] many of which were in the Adrianople region. Most land in the private ownership of Turks was in fact divided into small plots and rented to share-croppers, most of whom had previously farmed that land,[84] whilst the owners lived in the towns, perhaps appearing on their land only to supervise the harvest. Most of these chiflikchii were former tax-farmers, money-lenders, Janissaries, etc., but the height of their power and influence passed with the ending of the kurdzhaliistvo, the gospodari of the north-west, as ever, excepted. For most peasants who had not passed from spahi overlordship into the hands of a gospodar or a chiflikchiya, including most of those who did return to the central and eastern areas and many in southern Bulgaria and eastern Thrace, the reforms of the 1830s did bring important changes. Taxes had still to be paid and in many cases contributions had to be made to provide former spahis with pensions, but despite these burdens the peasant did become all but an independent freeholder,

the mirii land still belonged to the state but late in the
Tanzimat new regulations on inheritance virtually made these
lands private property.[85] And most Bulgarian peasant families
fell into this category; no more than one in fifteen of
Bulgaria's peasants were dependent on chiflikchiya[86] and 'the
main body of the peasant population of the pre-Liberation
Bulgarian lands consisted of small commodity producers with
their own land and their own implements'.[87] They were not
threatened by the chiflikchiya and dispossession, if it came,
was the result of oppressive taxation and usury combined with
antiquated and unproductive farming methods.[88] It was also
taxation and inefficient husbandry, rather than the prying
chiflikchiya, which caused land hunger, for heavy taxes in kind
could only be paid by farming greater areas, though land hunger
was a problem of the second rather than the first half of the
century for in the earlier years very large amounts of land
remained unused.

Though generalisation is predictably dangerous, most
Bulgarian peasants had holdings of medium size, that is between
thirty and a hundred dyunyuma, an area which was generally
sufficient to provide the basic needs of most families without
forcing them to employ outside labour. 56 per cent of the
peasantry were in this category[89] and the fact that most
peasants had sufficient land for their needs does much to
explain the absence of discussion of agrarian problems in the
writings of the early Bulgarian revolutionaries.

Differentiation amongst the peasantry was, however,
taking place, albeit slowly, and by the middle of the century
15.4 per cent of the land was concentrated in the hands of only
4 per cent of the population.[90] Differentiation there had long
been. Records of the late seventeenth and early eighteenth
centuries show clearly that a small number of villagers were
appreciably better off in terms of land held than their fellows,[91]
and in the middle of the century testamentary evidence from
around Sofia reveals a similar rich upper strata in the villages.[92]
By the end of the eighteenth century the local elder, or
chorbadzhiya as he generally became known, was to be encountered
in most Bulgarian communities. Much has been written and still
is being written on the origin and significance of the
chorbahzhii but it is safe to assume that in most cases the
chorbadzhiya was a member of one of the more wealthy and
influential local families.[93] By the middle of the nineteenth

177

century the general pattern was little changed with most
villages having a small number of well-to-do families.

In the initial stage of differentiation between peasants
in the village communities a vital role was played by livestock
ownership, for much of the wealth of the richer peasant was
based upon animal husbandry rather than more efficient or
extensive tillage of the soil. This was in large measure due
to the fact that except near the larger towns there was little
incentive for the accumulation of more land than was necessary
for subsistence; the extra produce would find no ready market
and an increased yield would mean paying more in tithes and in
land tax, the latter being directly proportional to the area of
land held.[94] On the other hand very soon after the conquest
large amounts of money were to be made in dzelepchiistvo, the
rearing of animals, usually sheep, and driving them on the hoof
to the centres of consumption, a trade which was dominated by
the Bulgarians. By the early nineteenth century this was a
highly organised business, the shepherds of Kotel, for example,
driving flocks of ten to thirty thousand sheep to graze on
pastures in the Dobrudja.[95] Such large enterprise was, of
course, the exception, but even on a more local level the
possession of enough sheep or cattle to sell regularly on the
open market was often the key to the accumulation of wealth,
more especially because in most small and many medium-sized towns
the urban Bulgarian was likely to have his own plots of land
which would provide staple crops but which would not be extensive
enough for the rearing of larger animals. Meat could thus
command a relatively high price in many towns and animals were
generally an easier and quicker path to wealth than cereals,
vegetables, etc.; that the majority of the labourers employed
by the monastery of Rila on its largest chiflik were shepherds[96]
was not entirely due to the nature of the terrain.

The importance of animal husbandry in the process of
differentiation is one of the conditions making the actual
amount of land held not an entirely accurate measure of peasant
wealth, as is the fact that holdings were divided at inheritance,
a practice which meant constant changes in the amount of land
contained in one holding or worked by an individual family or
family group.

A far better measure of peasant wealth is the value of
property held, this being defined as the amount of seed sown,
the area of vineyards etc. worked, the number of animals owned,

and, where appropriate, the value of any processing plant such
as a wine press, <u>rakiya</u> still, or mill. It is of course impossible to make a definitive survey but the few statistics which do
survive support the generalisations made above both with regard
to the gradual differentiation in the ranks of the peasantry
and to the importance of animal husbandry in this process. Let
us examine most thoroughly the case of Chuprene in north-west
Bulgaria, a village assessed for taxation in 1840 when details
of the wealth of individual households were recorded.[97] There
is no reason to suppose that the village was not typical of its
area, and it is interesting to note that this was a village
under <u>gospodar</u> control for it has been argued that differentiation in these and <u>chiflik</u> villages did not proceed as
rapidly as in villages on state lands.[98] The Chuprene data
may be tabulated thus:

Category based on value of property in groschen.	Number of households	Total value of property held in groschen	Average value of property per household in groschen	Relative size of average value as a proportion to overall av.prφ. per household	
propertyless	1 (0.96%)	–	–	–	
100 or less	4 (3.84%)	331 (0.33%)	83	0.086	
101 – 300	5 (4.80%)	860 (0.85%)	172	0.179	0.234
301 – 500	6 (5.77%)	2513 (2.51%)	419	0.435	
501 – 1000	54 (51.92%)	38048 (38.03%)	704	0.731	1.006
1001 – 1500	17 (16.34%)	20923 (20.91%)	1231	1.280	
1501 – 2000	6 (5.77%)	11335 (11.32%)	1881	1.964	
2001 – 3000	9 (8.65%)	19360 (19.35%)	2151	2.236	2.553
over 3000	2 (1.92%)	6675 (6.67%)	3337	3.468	
Total	104 (100%)	100,045 (100%)	962	1.000	

From further information, such as the amount of seed sown,
it is clear that the households with property between five and
fifteen hundred groschen in value were middle peasants with
holdings probably between thirty and one hundred <u>dyunyuma</u>, and
this group is overwhelmingly the most numerous. Nevertheless

179

taking those with property valued at more than fifteen hundred groschen we find that a mere seventeen households, 16.34 per cent of the total, have property worth 37,370 groschen, or 37.35 per cent of the total property; at the same time in the lowest group, those with property valued at less than five hundred groschen who form 15.38 per cent of the total number of households have only 3.7 per cent of the total assessed property (3,704 groschen's worth). This leaves the middle peasants as 68.26 per cent of the households (71 in absolute numbers) with 58.94 per cent of the property assessed. Closer inspection of the details of the richer households reveals that their property included many more animals, indeed Dimitrov, who discovered the Chuprene records, notes that 'the basic difference between this group and those below them is to be found in developed animal husbandry',[99] though their average holdings of arable land were also somewhat larger. In the richest of households, those with property worth more than 2,000 groschen we find not only slightly larger arable holdings and flocks but also a <u>rakiya</u> still or a mill.

Studies of tax registers for north-eastern Bulgaria in the 1860s reveal a generally similar picture with 56 per cent of the households holding 58 per cent of the land;[100] here, however, differentiation had progressed somewhat further in the inter-vening twenty years and the richer peasants were more prominent, 14 per cent of the households holding 33 per cent of the land, and, conversely, the poorer peasants were equally conspicuous with 28 per cent of the population having only 9 per cent of the land, an amount clearly insufficient for subsistence. Differ-entiation had progressed even further in the Dobrudja for here the middle peasants, though still in numerical terms equal to those in other areas - they were 53 per cent of the total - had only 40 per cent of the land, whilst the rich peasants who formed only 11 per cent of the population had 40 per cent of the land, leaving a large number of peasants with insufficient land or no land at all. Nevertheless, the latter is an exceptional case, and 'statistics from the Dobrudja must never be taken as valid for the other areas of north-eastern Bulgaria.'[101]

Despite obvious differentiation in Chuprene and elsewhere there was relatively little social tension within the Bulgarian villages. The differences in wealth were often overshadowed by the cultural division between the villages and their rulers and priests, and no-one had more interest in abolishing Turkish state power and thereby securing unfettered private ownership of land than the richest elements in the villages. But even leaving aside these larger issues social cohesion was strong; rich and poor peasants worked alongside each other in the large village fields and used the same methods, thus giving the appearance at least of a community of interests, but, more importantly, particularly in the first half of the century, there was, given the lack of incentive to increase landed holdings and the general availability of unused land, little competition between villagers for possession of land.

In Chuprene the analysis of households had listed 104 separate units, yet the tax registers of adult males revealed that there were 114 such units.[102] The missing ten were either completely landless or were members of a larger family unit or _zadruga_. Again it would be impossible to give a general picture of how widespread the _zadruga_ was at this time but the evidence to hand would suggest that large zadrugal groups were already far from common, and if we accept Dimitrov's argument that a _zadruga_ could only exist where five or six men were included in the household then the institution itself was weak and in Chuprene only six households could have been _zadrugas_; it is established that two at least of the rich households were _zadrugas_.[103] Yet this area of north-western Bulgaria was one of those where the _zadruga_ was at its strongest. In some places a number of nuclear families were to be found in the same household but these were patriarchal rather than zadrugal communities for here all wealth belonged not to the community but to its head; this institution, particularly appropriate to Moslem custom, persisted in some areas, such as the Rhodope mountains, both amongst Moslems and Christians.[104] Elsewhere the scanty data relating to family size suggests a decline in all types of larger household; families crossing into Romania from the area around Karnobat in 1828-29 were usually only four to six in number[105] and an investigation into ten devastated villages around Gabrovo almost fifty years later recorded that, 'As the average number of persons in a Bulgarian house or family has lately been made a subject of discussion, it may be of interest to note that the aggregate figure varies severally in the ten villages in question from four and a half to six.'[106]

If large collective familial units were in decline - or, if one accepts the notion of '_zadruga_ as process',[*] they were

[*] I am grateful to my colleague Mr. J. E. M. Thirkell for bringing this

then at a trough in their cyclical development- communal
cohesion was increasing,more especially in the emergence of the
communal councils which were assuming an ever more important
role in the cultural, economic and political development of the
Bulgarian villages. Crossing the Balkans in 1829 Major George
Keppel noted that 'The affairs of the Bulgarians are referred,
in each village, to a junta of old men, who may be considered,
in the absence of the Turkish authorities, as a sort of provisional government . . .'[107] This form of self-administration
was not new. Many villages had organised their own defence
during the kurdzhaliistvo and had thus acquired the habits of
and the taste for self-administration,[108] but the institution
was older than this and had been a particular feature of the
'specialist villages'. These were communities which had been
granted certain privileges, usually in the form of partial tax-
relief, in return for the performance of specific services, most
frequently, of an auxiliary military nature, for the Ottoman
authorities. These villages were not under spahi control and
central government did not intervene much in their affairs as
few taxes were collected and the villages were often in inaccess-
ible mountainous areas.[*] The result was that the villages
themselves were left to organise the fulfilment of their
specialist obligations and, by extension, they became responsible for collecting such taxes as were levied upon them. The
organising body in most such villages was the communal council
consisting usually of a number of prominent heads of households.
These examples were attractive to other communities and were
copied when circumstances permitted.[109] Likewise, in villages
with few Turkish settlers more responsibility inevitably fell
upon prominent local Christians.[110] The role played by the
communal councils increased rapidly in the early nineteenth
century as they concerned themselves not only with administrative and religious affairs, but also with owning and
renting shops, lending money, employing teachers, sending local
children abroad for higher education and a host of other
activities.
     During the eighteenth century as previous restrictions on
Christians in various professions fell into disuetude the

     important point to my notice.
[*] Many villages were made responsible for guarding mountain passes; some were
     required to provide birds of prey for the Sultan's falconry.

Christian element in Ottoman European towns increased.[111]
Christian maxala were established in many towns, some of which
had more than one Christian district, Turnovo, at the end of the
eighteenth century, for example, having Armenian, Greek and
Bulgarian maxala, the latter, significantly known as Novata (the
new) maxala, being the largest.[112] In most towns, however, the
Turks retained their majorities; Karlovo was still three quarters
Turkish at the end of the eighteenth century and towns such as
Shumen, an important garrison town, and Tatar Pazardzhik were
to remain predominantly Turkish until well into the nineteenth
century.[113]

The fundamental reason for the increasing Christian
settlement in the towns was the growth in trade between the
Balkans and the rest of Europe during the eighteenth century.
By the final quarter of the century Austrian imports, mainly of
manufactured items, were pouring into the Balkans whilst even
larger quantities of Balkan goods, mainly agricultural produce,
went in the opposite direction to complete an exchange which
was already worth one million piastres per annum;[114] at the
same time 60 per cent of the foreign trade of the Bulgarian
lands was with central and western Europe, much of it in cotton
and tobacco, for Serres was already producing 70,000 bales of
cotton a year, two thirds of which was being exported,[115]
though the established and traditional exports of wool, wax,
hides, leather, vegetable oils and rose oil all continued to
find markets.[116]

Most important of all export goods was aba, the coarse
woollen cloth used throughout the Balkans and the Ottoman empire
and a product of great importance in that, unlike cotton, it
spawned a native manufacturing industry. By the end of the
eighteenth century aba produced in Bulgaria was being sold as
far afield as Syria and even Hindustan, and so developed were
the weaving and processing of aba that ' . . . the entire
Plovdiv area from the end of the eighteenth century resembled an
enormous workshop producing not so much for immediate local
consumption as for the intermediate and distant markets of the
Ottoman empire.'[117]

With the great expansion of foreign trade came a quicken-
ing of local exchange the vitality of which was best represented
in the great annual fairs, particularly those at Uzundzhovo,
Turgovishte, Shumen and Sliven, which flourished at this time
and through which much inter-Balkan and a good deal of

183

international trade was conducted.[118]

A distinctive feature of the new and expanding concerns was that they were non-Moslem, and, as far as abadzhiistvo - the making and selling of aba - is concerned, predominantly Bulgarian,[119] though it is Greek names which predominate in lists of Serres cotton merchants.[120] The Turks had by tradition confined themselves to a few occupations, primarily those which demanded a minimum of effort, for example barbering and the selling of coffee, and those depending upon the processing of animal products - leather working, shoemaking, etc.,[121] although Turks did own some manufacturing plants in which they employed Christian labour, often extracting that labour as part of their rents, as, for example, in the iron furnaces of Samokov.[122] Nor were the Turks slow to see the profits which were to be made in the processing of tobacco though, here again, they generally appeared as owners and exploiters of labour.[123] However, in the making of aba and in the working of gaitan (decorative braid) that developed in the wake of the aba industry Christian predominance was undisputed. This was in no small measure due to the fact that the sale of the finished product and the purchasing of raw materials was, by guild regulation, the responsibility of the masters and journeymen themselves. In the autumn huge caravans of masters and journey-men wound their way south to Asia Minor, taking as long as a month to reach their destination and bringing with them both raw cloth and finished articles which they sold in large and small markets.

Meanwhile wives and children were left at home and even those of the richer masters would busy themselves making the belts and stockings which sold so well amongst the Turks and Arabs of Asia Minor.[124] Of great importance was the fact that the absence of the men left the women to exercise not only control over domestic affairs but also power and responsibility in the organisation of apprentices and any remaining journeymen as well as in the family plots which many craftsmen/manufacturers still retained; in Koprivshtitsa, Lyuben Karavelov noted, so deep-rooted had this system become that for a man not to leave the village either to trade or to go on pechalba (seasonal work in another area) was regarded as a loss of status for him and his family.[125] An occupation which allowed so public a recognition of female dominance beyond the household was one which obviously could not be equated with the Moslem

Weltanschauung.

It may well be that this partly explains why trading in general had never become a Moslem preoccupation and the Empire's traders had been the Jews, the Armenians, the Greeks and the Dubrovnik merchants.[126] By the second quarter of the nineteenth century a number of Bulgarian merchant houses were also emerging, such as those of Brakalov, Karaminkov and Stransky,[127] whilst even larger concerns were those of Tupchileshtov, the Gueshov brothers and Zolotovich, all of whom had houses in Istanbul though their original base of operations had been outside the Empire, usually in Wallachia or Southern Russia.[128]

In Bulgarian urban communities, however, more people were concerned with production than with exchange. For the most part the methods of production were little if any changed from those used for centuries and even in *aba* making where technological change did take place - the introduction of the iron spinning-wheel in the late eighteenth century was of great importance - the old continued to exist alongside the new, and

' . . . in the early nineteenth century *abadzhiistvo* was found in different areas and at different stages of development; there were *abadzhii* who worked on orders in their own workshops and even those who had no workshop and sewed in the home of the customer. Others, catering for local needs, sold their goods individually in neighbouring fairs. The greatest expansion, however, in the first half of the nineteenth century was in tailoring which worked principally for mass sale in the market.'[129]

Nor did the *aba* and *gaitan* manufacturers suffer, as did other textile producers, from foreign competition, at least not until after the Crimean war.[130]

In all trades, no matter what their stage of development, the *esnaf* or guild played a dominant role. Guilds had been long established in the Balkans and so keen were the Ottoman authorities that trades should be organised that in Istanbul in the seventeenth century there was even an *esnaf* for thieves and highwaymen.[131] Originally primarily if not exclusively Moslem the ethnic composition of the *esnafs* naturally reflected the penetration of Christians into various trades in the eighteenth century or even earlier, as in the case of the goldsmiths of Turnovo,[132] though in many cases it is impossible to establish which race or religion dominated a particular trade.

It was the function of the guild to regulate the production

185

of a particular article within a particular town, the surrounding villages soon coming under the sway of that town if the
trade in question were flourishing. The esnaf was expected to
defend the interests of its own members against competition from
outside, a famous instance of this being the decision of the
Plovdiv dyers in 1792 to fine any master sending cloth to
Karlovo for dyeing; in 1800 the dyers of the two towns agreed
that they should not take in work from each other on pain of a
250 groschen fine.[133] Esnafs frequently provided a number of
services for their members. Credit could be extended to masters
and even to non-members at times, though it was seldom cheap
with rates varying from twelve to 50 per cent; esnaf funds would
also be spent on celebrations for all members and their families
on the name-day of the guild's patron saint, welfare payment
might also be made to those in distress whilst gifts to Ottoman
officials were usually accounted a wise investment. All esnafs
maintained at least one room in a near-by monastery and some
built esnaf centres for the use of their members, and in many
towns the Christian community as a whole benefited from the
endowment and upkeep by the esnafs of schools or churches, more
especially in the period after 1825. In some communities the
Christian esnafs were in close co-operation with the local
church and commune leaders and these institutions between them
administered much of the internal affairs of the Christian
community, the masters of various guilds in Plovdiv, for example,
agreed in 1818 to meet every Wednesday and Friday in the home of
the Metropolitan to settle any inter-Christian disputes.[134]
Other guilds even performed administrative functions for the
state, those in Sofia in the early nineteenth century being
responsible for collecting taxes from their members.[135]

The guilds were divided into the traditional structure of
master, journeymen and apprentice, the latter serving usually
for three years, the first two of them without pay; though they
were guaranteed days off for religious festivals and guild
assemblies there was no regulation of the working hours of
journeymen or apprentices, the latter sometimes being treated as
little more than unpaid domestic servants or labourers on the
family plot.[136] The senior official was the 'grand master',
istibashi or purvomaistor, who in some associations had the
assistance of a deputy, the igitbashi. These officers were
elected by the longzha, lodge, an assembly of all the guild's
masters from whose ranks the senior posts were filled. The

186

lodge also decided upon the election of new masters, the regulation of prices, the settlement of disputes between members, the granting of credit, the admission of new apprentices and the promotion of others to journeymen status, the punishment of those who had contravened guild rules, etc.[137] The lodge clearly had extensive powers, though these were undermined in later years by the emergence in many trades of a small number of very successful and powerful masters. There was also a general assembly of the guild in which all members could express their opinions and that this was still a living institution in the early nineteenth century was shown in 1817 when over a thousand members of the Plovdiv aba guild attended what was the largest guild assembly ever recorded.[138]

In earlier years guilds, Christian as well as Moslem, had had to rely ultimately on Ottoman state power for the enforcement of guild decisions, but as the Christian guilds became more powerful they became more independent of the Turkish authorities and moved into a much closer relationship with their own church officials. The example of the Plovdiv guilds is not singular and the growing association of the guilds and the Church later had important effects upon the cultural development of the Bulgarians both in increasing the sense of separateness from the Turkish state and in dividing the mass of the Bulgarian town dwellers from those leading guildsmen who were in close collaboration with the Greek ecclesiastics. In some centres the differences between Greek and Bulgarian were first aired in the guilds, though again this is a later development and it was not until the 1850s that mounting disagreements over education and religion forced the Plovdiv aba guild to divide into separate Greek and Bulgarian organisations.[139]

Inevitably the disorders of the late eighteenth and early nineteenth centuries affected trade and manufacturing. Towns in the central mountains suffered during the kurdzhaliistvo but these setbacks were temporary. The very insecurity of the disorders had caused a noticeable influx of Bulgarians into some towns and they both intensified the trend towards the Bulgarianisation of the towns and provided a large pool of labour for when economic recovery came. And recovery was not long delayed. By 1810, with the disorders only just beginning to show signs of declining, there were indications of a revival of internal trade, particularly between towns and the surrounding countryside, whilst later in the decade even centres such as

187

Karlovo, twice burned during the kurdzhaliistvo, and Koprivshtitsa were once again thriving.[140] The authorities were naturally anxious to stimulate trade and in 1819 issued new trading regulations from which 'it was clear that the rights of Christian merchants were to be carefully protected'.[141]

This trend continued during the 1820s and was only slightly impaired by the war of 1828-29. For the aba makers the 1820s saw a particularly important development with the creation of a regular Ottoman army for it was to them, especially those of Sliven and Plovdiv, that the army turned for cloth and ready-made uniforms. In 1828 Sliven was asked to provide 10,000 uniforms and two years later this and other towns, Plovdiv included, were supplying 70,000 bales of cloth to the army.[142] So profitable did this trade become that it was here that Bulgaria's first real factories appeared, the first being built with state help in Sliven in 1836 by the abadzhiya, Zhelyazkov, and a second and more successful enterprise being established in Plovdiv in 1848 by Gyumyushgerdan.[143]

Despite the general increase in trade and the appearance of the first signs of factory production the guilds remained dominant and in the very year Gyumyushgerdan set up his factory the government concluded its first formal agreement with the aba guilds.[144] In most occupations the persistence of the esnafs was due to the backward nature and small scale of the manufacturing, for even in aba making most abadzhii worked alone or with one or two apprentices and only a few masters had five or six; at the same time the economic and cultural idiosyncracies of the Ottoman empire also helped to maintain the guilds' power and usefulness. If in a few trades the pressure of modern economic impulses did force some journeymen to become dependent upon, or even labourers for, local merchants then these were exceptions and such developments within a single trade were uneven.[145]

The persistence of the esnaf and the prevalence of small scale production with which it is naturally associated did not mean that social differentiation was not taking place in the Bulgarian urban communities, though, of course, an alien state and a suspicious church produced cultural pressures which retarded social fission, more especially as the wealth of some Turks was far in excess of that of even the richest Bulgarian; Husseyin Paşa, the suppressor of the Janissaries and later governor of Vidin, had wealth of literally fabulous proportions[146] and high ranking Ottoman officials could earn in one month sums which a leading Bulgarian merchant or manufacturer could not hope to accumulate in a year.[147]

It was not, however, that disparities of wealth had not arisen amongst the Bulgarians. Even in the eighteenth century most Bulgarian villages and small towns could point to their own small, wealthy élite, a sure sign of which was the growing number of Bulgarian names to be found, especially from the late eighteenth century, in the lists of founders and benefactors of churches.[148] These new men, whose money had been made in tax-collecting, money-lending, trade, manufacturing, etc., still retained the social practices of contemporary Ottoman society and seldom showed any signs of wishing to break out from that traditional social and economic mould.[149]

This was reflected in an unwillingness to adopt European habits of dress, eating, etc., and also in an unswerving commitment to existing institutions and their established practices. In 1789 the Plovdiv aba guild decided that it would punish any master taking as his partner any person who had not undergone the traditional preparation for that status, a clear indication that people with money were trying to buy their way into the top of the guild hierarchy.[150] Yet within that hierarchy there were signs that a new wealthy élite was being established. The masters of the Plovdiv aba guild recognised solidarity amongst themselves by charging their sons only half the fee paid by others on becoming journeymen.[151] By the 1820s in the same guild the post of purvomaistor, which had once been rotated annually, was being held by the same man for four or five or even in one case for ten years without a break.[152] By the 1840s the accumulation of wealth by a small élite was further represented in the building by this group of larger and more elaborate homes, a new phenomenon in the Bulgarian community and one which was not everywhere encountered for the inhabitants of Koprivshtitsa joked that Sofiotes who visited the town usually crossed themselves every time they passed a merchant's house for so imposing and opulent was the building that the visitors assumed it must be a monastery.[153] In towns where trade and manufacturing did prosper it was not only the merchants' homes which reflected increasing affluence for in many communities new public buildings were also erected - schools, more elaborate churches, clock towers, covered markets, etc.[154]

189

Whilst the wealthy few might sometimes bring architectural distinction to a Bulgarian community and inevitably assumed a leading place within its administration most members of that community remained poor. During the first half of the nineteenth century there was a constant drift from the village to the town, and in many cases the town was not the end of the journey for thousands of Bulgarians left the country for Serbia, Romania, Russia and even farther afield.[155] The new emigrants into the towns provided a ready supply of labour for the workshops of the craftsmen and, when they eventually appeared, for the new factory owners; Gyumyushgerdan opened his factory in a village well-known for its weaving traditions yet he chose to take almost all his employees from the cheap pool of labour in the towns of Pirdop, Plovdiv and Tatar Pazardzhik.[156]

The towns provided not only most of the work force for the few early factories when they eventually appeared but also a large proportion of the native Bulgarian intelligentsia,[*] though here too we are concerned with a phenomenon which was only beginning to appear towards the end of the period under review. The teachers, priests, etc. who formed that intelligentsia came to a large extent from parents who were craftsmen in workshops, traders, or priests and their training owed much to the development of communal councils.[157]

If there were clear differentiations of wealth in the Bulgarian towns by the second quarter of the nineteenth century there was as yet very little concentration of wealth into single spheres of activity. Gyumyushgerdan's money came from aba-making and trading and even when he had established his factory he retained possession of a number of chifliks, large flocks of sheep and herds of cattle, and a few mills and vegetable-oil processing plants.[158] As late as the 1850s the head of the great merchant house of Tupchileshtov in Istanbul still involved himself with buying the right to collect taxes, with money lending and with other concerns[159] whilst even in the 1860s and 1870s the wills of leading members of the Elena chorbadzhii show a very wide distribution of economic activity.[160] It would be reasonable to suppose that in earlier decades and in small or medium-sized Bulgarian communities similar

[*] Native in the sense that they emerged within communities in Bulgaria rather than within Bulgarian communites in exile in Romania or Russia.

190

phenomena could be observed and although precise data is
extremely difficult to secure we do have a detailed description
of one such community in the 1840s, that of the Bulgarian quarter
(maxale) in the town of Lom on the Danube.[161]

Of the three hundred and sixty three men whose income and
occupations are recorded thirty four (9.37 per cent) were to be
found in the highest income bracket, that of over one thousand
groschen per annum, and these thirty four consisted of thirteen
manufacturer/craftsmen, fourteen merchants and seven farmers.
In the medium group, classified as those earning between three
hundred and one thousand groschen per annum, were to be found
ninety-six men (26.4 per cent). Forty-five of these were
manufacturer/craftsmen and this was 60 per cent of the total of
seventy-five men classified as manufacturer/craftsmen. Thirty-
three of the ninety-six men in the middle income group were
farmers, this being 43.4 per cent of the total number of
farmers (seventy-five); fifteen of those in the middle income
group were merchants, this representing 45.5 per cent of the
total number of merchants (thirty-three). To complete the
ninety-six in the middle category were one journeyman and,
surprisingly, two men whose income depended on wage labour. The
vast majority of the Bulgarians in Lom, two hundred and twenty
or 60.7 per cent of the total, could be classified as poor for
their earnings were less than three hundred groschen a year.
Within this category fell all those employed as wage earners in
handicraft/manufacturing or in agriculture, thirty-six of the
seventy-six independent farmers, all the fishermen and sailors,
fifteen of the seventeen independent craftsmen, and twenty-six
of the twenty-eight journeymen.

This concentration in the lowest income bracket is not
surprising but an examination of the sources of wealth of the
richest does provide some interesting revelations. Of the four
richest men in the register, those with an income of over two
thousand groschen per annum, three are classified as merchants
and one as a manufacturer. One of the merchants was Todor, son
of Petko. Classed as a bakalin (grocer, or seller of food) he
had a total yearly income of 3,170 groschen of which his
grocery dealings provided 2,000 groschen, the remainder being
made up as follows:

Renting two other grocery stalls in his
                                    ownership   ....   400 gr.

191

A rakiya still	....	250 gr.
Vineyards, 14 dyunyuma	....	210 gr.
Meadows producing fifteen bales of hay	....	210 gr.
Beehives	....	100 gr.

A similar pattern is revealed in the income of Kamen, son of
Stan. Classified as an inn-keeper his income reached almost
two thousand groschen even without his main trade and was
derived from the following sources:

Three corn fields	....	304 gr.
Milking ewes	....	840 gr.
Rams and sheep	....	140 gr.
One milch cow	....	25 gr.
Two mares	....	60 gr.
Two rakiya stills	....	500 gr.
Vineyards, 6 dyunyuma	....	90 gr.

The sources of income for those receiving between one
thousand and one thousand five hundred groschen per annum are
not dissimilar, with once again a considerable mixture of
sources, one farmer, for example, running a tavern from which he
earned more than from his land and in which he lived although he
did not own it. Here too there was very widespread ownership
of vineyards and more than half of the manufacturing craftsmen
still owned vineyards, this being 'the indispensable attribute
for a respected member of the esnaf'.[162] Indeed , more
manufacturers owned their own vineyard than owned their own
workshop or stall, dyukyan; of the seventy-five guild masters
only nineteen owned their own dyukyan whilst forty-five had their
own vineyards. The ownership pattern for the dyukyani is itself
revealing. There were in the town fifty-one dyukyani and thirty-
four dyukyani owners, seventeen Turkish owners who between them
had twenty-seven dyukyani, fifteen Bulgarian with a total of
twenty-two dyukyani, and two dyukyani owned by vakufs. Amongst
the Turkish owners there was not one who described himself as
a manufacturer or trader, they were in fact all mollahs, ayani
or their relations. The picture amongst the Bulgarians was very
different and nearly all owners were involved in manufacturing
or trading, sometimes owning more than one dyukyan in their own
trade, especially those in tavern-keeping and grocery, and
sometimes owning ones for entirely different trades, as for

192

example, the potter who owned a rug-making workshop; two
businesses, a tavern and a jewellery workshop, were owned by
inhabitants from nearby villages and leased to townsmen, and
one dyukyan, it is not known of what sort, was owned by a priest.
The dyukyani owned by Turks were eight worked by shoemakers,
four by leather workers, four by tailors, three by dyers, two
by abadzhii, two for use by grocers, two for confectioners,
one jewellery workshop, one for a candlemaker, one pottery, and
one tavern; the Bulgarian-owned workshops were six grocery
stalls, five taverns, three rug-making workshops, two potteries,
two jewelmakers' shops, one leather working and one shoemaking
establishment.

Assuming that the Bulgarian maxale of Lom was similar to
that in other towns, and there is no reason to suppose otherwise,
we see a clear pattern with an accumulation of wealth in
relatively few hands but with the sources of that wealth being
still remarkably diversified. It is also clear that in such
relatively small communities in the 1840s the Turks were still
holding on to their old trades, but, more often than Bulgarians,
they were owners of, but not participants in, the business
concerned. The Bulgarians, meanwhile, were still tending to
concentrate in those activities associated primarily with the
transitional stage between village and town, especially catering
and the sale of food, this itself being an indication that
capital accumulated in the village was not being used there but
in nearby towns.

* * * * *

Bulgarian society in the first half of the nineteenth
century was still dominated by established institutions and long-
standing cultural habits. The forces which would soon undermine
these institutions and alter these habits were already operating
though not as yet to any great effect.

For the historian there remains the problem of establishing a clearer and more definite picture of social institutions
in this period and this paper will have served its purpose if
it provokes further research and more discussion on a theme
which, though extremely complex, is of great importance and
interest.

1. For a useful periodisation of this time of troubles see Vera Mutafchieva,
'"Kyrdzhaliiskoe Vremya". Opyt periodatsii kyrdzhaliistva', Etudes
Balkaniques ix (1973) 100-120. In the 1950s the Bulgarian historian Sht.
Atanasov attempted to represent the kurdzhaliistvo as a national rebellion,
see his Koi se bili kurdzhaliite i protiv kogo se borili te? (Sofia 1955),
and his Selskite vustanie v Bulgariya kum kraya na xviii i nachaloto na xix
v i susdavane na Bulgarskata zemska voiska (Sofia 1958). This view was never
widely accepted.

2. For the reforms see Bernard Lewis, The Emergence of Modern Turkey (London
1968) 75-111; F. E. Bailey, British Policy and the Turkish Reform Movement
(reprint edition, New York 1970) especially chapter iv; R. H. Davison,
Reform in the Ottoman Empire, 1856-1876 (Princeton, N.J. 1963), and
Stanford J. Shaw and Ezel Kural Shaw, History of the Ottoman Empire and
Modern Turkey vol. 2 (Cambridge 1977) 1-171 passim, and especially 58-133.

3. For a collection of over 3,000 references to and extracts from sources
on the population of the Bulgarian lands see Dr. Nikola B. Mikhov,
Nasenlenieto na Turtsiya i Bulgariya prez xviii i xix v. 4 vols (Sofia
1915-35). (I have been unable to consult the first volume of this impressive
compendium as it is missing from the British Library.) Unfortunately Mikhov's
efforts serve as well to confuse as to clarify for widely varying estimates
of the population of the Bulgarian lands are to be found. The most
authorative would suggest that on the eve of the Russo-Turkish war of 1828-
29 the population of the area was just over four and three quarter million,
see M. Jomard, 'The Numerical Force of Turkey', The Asiatic Journal and
Monthly Register for British India and its Dependencies xxvi (1828) 63.
(Mikhov, iii 233) This source allows 2,800,000 inhabitants for Rumelia,
including Istanbul, 1,440,000 for Bulgaria and 1,160,000 for Macedonia.
Equally authorative figures for the middle of the century are less easy to
find and the best general indication is that given in the Almanach de l'Empire
ottoman pour l'année 1850 (Galata 1850) which estimates the total population
for Rumelia, Thessaly, Bulgaria and Thrace as 5,000,000. (Mikhov ii 3-4.)
There are widely divergent figures in G. F. Bowen, Mount Athos, Thessaly
and Epirus; A Diary of a Journey from Constantinople to Corfu (London 1852)
249-52; Bowen could muster only 2,630,000 inhabitants for Bulgaria, Thrace,
Macedonia and Thessaly, (Mikhov, ii 47-8) though E. H. Michelson, The
Ottoman Empire and its Resources (London 1854) 138, populated Bulgaria alone
with 4,000,000 souls with another 2,600,000 in Rumelia and a further
1,800,000 in Thrace. (Mikhov, ii 189.) Much of this confusion came from a
lack of clearly defined geographic or administrative units but in the face
of such unrestrained confusion one might choose to rely on Gibbon who had
reckoned the population of Greece and European Turkey at 6,000,000, see
The History of the Decline and Fall of the Roman Empire, Bohn's British

Classics series, 7 vols (London 1869) i 57n[*]; as Bohn remarks in a gloss,
'Gibbon's estimate . . . is probably more correct than many calculations
that have been made', and, of course, whilst being no less accurate than
many later writers Gibbon is still a good deal more readable than most of
his successors.

4. Most contemporary travellers comment on this racial mixture. For the
limit of Greek settlement see J. A. Blanqui, Voyage en Bulgarie pendant
l'année 1841 (Paris 1845) 209. For the presence of Arabs and Tatars see
Elena Grozdanova, 'Za demografskoto sustoyanie na karnobatsko i aitsko prez
xvii-xviii v.', Istoricheski Pregled xxxiii (1976) 81-8, 85-6.

5. Summaries of this system are to be found in Mercia Macdermott, A history
of Bulgaria, 1393-1885 (London 1962) 26-31; see also, D. Kosev, D. Dimitrov,
et. al. eds., Istoriya na Bulgariya i (Sofia 1954) 245-50. (This work
cited hereafter as Ist. Bulg..)

6. See Zina Markova, 'Za ikonomichiskiya gnet na fanariotskoto dukhovenstvo
i borbata na bulgarskiya narod sreshtu nego do krimskata voina', Izvestiya
na Instituta za Istoriya xxi (1970) 203-18. The church taxes were of
various types, eighteen of which have been identified by M. Dimitrov,
'Narodnite masi v Bulgariya prez epokhata na vuzrazhdaneto - nachalo na
bulgarskata demokratsiya', Filosofska Misul ii (1947).

7. Though Lewis talks of under a thousand timars in European Turkey by the
1830s, (Lewis, op. cit., 92) a commentator who visited the area late in the
1790s refers to 914 ziamets and 8356 timars, see G. A. Olivier, Voyage dans
l'Empire ottoman, l'Egypte et la Perse 3 vols (Paris 1861) i 166-8.

8. Price movements were as follows, the year 1456 being taken as the base
of 100. Manufactured goods 1770-79: 142, 1780-89: 484, 1790-99: 252.
Figures in the same three decades for cereals and animal products were
227, 250 and 262, and 206, 269 and 276 respectively. See Lyuben Berov,
'Dvizhenieto na tsenite na Balkanite prez xvi-xix v. i evropeiskata
revolutsiya na tsenite', Istoricheski Pregled xxxi (1975) 92-102, see
especially 99. The producer of cereals was further inconvenienced by an
official prohibition on the export of wheat but generally this official ban
was no more resistant to bakshish than other Ottoman regulations, see Olivier,
op. cit., i 204.

9. See Strashimir Dimitrov, 'Za agrarnite otnosheniya v Bulgariya prez xviii
v.', in D. Kosev et. al. eds., Paisii Khilendarski i negovata epokha, 1762-
1962 (Sofia 1962) 129-165, particularly 151-5. (This work hereafter cited
as Dimitrov, 'Agrarnite otnosheniya'.)

10. Khristo Khristov, 'Kum vuprosa za zagrabvaneto na selskite zemi i
izdavaneto na chiflitsi i gospodarlutsi v evropeiska Turtsiya prez xviii i
xix v.', Izvestiya na Instituta za Istoriya xiv-xv (1964) 151-162,
particularly 159. (This work hereafter cited as Khristov 'Zagrabvaneto'.)

The traditional Marxist interpretation was first laid down by Dimitur
Blagoev; see, for example, his Prinos kum istoriya na sotsialisma v
Bulgariya, first published in Sofia in 1906. (The latest edition was
published in Sofia in 1976 and p.33 of that edition gives an expression of
the traditional view.) Blagoev's ideas were strongly presented in the first
decade after 1944 by Zhak Natan; see, for example, his 'Klasi i klasovi
otnosheniya v epokhata na bulgarskoto vuzrazhdane', Istoricheski Pregled i
(1945) 34-48, and 'Otnovo po vuprosa za klasite i klasovite otnosheniya v
Bulgariya prez vuzrazhdaneto', Istoricheski Pregled vii (1950-51) 464-482.
The latter article is intended to counter the somewhat revisionist interpretations of Dimitur Kosev, as presented in his 'Klasovite otnosheniya v
Bulgariya prez vuzrazhdaneto', published in the same number of Istoricheski
Pregled (443-463); a further statement of Kosev's views came in his Lektsii
po nova bulgarska istoriya (Sofia 1951). The traditionalists received
strong support from the Soviet historian N. G. Levintov, 'Agrarnye
otnosheniya v Bolgarii nakanunye osvobozhdeniya i agrarnyi perevorot 1877-
1879 godov', in L. B. Valev, S. A. Nikitin, and P. N. Tret'yakov eds.
Osvobozhdeniye Bolgarii ot turetskogo iga; sbornik statyei (Moscow 1953)
139-221. Levintov, intent upon proving the emergence of a Bulgarian kulak
class and establishing chiflikisation as a necessary part of, and preliminary
to, the appearance of a capitalist phenomena, concentrated his researches
on the 1860s and himself admitted that the evidence was tenuous, especially
in earlier decades: 'Descriptions of two or three regions based upon what
their inhabitants could recall, a few descriptive remarks in the memoirs
of activists in the era of national revival, and, above all, Ottoman
agrarian legislation, these are virtually all the sources we have for the
history of agrarian relations in Bulgaria from 1830 to 1870', 142. Kosev
was not overawed by his Soviet colleague, witness his 'Kum izyasnyavane na
nyakoi problemi ot istoriyata na Bulgariya prez xviii i nachaloto na xix
v.', Istoricheski Pregled xii (1956) 26-62. (This work hereafter cited as
Kosev, 'Izyasnyavane'.)

11. Hristo Hristov, 'The Agrarian Problem and the National Liberation
Movement in the Balkans', Actes du premier Congrès des Etudes balkaniques et
sud-est européennes, part iv, Histoire xviii-xixe ss. (Sofia 1969) 65-70,
particularly 66. (This work cited hereafter as Hristov, 'Agrarian Problem'.)

12. Kosev, 'Izyasyavane', 33-4; see also Strashimir Dimitrov, 'Kum vuprosa
za otmenyavaneto na spakhiiskata sistema v nashite zemi', Istoricheski
Pregled xiii (1956) 27-58, particularly 34. (This work cited hereafter as
Dimitrov, 'Otmenyavaneto'.)

13. Khristo Khristov, Agrarnite Otnosheniya v Makedoniya, (Sofia 1964) 41-4.
(This work hereafter cited as Khristov, Makedoniya.)

14. See Marta Bur, 'Kum istoriya na stopanska i stroitelnata deinost na

rilskiya monastir, 1833-48g.', <u>Izvestiya na Instituta za Istoriya</u> xxii
(1972) 227-261, passim.

15. Herbert Wilhelmy, <u>Hochbulgarien; die ländliche Siedlungen und die</u>
<u>bauerliche Wirtschaft</u>, no. iv of the <u>Schriften des Geographischen Instituts</u>
<u>der Universität Kiel</u>, ed O. Schneider and H. Wenzel (Kiel 1935) 181.

16. For the development of the dispersed village from a number of original
<u>zadrugas</u>, see ibid. 95 et. seq.. Excellent descriptions of dispersed
villages, including lists of numbers of households in each <u>maxale</u> and of
<u>maxale</u> in individual villages can be found in F. Kanitz, <u>Donau-Bulgarien und</u>
<u>der Balkan. Historisch-Geographisch-Ethnographische Reisestudien aus den</u>
<u>Jahren 1860-1879</u> 3 vols, (Leipzig 1881) 214, 223-5, 256-7.

17. For descriptions of <u>izpolicharstvo</u> see <u>inter alia</u>, Zhak Natan,
V. Khadzhinikolov, L. Berov, <u>Ikonomikata na Bulgariya</u> i, <u>Ikonomikata na</u>
<u>Bulgariya do sotsialisticheskata revolutsiya</u> (Sofia 1969) 212-3. (This
work hereafter cited as <u>Ikon. Bulg</u>..) See also Ivan Sakazov, <u>Bulgarische</u>
<u>Wirtschaftsgeschichte</u> (Berlin and Leipzig 1929) 195-7.

18. See <u>Ikon. Bulg</u>., 212; Sakazov, op. cit., 191-3; and Fani G. Milkova,
'K kharakteristike kesimskoi formy ekspluatatsii krest'yan v bolgarskikh
zemlyakh do osvobozhdeniya', <u>Actes du premier Congrès des Etudes balkaniques</u>
<u>et sud-est européennes</u>, iv, Histoire xviii-xix ss. (Sofia 1969) 71-6.

19. Strashimir Dimitrov, 'Chifliiskoto stopanstvo prez 50-70 godini na
xix vek', <u>Istoricheski Pregled</u> xi (1955) 3-34, particularly 22. (This work
hereafter cited as Dimitrov 'Chifliiskoto stopanstvo'.)

20. <u>Ikon. Bulg</u>., 26.

21. Ibid., 213.

22. Sakazov, op. cit., 195.

23. <u>Ikon. Bulg</u>. 226. See also the sparkling short essay by Tsvetana
Georgieva, 'Za genezisa na burzhoaznite elementi v sotsialnata struktura
na Bulgarite', <u>Istoricheski Pregled</u> xxxiii (1977) 87-90, especially 88-9.

24. Dimitrov, 'Chifliiskoto stopanstvo' 20.

25. Khristov, <u>Makedoniya</u> 92.

26. Dimitrov, 'Otmenyavaneto' 33.

27. Kosev, 'Izyasyavane' 49-50 and Khristo Khristov, 'Nyakoi problemi na
prekhoda ot feodalizum kum kapitalizma v istoriyata na Bulgariya',
<u>Istoricheski Pregled</u> xvii (1961) 83-107, particularly 87-8. (This work
hereafter cited as Khristov, 'Nyakoi problemi'.) Information on south-
west Bulgaria and on the <u>kesim</u> system in general is nearly all derived from
K. Irechek and M. Sarafov, <u>Raport na Komisiyata izpratena v kiustendilskiya</u>
<u>okrug za izuchi polozhenieto na bezzemnite selyani</u> (Sofia 1880).

28. Strashimir Dimitrov, <u>Vustanie ot 1850 godina v Bulgariya</u> (Sofia 1972)
21-2. The inclusion of new material in this work makes it a replacement of,
rather than a supplement to, his <u>Vustanieto na selyanite v severozapadnite</u>

Bulgariya prez 1850 godina (Sofia 1961). (The former and more complete work cited hereafter as Dimitrov, *Vustanie*.)

29. Dimitrov, *Vustanie* 22.

30. Ibid., 26-7.

31. Ibid., 23.

32. Ibid., 22.

33. Ibid., 23.

34. Ibid., 26.

35. Ibid., 27-9; and Strashimir Dimitrov, 'Iz istoriyata na revolutsionnoto dvizhenie v nishkiya vilaet prez 1850g.', *Izvestiya na Instituta za Istoriya* xvi-xvii (1966) 407-22.

36. 'Presque toutes les populations des campagnes sont chrétiennes', Blanqui, op. cit., 209.

37. Strashimir Dimitrov, 'Selo Chuprene prez xix vek (do Osvobozhdenieto)', in *V. pamet na Akademik Mikhail Dimitrov* (Sofia 1974) 23-37, particularly 24. (This work cited hereafter as Dimitrov, 'Chuprene'.)

38. Dimitrov, *Vustanie* 27.

39. Dimitrov, 'Chuprene' 25-6, and Khristov, 'Zagrabvaneto' 161.

40. Ivan Undzhiev, *Karlovo: istoriya na grada do Osvobozhdenieto* (second edition, Sofia 1968) 48.

41. So inefficient was the new system that within two years tax-farming had been reintroduced, see Davison, op. cit., 44.

42. See Mark Pinson, 'Ottoman Bulgaria in the First Tanzimat Period - the Revolts in Nish (1841) and Vidin (1850)', *Middle Eastern Studies* xi (1975) 103-146, especially 117.

43. *Ikon. Bulg.*, 222.

44. Ibid., 212.

45. Khristov, 'Zagrabvaneto' 155-6. Similar cases were reported from Macedonia.

46. Pinson, loc. cit., 128-9.

47. Hristov, 'Agrarian Problem' 62.

48. See Virzhiniya Paskaleva, 'Avstro-bulgarski turgovski vruzki v kraya na xviii i nachaloto na xix v.', *Istoricheski Pregled* xiv (1958) 83-92, (this work cited hereafter as Paskaleva, 'Avstro-bulgarski'), and see also the same author's 'Razvitie na gradskoto stopanstvo; genezisut na bulgarskata burzhuaziya prez xviii v.', in D. Kosev et al. eds. *Paisii Khilendarski i negovata epokha, 1762-1962* (Sofia 1962) 71-128, especially 180-2. (This work cited hereafter as Paskaleva, 'Razvitie'.)

49. Paskaleva, 'Razvitie' 81.

50. Khristov, *Makedoniya* 44-5.

51. Dimitrov, *Vustanie* 25 and Khristov, *Makedoniya* 51.

52. Khristov, *Makedoniya* 51.

198

53. For derudedzhiistvo, see ibid., 35-8, and the same author's 'Nyakoi problemi', 90.

54. Ibid., 91.

55. Petur Koledarov, 'Naródniyat sustav na Dramsko do sredata na xix v.', Izvestiya na Instituta za Istoriya x (1962) 147-189, particularly 148.

56. Kosev, 'Izyasyavane' 43.

57. Khristov, Makedoniya 21 and 99.

58. Strashimir Dimitrov, 'Za klasovóto razsloenie sred selyanite v severoiztochna Bulgariya prez 70te godini na xix v.', Izvestiya na Instituta za Istoriya viii (1960) 225-271, especially 231-2. (This work cited here-after as Dimitrov, 'Razsloenie'.)

59. Wilhelmy, op. cit., 178.

60. Nikolai Todorov, 'Novi danni za agrarnite otnosheniya u nas prez 60te godini na xix v.', Istoricheski Pregled xiv (1958) 102-113, especially 105. (This work cited hereafter as Todorov, 'Novi danni'.) Todorov's perceptive article undermines Levintov's arguments.

61. Hristov, 'Agrarian Problem' 67.

62. Ikon. Bulg., 211. Khristov, 'Nyakoi problemi' 91, gives a much higher estimate, one of 25 to 33 per cent.

63. Wilhelmy, op. cit., 178.

64. Todorov, 'Novi danni' 106.

65. Khristov, 'Nyakoi problemi' 91.

66. Strashimir Dimitrov, 'Kum istoriyata na chiflikchiistvoto v rusensko', Istoricheski Pregled xiv (1958) 84-98, especially 93-8.

67. Ikon. Bulg., 219.

68. Nikolai Todorov, 'Po nyakoi vuprosi za ikonomicheskoto razvitie i za zarazhdaneto na kapitalizma v bulgarskite zemi pod tursko vladichestvo', Istoricheski Pregled xvii (1961) 87-105, especially 98. (This work here-after cited as Todorov 'Ikonomicheskoto razvitie'.)

69. Traian Stoianovich, 'Land Tenure and Related Sectors of the Balkan Economy, 1600-1800', Journal of Economic History, xiii (1953) 398-411, especially 402.

70. Ikon. Bulg., 224.

71. See Virzhiniya Paskaleva, 'Za nyakoi osobenosti i faktori v obrazuvaneto na bulgarskata natsiya prez purvata polovina na xix v.', Izvestiya na Instituta za Istoriya xvi-xvii (1966) 423-452, especially 434 and n.40. (This work cited hereafter as Paskaleva 'Osobenosti'.) It may not be without significance that this area contained a relatively high proportion of Moslems, see Grozdanova, loc. cit., 81.

72. See the Paskaleva reference quoted in the preceding note.

73. Ibid., and Khristov, 'Zagrabvaneto' 154.

74. Khristov, 'Nyakoi problemi' 97.

75. Konstantin Veliki, 'Izselvaneto ot Karnobat vuv Vlashko prez 1830g.', Izvestiya na Instituta za Istoriya xvi-xvii (1966) 453-466, especially 460-1.

76. Ikon. Bulg., 213.

77. Ibid., 226.

78. Ibid.

79. Khristo Khristov, 'Kum vuprosa i klasovite otnosheniya v bulgarskoto za klasite obshtestvo prez Vuzrazhdaneto (proizkhod sotsialna prinadlezhnost i rolya na chorbadzhiite)', Isvestiya na Instituta za Istoriya xxi (1970) 51-85, especially 68. (This work cited hereafter as Khristov, 'Klasite'.)

80. Khristov, Makedoniya 99-101, and 'Nyakoi problemi' 98.

81. Ikon. Bulg., 226.

82. Nikolai Todorov, 'Za naemniya trud v bulgarskite zemi kum sredata na xix v.', Istoricheski Pregled, xv (1959) 3-35, especially 24-30 passim. (This work cited hereafter as Todorov, 'Trud'.)

83. Todorov, 'Ikonomicheskoto razvitie', 98.

84. At the beginning of the nineteenth century 95 per cent of the chiflik peasants in Macedonia were farming the same land that their families had used for generations and were probably to continue using for generations to come. Khristov, Makedoniya 93.

85. Ikon. Bulg., 210; see also Fani Milkova, Pozemlenata sobstvenost v bulgarskite zemi prez xix vek (Sofia 1969) 40-1.

86. Ikon. Bulg., 214.

87. Todorov, 'Ikonomichesko razvitie', 98.

88. Ibid.

89. Ikon. Bulg., 227.

90. Ibid.

91. Dimitrov, 'Agarnite otnosheniya', and also Strashimir Dimitrov and Rusi Stoikov, 'Sotsialnata diferentsiatsiya sred selyachestvoto v turnovsko kum kraya na xvii i nachaloto na xviii v.', Izvestiya na Instituta za Istoriya, xiv-xv (1964) 183-194.

92. Paskaleva 'Razvitie', 102-3.

93. The most interesting recent contribution to the debate on the chorbadzhiya is Georgieva's brilliant essay quoted in note 23 above. Her argument is that the relationship between the large flock owners and the shepherds who were allowed to graze a few animals of their own with the large flocks of their employers was one of absolute economic dependence not merely that of employee to employer. It was in fact a relationship similar to that between a Janissary commander and his men and therefore when such a relationship appeared amongst the shepherds and the flock owners they appropriated the only known term to describe such a relationship, and thus the flock owner became a chorbadzhiya. It was, says Georgieva, in the sheep-rearing areas that the word was first used in this new sense, spreading

200

thereafter throughout the Bulgarian communities, urban and rural.

94. Georgieva, loc. cit., 88.

95. Ikon. Bulg., 215.

96. Bur, Loc. cit., 248-9.

97. See Dimitrov, 'Chuprene'.

98. See, for example, Khristov, 'Klasite' 59-60.

99. Dimitrov, 'Chuprene' 28.

100. Dimitrov, 'Razsloenie' 265.

101. Ibid., 242.

102. Dimitrov, 'Chuprene' 26-7.

103. Ibid.

104. Tamyana An. Koleva, 'Semeistvo i semeini otnosheniya u rodopskite Bulgari', in Tsv. Ramanska (ed. in chief), Narodnostna i bitova obshtnost na rodopskite Bulgari (Sofia 1968) 151-69, especially 152-6.

105. The average was 5.2, taken from 3220 people in 614 families. Veliki, loc. cit., 457.

106. British Parliamentary Papers, Turkey (1877) No. 15, xcl, document no. 51, enclosure 2.

107. Major George Keppel, Narrative of a Journey across the Balkans i (London 1831) 307.

108. See Virzhiniya Paskaleva, 'Za samoupravlenieto na Bulgarite prez Vuzrazhdaneto', Izvestiya na Instituta za Istoriya xiv-xv (1964) 69-84; and V. Mutafchieva, 'Feodalnite razmirnitsi v severna Trakiya prez kraya na xviii i nachaloto na xix v.', in D. Kosev, et al. eds, Paisii Khilendarski i negovata epokha, 1762-1962 (Sofia 1962) 167-212 passim.

109. The standard work on the Bulgarian communes is Khristo Khristov, Bulgarskite Obshtini prez Vuzrazhdaneto (Sofia 1973). (This work cited hereafter as Khristov, Obshtini.) Some of the main themes of this book are summarised in the same author's 'Communities and the Bulgarian National Revival', in Thomas Butler ed, Bulgaria Past and Present (Columbus, Ohio 1976) 3-14.

110. The obvious example is that of Elena where no Turkish settlement took place and whose chorbadzhii became famous, perhaps infamous. See Georgi Pletnyov, 'Sotsialna prinadlezhnost na elenskite chorbadzhii prez Vuzrazhdaneto', Istoricheski Pregled xxxi (1975) 69-74.

111. The standard text on the Balkan city is Nikolai Todorov, Balkanskiyat Grad, XV-XIX vek (Sofia 1972), see especially 127-140.

112. Paskaleva, 'Razvitie' 97-8.

113. See Ivan Sakuzov, 'Razvitie na gradskiya zhivot i na zanayatite v Bulgariya prez xviii i xix vek', in Bulgariya 1000 godini, 927-1927 i (Sofia 1930) 685-703, especially 689-90.

114. Paskaleva, 'Avstro-bulgarski' 83.

115. See Sakuzov, loc. cit., 691, and, for tobacco, Boyan Besevliev, 'Wirtschaftskarte des europäischen Teils von osmanischen Imperium im 18 Jahrhundert', Etudes Balkaniques vii (1971) 92-104, especially 97.

116. Bulgarian sesame seed oil sold in Marseilles in 1842 alone was worth ten million francs. Blanqui, op. cit., 232.

117. Todorov, op. cit., 200.

118. Paskaleva, 'Razvitie' 79-80; for a picturesque description of Uzundzhovo see Blanqui, op. cit., 252-7; for the fair at Turgovishte see Stefan Velikov, 'Turgovishte prez Vuzrazhdaneto', Istoricheski Pregled xxxii (1976) 93-106, passim.

119. Paskaleva, 'Razvitie' 87-101, passim.

120. See Konstantin Veliki, Za turgoviyata na bulgarskite gradove s Avstriya v kraya na xviii i nachaloto na xix v.', Istoricheski Pregled xv (1959) 61-76, especially 66.

121. Sakuzov, loc. cit., 686.

122. Kosev, 'Izyasyavane' 35; Paskaleva, 'Razvitie' 101-3.

123. Sakuzov, loc. cit., 694.

124. See Nikolai Todorov, 'Za nyakoi promeni v kharaktera na tsekhovata organizatsiya u nas prez purvata polovina na xix v.', Istoricheski Pregled, xiv (1958) 44-76, especially 71. (This work cited hereafter as Todorov, 'Tsekhovata organizatsiya'.) See also Todorov, op. cit., 198 et seq.

125. Quoted in Mikhail Arnaudov, Lyuben Karavelov; zhivot, delo, epokha, 1834-1879 (Sofia 1972) 13-14.

126. The classic treatment of the Balkan Christian merchant is Traian Stoianovich, 'The Conquering Balkan Orthodox Merchant', Journal of Economic History, xv (1960) 234-313.

127. Paskaleva, 'Razvitie', 111-5, and the same author's 'La mer noire et son littoral a l'époque de la domination ottomane sur les terres bulgares', Bulgarian Historical Review, iii (1975) 78-94.

128. Paskaleva, 'Osobenosti' 428. See also above

129. Todorov, 'Tsekhovata organisatsiya' 54.

130. Todorov, 'Trud' 24.

131. Gulub D. Gulubov, 'Dva turski dokumenti ot xvii v. za stopanskata i obshtestvenata deinost na bulgarskite zanayatchii', Izvestiya na Instituta za Istoriya xviii (1967) 289-297, especially 289.

132. Paskaleva, 'Razvitie' 94.

133. Ibid., 111-5; Todorov, 'Tsekhovata organisatsiya' 60-2; Todorov, op. cit., 212-3.

134. Ivan Snegarov, 'Po vuprosa za klasite i klasovite otnoshenie prez Vuzrazhdaneto', Istoricheski Pregled viii (1951-52) 202-210, especially 209-210.

135. Khristov, 'Klasite' 64. Some esnafs were also connected to the

Church and individual esnafs often made themselves responsible for
providing specific items of building material or decoration for new churches,
see Nikolai Zhechev, 'Velchovata zavera', Istoricheski Pregled xxi (1975)
63-80. Other esnafs took small churches and graveyards into their protection,
see Konstantin Irichek, Putuvane po Bulgariya (Sofia 1974 edition) 72. For
other activities undertaken by esnafs see Manyo Stoyanov, 'Bulgaro-grutsko
kulturno sutrudnichestvo v Plovdiv prez purvata polovina na xix v.', in
V Pamet na Akademik Mikhail Dimitrov (Sofia 1974) 223-232.

136. Sakuzov, loc. cit., 697.

137. Ibid.

138. Todorov, op. cit., 210.

139. Stoyanov, loc. cit., 225.

140. Todorov, 'Tsekhovata organizatsiya' 51-2 and Undzhiev, op. cit., 46-7.

141. Oya Komen, 'The Advent and Consequences of Free Trade in the Ottoman
Empire', Etudes Balkaniques vii (1971) 47-55.

142. Todorov, 'Tsekhovata organizatsiya' 51.

143. Todorov, 'Trud' 7.

144. Todorov, op. cit., 200 et seq.

145. Virzhiniya Paskaleva, 'Die Entwicklung der städtischen Wirtschaft in
den Balkanländern in der ersten Hälfte des xix Jahrhunderts (Vergleich und
Probleme)', Actes du premier Congrès international des Etudes balkaniques et
sud-est européennes iv Histoire xviii-xixe ss. (Sofia 1969) 43-53, especially
46-8.

146. Blanqui, op. cit., 136-8.

147. Todorov, 'Trud' 12-7.

148. Paskaleva, 'Razvitie' 98.

149. Western furniture etc. began to be used by the richer urban elements
from the second quarter of the nineteenth century, though women did not
copy western fashions in clothes until the 1850s. See Nikolai Todorov,
'The City in the Bulgarian Lands from the Fifteenth to the Nineteenth
Century', in Thomas Butler ed, Bulgaria Past and Present (Columbus, Ohio
1976) 15-31, especially 27.

150. Paskaleva, 'Razvitie' 108.

151. Ibid.

152. Todorov, 'Tsekhovata organizatsiya' 70-3.

153. See Arnaudov, op. cit., 14. Blanqui found new towns to his taste and
was especially censorious of Plovdiv on account of its dilapidated bridge
and because 'des cadavres de chiens et de chats, des débris de boucherie,
des immondices fétides obstruaient la grande avenue du pont'. Blanqui, op.
cit., 250.

154. Paskaleva, 'Osobenosti' 432.

155. For emigration see, inter alia, Todorov, 'Trud' 31 and the same author's

'Tsekhovata organizatsiya' 100.

156. Todorov, 'Trud' 19.

157. Paskaleva, 'Razvitie' 125.

158. Todorov, 'Trud' 12-7, 19.

159. Khristov, Obshtini 27.

160. See Pletnyov, loc. cit., 72-3.

161. Nikolai Todorov, 'Bulgarskoto naseleniye v grad Lom prez 40te godini na xix v.', in Aleksandur K. Burmov, Dimitur Angelov, Ivan Duichev, et al. eds Izsledvanie v chest na Marin Drinov (Sofia 1960) 579-592.

162. Ibid., 569.

9

MONTENEGRIN SOCIETY 1800-1830

ALAN FERGUSON

'Better one day with a falcon than a hundred years with a crow.'
(Montenegrin proverb)

The Serbs of Montenegro[1] had enjoyed complete, if unrecog-
nized, independence of the Ottoman Empire for over forty years
when the War of Greek Independence began. Ottoman rule over
them, between the collapse of the native Crnojević dynasty in
the early sixteenth and the re-assertion of a desire for
independence in the early eighteenth century, had been at best
tenuous. Under a series of governors and bishops of varying
degrees of ambition and talent, Montenegro had progressed by the
start of the nineteenth century to a condition in which any
suggestion of a return to Ottoman rule was treasonable. The
European powers might refuse formally to recognize the independence of the Montenegrin lands, as they steadfastly did until
the Treaty of Berlin in 1878; the Porte might insist that
Montenegro was still an integral part of the Ottoman Empire, a
territory in revolt but nonetheless a kadılık of the sancak of
Scutari (Shkodër); in practice the refusal of the Montenegrins
to admit Ottoman administrators and pay tribute or other taxes
testifies to the region's actual status. It is incorrect, however, to surmise from this that liberation from Ottoman rule
implied a desire for the creation of a Montenegrin state in its
stead: untypically for the Balkans in the age of national
re-affirmation, in the Montenegrin context the two were not
synonymous. Living in separate tribal communities, the
Montenegrins were no more willing to surrender their anarchic
freedom to domestic central authority than they had been to
'the Turk'.[2] The leitmotiv of Montenegrin history even until
the territory's inclusion in the Kingdom of the Serbs, Croats
and Slovenes in 1918 was to be friction between the development of central government and the resistance to it of local,
tribal forces. Political authority was unwelcome at any but a

205

tribal level. In 1830 Montenegro had no army, police force,
national administration, constitution or secular schools just
as, in rejecting the concept of a regulated, ordered state, its
inhabitants also refused payment of the taxes necessary for its
functioning. If, 'nations borrow only what they are nearly in
a condition to have invented themselves'[3] Montenegro was not a
ready debtor. That its bishops and few tribal headmen who had
had experience of European civilization might counsel the introduction of its outer trappings was of no consequence to the
mass of the population. The foreigner, with the sole exception
of the Russian, was regarded by it with suspicion at best and
undisguised hostility at worst.

If not a state[4] the loose federation of tribes was a
beleagured society. Encompassed and isolated, on three sides
by the Ottoman Empire in the Herzegovina, the sancaks of Novi
Pazar and Scutari, on the fourth by Austrian Dalmatia, which
separated it from the Adriatic, Montenegro displayed a psycho-
logical outlook not dissimilar to that of Albania in recent
history: the mentality of the state of siege, the imagined or
actual territorial ambition of neighbours, and confidence in a
distant, apparently beneficent but not wholly reliable, great
ally. In that the tribes felt themselves encircled by hostile
forces their situation was markedly different from that of the
Serbians. The latter had, and on more than one occasion made
use of the opportunity of retreating to Habsburg territory in
numbers, in the face of advancing Ottoman troops. Furthermore,
as Serbia lay on a major line of communication between the
Habsburg and Ottoman Empires, the Serbians came under indirect
but definite Central European economic, political and cultural
influences. As Austria's Serbs played an important role in the
maintenance of the Empire's Military Frontier, the concept of
their being 'a bulwark of civilization' and 'rampart of
Christendom' was deeply implanted in them. None of these factors applied in the Montenegrin case: no line of retreat existed
nor did possibilities of cultural and political cross-
fertilization. Montenegro was little stimulated by contacts,
economic, political or cultural, with the Habsburg Empire,
while the latter's proximity and Roman Catholicism provided a
constant source of suspicion. The Montenegrins had few exact
co-nationals[5] on adjacent Habsburg territory and conducted little
trade with them.

In spite of its relative economic and social primitivity,

or perhaps because of it, Montenegro played a disproportion-
ately great role in the re-assertion of the Serbian liberation
idea in the early nineteenth century. Its uncompromising
resistance to Ottoman attempts to re-incorporate it in the
imperial order, its defence of Orthodoxy and legendary readiness to offer and give refuge to Serbians displaced or for any
reason in flight from Ottoman territory, gave it a unique
practical and spiritual significance in Serbian history. Mount
Lovćen, by which the core of Old Montenegro lay, was looked upon
as a totem of freedom from Islam even by Serbians who had already
shed the tribal mentality. Once the myth of Montenegrin freedom
had been created, the fact that the area had paid harac for
eighty years in the seventeenth century and was subsequently
forced to do so periodically, as during the incursion of Mahmut
Paşa Bushatli of Scutari in 1785[6], was incidental. The poet
Bishop Njegoš was merely encapsulating a truism when he wrote
that 'whatever would not be enchained, fled and gathered in
these mountains'.[7]

By the final years of the reign of Bishop Peter I (1782-
1830) Montenegro was a definable though small indentation into
Ottoman Europe. With no outlet of its own onto the Adriatic,
it stretched north-east, inland, from close above the Austrian
port of Kotor. Resembling in form a figure eight, its lower,
south-western section was known as Old Montenegro (Stara Crna
Gora), its upper, north-eastern half as the Highlands (Brda).
The dimensions of Old Montenegro, whose southern tip bordered
on Lake Scutari, were twenty-five by forty miles; the Highlands
were slightly larger. At most the territory reached fifty
miles inland. The neck of land joining the two sections was
fifteen miles across. At both its ends stood Turkish fortresses:
Nikšić to the North, Spuž to the south. The land was predominantly mountainous, rising sharply from near sea-level to 1,700
metres within four miles, and over 2,000 metres in the Highlands. It contained no town or fortress: Grahovo, Nikšić,
Kolašin, Podgorica, Spuž and Žabljak lay close outside its
frontiers. The capital of Montenegro, if it can be so called,
was the monastery of Cetinje, which was also the bishop or
Metropolitan's seat.[8] This and the handful of buildings around
it, one of which was the territory's only inn, was the focal
point of Montenegro. Assemblies of headmen were invariably
convened there. Montenegro's roads were merely tracks with
barely enough space for two laden mules or women to pass in the

mountainous districts. With more than a little wit, the
Russian captain and geologist Kovalevskii remarked in 1841 that
'for the Montenegrins the road is everywhere'. The condition of
Montengro's roads was a frequent source of complaint to travellers. The French Captain Vialla de Sommières explained 'I have
used the expression "road" to denote the places by which one
enters Montenegro, but in truth the word is unsuitable and I am
unable to find one to express my ideas precisely'. The Russian
consul in Dubrovnik Gagić noted that he found it easier to
maintain relations with Mexico and Peru than with Montenegro.
And what is as eloquent of the Montenegrin mentality as of the
state of communications on their territory, when Marshal Marmont
offered to undertake the construction of a road through
Montenegro from Kotor to Nikšić in the Herzegovina at the
expense of the French Empire, the reply of the headmen's assembly was that they already found their roads quite satisfactory.
The one route of more than local importance was that along the
valley of the river Zeta between Nikšić and Spuž, which
connected the paşalık of Herzegovina and the sancak of Scutari.
This was commonly sealed off by the Turks in times of crisis.

Apart from Montenegro's geo-political situation, the
general inhospitableness of habitat was a major cause of the
region's primitivity. There were notably wide local variations
in both its climate and physical formation. Nowhere was the
climate dry, but the porous limestone base of much of the
region rendered it arid. As a treasured commodity, fresh
water was used primarily for culinary purposes and the watering
of flocks and cattle. In the uplands, milk, whether of goats
or cattle, and thawed snow were more often drunk than fresh
water. Cetinje had a single spring. Away from the rivers,
only in the lowlands near the tip of Lake Scutari and Crmnica
was there fresh water in any great supply, but even there
certain apparently fresh springs were shunned in the summer.
The climate varied from the Mediterranean nearer the coast, to
the Alpine deeper in the Dinaric range. The districts of
Crmnica and the Zeta valley contained the only fertile soil in
Montenegro. Elsewhere, even in river valleys meadows were
practically unknown. In the Middle Ages Montenegro had been
well forested but this natural wealth had been over-exploited by
the Venetians for shipbuilding and by the Montenegrins themselves for fuel and the erection of shelter. In 1881 the
Russian scholar Rovinskii noted having seen trees felled so

that flocks might feed on their foliage. During Peter I's
reign, the only restriction on the felling of trees related to
those providing shade by the roadsides. Deforestation resulted
in the pasture-line being somewhat lower than it had been in the
fifteenth century. The main areas of human habitation were on
plateaux, in mountain valleys and on their slopes, with
considerable movement with flocks from season to season. It was
unusual for a shepherd to descend a mountain in summer or ascend
it in winter without good cause. The quality of pasture was
irregular, even at the same height, because of differing degrees
of shelter and the direction of slope. Montenegro was poorly
endowed with rivers, and since most of those flowing through it
continued into Ottoman territory, their banks were not widely
used for cultivation. The additional danger of seasonal inunda-
tion served as a conclusive deterrent. In short, Montenegro was
not rich in natural wealth. The one fertile plain of substantial size, that of the lower Zeta around Podgorica, was held by
the Turk. As the Montenegrin proverb had it, 'the Latins took
the sea, the Turk the field'.

The population of Montenegro, including the Highlands,
was estimated in 1834 to be 20,000 rifles, or 100,000 people.[9]
As youths bore arms from the age of about fourteen, this
estimate would indicate that the ratio of men to women was
approximately 1:3, reflecting high male mortality in clashes
with the Turk and in the blood feud. In the reign of Peter I
it was still considered dishonourable to die from natural
causes, 'in bed like a woman'. On learning of a tribesman's
death, the proper reply remained: 'Who killed him?'. In the
event of his not having perished as a warrior, the retort was:
'God, the old executioner'. Peter I was of the opinion that for
fifty years the population had shewn no natural increase[10] and
acknowledged this while attempting to arrange the migration of
some 20,000 Montenegrins to Western Russia where he hoped they
might form a new military frontier. Had he wished to stress
the urgency of his request, this information, unless reliable
and already known to St. Petersburg, would not have been
rehearsed. Lacking urban settlements and having 100,000
inhabitants, Montenegro was a densely populated region. Given
the high mortality from domestic and foreign conflict, periodic
famine and barbaric conditions of sanitation and hygiene, the
population, which was as great as at any time in Montenegro's
previous history, had undoubtedly been augmented by the influx

of individuals, families and tribes from Ottoman territory. The
only authoritative statistics concerning the relative density of
population in the four nahije /ñahiye7 or districts of Old
Montenegro and in the Highlands were compiled in 1805 by the
Russian Brigadier Stefan Sankovskii, who had been sent to
Montenegro by Tsar Alexander to assess its military capability.
His findings were that the tribesmen were evenly distributed,
with a slightly greater density in Crmnica.[11] Significantly, as
well as being a fertile district, Crmnica was separated from
North Albania by a range of mountains. It is not unreasonable
to argue that the population, when not subject to plague or
famine, was the maximum that the land could then support.[12] The
view that Montenegro possessed insufficient land and produced
too little food for its population was expressed at a headmen's
assembly as early as 12 May 1805.[13] Before the national
liberation idea became imperative, basic physiological and other
elementary needs provoked frequent raids into adjacent territory,
whether inhabited by Orthodox, Catholic or Moslem.[14] The
periodic migration of related social units to Serbia, Russia,
Naples, Hungary and even the Ottoman lands is a clear indication
that basic needs were not fully met by organized or isolated
military activity.[15]

Notwithstanding the attempts of Peter I and his
predecessors in the eighteenth century to introduce a central
political authority, in 1830 Montenegro appeared a solidly
tribal society. Following the collapse of state and consequent
disappearance of nobility and serfdom with the approach of the
Ottomans, Montenegrin society had reverted to a pre-feudal
structure. The reason for the reversion, determined by
habitat, was the same as caused the segmentation of the primitive horde: the need to gain access to the major sources of
food supply. A division of labour was made necessary by the
low level of production. If tribal society may be categorized
according to the primary mode of food production[16] most of the
Montenegrin tribes had reached the higher pastoral level, of
stock-raising supplemented by agriculture, while those nearer
the Adriatic littoral had reached the highest agricultural
level, of field tillage supplemented by stock-raising.
Montenegro was approaching, but had not yet reached the thres-
hold of transition from tribal society to state. In his last
years Peter I was convinced that his efforts in establishing law,
effective administration and security had been in vain. 'If I

lived among the Turks I would not have to bear the travail
which I suffer at the hands of the Montenegrins . . . My
heart has shrivelled from your misdeeds and my old age has been
embittered.'[17] Objectively the economy was not yet predominantly
monetary but natural, based on barter and exchange. What
currency did circulate was Venetian and Austrian. This was also
used in transactions with the Turks.

Society was wholly segmented, in the 4 nahije of Old
Montenegro into 24 tribes (plemena) and in the Highlands into
7. Each of these was subdivided into villages (sela) or more
often brotherhoods (bratstva), and further into the final
social unit, the household (kuća). Before the formation of the
state and thereafter the development of a sense of citizenhood,
primary loyalty was due to brotherhood and tribe. Territorially
this meant localism and particularism. The importance of the
individual resided pre-eminently in his significance as a
brotherhood or tribal member. The component strands of this
communistic society were entwined in a complex pattern in which
all action was based on co-operation or competition, reciprocity
or rivalry. Collaboration was the cornerstone of the brotherhood members' activity. Brotherhoods collaborated in production
yet vied for prestige. They were linked by intermarriage or set
in opposition by the blood feud. The tribal system had a
dynamic uniquely its own, determined by communal self-interest
calling now for co-operation, now for competition. It was not
until conditions developed for the accumulation of private
property in a money economy later in the century that the
balance of tribal society was destroyed. By 1830 there had been
no significant accumulation of private capital. Variations in
the size of flocks or the number of cattle owned marked the only
differences in wealth and these did not engender distinct social
stratification. Conflict between those who produced and those
who enjoyed wealth did not therefore emerge as a cause of
domestic friction, but neither did it make possible the
technical and cultural transition from barbarism to civilization witnessed elsewhere in the Balkans.[18] Conflict as a
driving force of human activity was evident, but manifested
itself between tribe and tribe, brotherhood and brotherhood,
tribe and 'Turk', man and nature. The tribal system was deeply
entrenched, preserved by a keen sense of kinship, itself based
on the ancestral cult. Exogamy was strictly enforced, the
intermarriage of descendants being forbidden to the eighth

degree.[19] Membership of the brotherhood was determined by patrilineal descent, which made the communal order strongly patriarchal.

The affairs of the tribes and their components were regulated at various levels and more or less effectively, depending on whether brotherhoods or tribes were 'in blood', by the assembly of headmen (<u>zbor glavara</u>), district (<u>nahijski</u>), tribal (<u>plemenski</u>) and village assemblies (<u>seoski skupovi</u>). Matters of interest to particular social units would be debated, resolved and ratified by the appropriate gathering. Insoluble local disputes and questions touching inter-tribal interest would be brought before the headmen's assembly. Like all the others, it was convened irregularly as the need arose. While the bishop was solely responsible for the conduct of foreign policy, his authority in domestic affairs was no greater than that of the headmen. By virtue of his ecclesiastical position, the sanction of excommunication could be invoked by him, but as temporal ruler, in the absence of an executive he could do little more than appeal, counsel, or threaten concerted tribal action against an offending party. The attitude of the headmen was crucial, since their consent was essential for any far-reaching action by the bishop. By 1830 the office of headman, like that of bishop, had become hereditary. Headmen, however, received no remuneration for their services, had no practical means of asserting authority, were not visibly differentiated from their fellow tribesmen except in that they were served first at meals and enjoyed the privilege of being first in battle. They could not, therefore, become an oligarchy. On the contrary, forces of natural democracy persisted. Any male Montenegrin capable of bearing arms had the right to attend and speak at any gathering from his village assembly upwards. No less than 2,000 Montenegrins, mostly Highlanders, attended an assembly on 12 May 1805.[20] Eloquence rather than erudition was a respected gift among the tribesmen and the power of persuasion rather than coercion was acknowledged. Customary rules of debating procedure which forbade the interruption of any speaker were properly observed. Since, as the perceptive Karadžić remarked, it was not easy to persuade a Montenegrin to do anything save battle, 'greater entertainment than any dancing or merriment,'[21] assemblies were known to continue for several days. The functioning of the tribal system did not depend on merely the acquiescence of its member units, but required their active participation in it. The importance of the assembly institution cannot, therefore, be over-emphasised.

In 1830 tribal mentality remained, like the assembly system, vital and resilient.[22] Indicators of tribal awareness reflected in custom were numerous. Totemism and taboo, which continued into the twentieth century, formed integral features of communal life. Totemism was evident in the belief in the vila or nymph, normally associated with natural geographical features; the name taboo in the reluctance to address one's spouse directly by name; the food taboo in the refusal to eat horsemeat, frogs, and, among certain tribes, beef and veal, even in times of famine; the taboo on the forging of metal, especially iron, in the concomitant degradation of the smith.[23] The taking of physical trophies in battle, notably the head or at least the nose of one's victim, was considered natural and desirable.[24] The donning of his clothing, if possible, was also thought normal. The Montenegrin who wore the uniform of the late General Delgorgue in the campaign against the French in Dalmatia did so as much for symbolic as for practical purposes. Similarly, the recovery of at least the head of a member of one's household fallen in battle was a sacred duty. Such phenomena as the totem, taboo and trophy together bear witness to the existence of a definite tribal morality. Simplistically commented upon by progressive historians as examples of barbarity, such practices were not primarily inhuman. The same moral code imposed the obligation to behead a fellow tribesman so seriously wounded in conflict that he could not be carried, and forbade the severance of the heads of adversaries who surrendered prior to the commencement of hostilities. The torture or other maltreatment of those who so surrendered were unknown among the tribesmen. Instant death in battle was held more noble and honourable than the ignominy of falling prisoner.[25] Montenegro had no prison during the reign of Peter I. His successor Bishop Njegoš held institutionalized confinement in like contempt and expressed disgust at the condition of the prison in Venice. Both bishops shared with their fellow tribesmen the view that heroic death and, paradoxically, the act of inflicting a speedy death heroically (junački) were to be preferred.[26] These were but particular facets of the morality of humanitas heroica (čojstvo i junaštvo), determined by the struggle for survival and based on customary ethical principles.[27]

213

When tribal consciousness exerted itself in joint tribal action in the common interest, the Montenegrins were an effective military force. More frequent, however, were instances of inter-tribal dispute and, most seriously for the domestic weal, the blood feud (osveta). In this, the Montenegrin tribes closely resembled the Albanians. If an individual were killed by the member of another brotherhood,[28] tribe or district, the fellow members of the victim's brotherhood, tribe or district were bound to avenge the murder immediately, regardless of considerations of provocation or guilt. The very terminology of the blood feud (osvetiti, osveta, osvetnik), based on the adjective 'sacred' (sveti), indicates the moral and spiritual nature of this obligation. If the offender himself could not be found, any other male member of his brotherhood, tribe or district might be killed in his stead; the more eminent the surrogate victim the greater the satisfaction. The social group to have suffered the last loss was bound by the same obligation. In this way a vendetta would develop. Feuds continuing for decades and resulting in more than fifty deaths or fighting on a large scale were not uncommon.[29] The process could be halted only by the satisfaction of honour through recompense,[30] following initially the mediation of the bishop or an appointee of his, and subsequently the judgment of a court of assessors nominated by both parties. At no point was murder treated formally as a crime. The aim of the so-called Court of Good Men (Sud dobrih ljudi) was to satisfy both parties by balancing the blood account. The dispute would be concluded by the original murderer's kinsfolk entertaining the aggrieved party and inviting one of its number to become spiritual guardian to one of the murderer's survivors. Generally, the greater the territorial dimensions of the feud, the easier it proved to effect a reconciliation. Local disputes were more problematical as, out of a sense of honour, brotherhoods were less willing to be paid off for the murder of any of their number by a neighbour. That the blood feud had become endemic among the Montenegrins by the start of the nineteenth century can be seen in the extended name structure of the individual, which indicated not only Christian name, patronymic and brotherhood, but the tribal branch name if the tribe had offshoots, and tribe proper (e.g. Djiko Milov Martinović Bajica Cetinjanin). It served as a personal key to a man's sequence of allegiances, and to a potential enemy it was an indication of the other's suitability as a victim.

If manslaughter was the most frequent cause of feud, the abduction of girls and women was a more localised, but no less dishonourable offence. It brought disgrace not only on the family of the abducted, but the brotherhood or village which let her be taken. Exogamy through the arranged marriage was still customary as one of the principal supports of tribal society, erasing the possibility of incestuous alliances and strengthening inter-tribal relations.[31] Nevertheless, the high mortality of men in middle age led to not a few Montenegrin youths being fatherless. If a dowry of substance could not be offered, or if one had been offered and rejected, abduction with the assistance of friends might be seen as the only alternative. In such cases the girl or woman might be dragged by the hair and 'beaten as an ox among cabbages'.[32] Furthermore, not all women were glad to be treated as chattels and, having formed a free emotional attachment, might agree to elopement. This was also sufficient justification for the taking of blood.[33]

The blood feud represented a great obstacle to the establishment of public security in Montenegro and hindered the area's economic progress as much as threats of re-conquest by the Turk. Peter was to grapple with this widespread and deep-rooted phenomenon throughout his reign. There are no data as to its precise intensity at any given time, but estimations can be made on the basis of fragmentary evidence. Milaković, a near contemporary of the bishop, secretary to his successor and not normally given to exaggerating the disorder of Montenegrin society, acknowledged that 'veritable anarchy continued until the end of the bishop's /Peter I's/ life. There was not a single nahija or region of the Highlands whose inhabitants were in mutual peace, and hardly could one find a single tribe in which there was no internal warfare or bloodshed between brotherhoods.'[34] Some statistical data were recorded by Medaković, another secretary and close collaborator of Njegoš'. In 1786 Peter made a circuit of Montenegro in an attempt to settle disputes by mediation. Medaković wrote[35] that the bishop learned of 75 'dead heads' in Čevo and 71 in Velestovo. From a misguided sense of patriotism Medaković declines to give further figures. If in these two localities 146 heads were to be recompensed, it is probable that in all Montenegro there were a thousand local or regional armed disputes, in which a quarter of the total number of brotherhoods was involved.[36]

It was not climatic conditions alone which made 1787 a year of
famine in Montenegro, since flocks could not be safely grazed
or fields tilled when tribesmen were involved in punitive
expeditions or preoccupied with self-defence. While tribal
consciousness provided a constructive factor in the maintenance
of common independence, tribal morality was disruptive of the
quality of that independence.

As in the development of previous tribal societies, the
tendency in Montenegro was for high office to become hereditary.[37]
Because the bishop was bound to remain celibate, the succession
was not within a single family but a brotherhood, passing most
often from uncle to nephew. By the mid-eighteenth century the
tenure of this office had come to reside and, until 1852, with
short interruptions remained, in the Petrović brotherhood of
the Njeguši tribe.[38] The succession was formally subject to
ratification by the tribal headmen who retained the right,
although it was never employed, to reject an unsuitable nominee.
Parallel to this tendency towards hereditary succession in
ecclesiastical office and the consequent concentration of high
spiritual authority in one brotherhood, but not simultaneous
with it, went an accumulation and transfer of temporal power.
At the time of Peter's accession to the metropolitan's seat in
1784, upon the death of Arsenije Plamenac, there was a distinct
division between spiritual and secular authority. The latter
was exercised by a governor, also of the Njeguši tribe, but of
the Radonjić brotherhood. The office of <u>guvernadur</u> had been
established in the early eighteenth century by the Venetian
Republic, to represent its local trading interests. Tenure of
it passed from the Vukotić brotherhood and became hereditary
in the Radonjić brotherhood in the mid-eighteenth century. In
the absence of any other temporal authority, the prestige which
attached to the governorship brought with it perceptible
political influence.[39] In 1784 it was the governor who presided
over the headmen's assembly. The next 50 years witnessed a
gradual usurpation of temporal authority by Bishop Peter in a
series of shrewd and ultimately effective attempts to bring
into question the governor's allegiance to the tribes.[40] As
the bishop's political ploys fall outside the scope of this
article, suffice it to note that between 1784, when the governor,
Jovan Radonjić, was the only temporal authority in Montenegro,
1796, when he led one half of the Montenegrin army and the
bishop the other against the army of the vizier of Scutari

Kara Mahmut Paşa Bushatlı, and 1830, by which time the governor
Vuko Radonjić's authority had been all but extinguished,[41] there
was a gradual but constant concentration of temporal authority
in the hands of the bishop. If the bishop's methods are not of
direct relevance here, the reasons for the headmen's approval
of the process outlined are of importance for an understanding
of the mentality of a mature tribal society.

Religious affiliation had been accepted as the sole
indicator of nationality since before the Ottoman conquest. The
Orthodoxy of the Montenegrins, whether based on the authority of
the Patriarchate of Peć or, as since 1767, institutionally
autonomous, was the only remnant of pre-Ottoman independence.
In this it held a strong emotional attraction and was, moreover,
embodied in the person of the bishop. That the tribesmen were
not dogmatic or pious did not affect their reverence for the
symbol of the only indicator of the common Serbian origin which
underlay tribal individuality. Furthermore, since the time of
Peter the Great, Russia had been regarded by the tribesmen,
quite unjustifiably in the light of experience to the contrary,
as a distantly related, sympathetic ally and potential protector.
Linguistic affinity and shared Orthodoxy were the major
determinants in this. Bishop Peter took pains to cultivate his
image as the link between the tribes and the ally, even when
treated with disdain by Russia in the 1780s and abandoned by it
in 1805-6, when the Austrian-held Bay of Kotor passed to the
French, and in 1814-15, when it was returned to Austria. The
fruitlessness of his foreign policy did not result in personal
unpopularity. Clearly, Russia, as against the Tsar, remained
an object of sentimental attachment to the headmen, and being
distant, unlike the Habsburgs and Ottomans, posed no threat of
conquest. As the apparent head of Russophile tendencies, Peter
was less likely to undermine tribal autonomy than the governor.
The conclusive factor in his ascendancy through the gravitation
of temporal authority towards him, with the headmen's approval,
was less obvious, more devious, perhaps unconscious, but
symptomatic of tribal mentality. It lay in Peter's inability
to maintain more than sporadic domestic peace, to enforce law
and order, or forge supra-tribal interdependency except in time
of external threat. In denying the authority of the governor
and transferring it to the bishop, the headmen were choosing
the less perilous course. The bishop's useful and necessary
role of mediator in feud and commander-in-chief in war could

continue without his disposing of practical means of forcing political unity among the tribes.[42] It was widely known that Peter had financially ruined himself and pawned his cross, mitre and other regalia in order to purchase grain in   years of famine and munitions during the campaigns against the French. This redounded to his moral credit as the exhibition of altruism and, together with his political impotence, made him the preferable option. It was not without irony or a trace of hypocrisy that the canonisation of Peter four years after his death was enthusiastically received by the tribesmen who had more than once fired over his head during his attempts to reconcile them.[43]

Peter's first efforts to forge a sense of Montenegrin unity by transferring the execution of legal sanctions from tribal to central authority were made in 1796. He had been convinced of the timeliness of introducing written legislation based on adapted customary law by two multi-tribal victories earlier in that year over Mahmut Paşa's army, at Visočica in the Highlands on 11 July, and at Krusi in Old Montenegro on 3 October. These denoted an apparent increase in the sense of inter-tribal dependency since 1775, when the tribesmen of Old Montenegro had not gone to the assistance of the besieged Highlanders. The codex of 1796, known significantly as the Constraint (stega)[44] and supplemented in 1798 and 1803, was clearly intended to eradicate the blood feud, by making the murder of a fellow Montenegrin or Highlander a punishable offence; to isolate offenders by forbidding the provision of shelter by their tribe;[45] to create supra-tribal unity by making treason a grave crime;[46] to discourage raids by declaring theft from Old Montenegro, the Highlands, the littoral and Austria a culpable offence. The codex further envisaged the establishment of a court, to be known as the kuluk (corvée). As there was no revenue from taxes, headmen were to be obliged to serve on it without remuneration. In the supplement of 1803 Peter attempted to introduce the payment of a modest but revolutionary tax (mirija) of 60 para per household, to be delivered annually by district headmen to the monastery at Cetinje.

The stega served more as an enumeration of the most common crimes in Montenegro than as an effective piece of legislation. Having once ratified it at their assembly, the headmen proceeded to ignore it and judge according to tribal law

218

in local councils of elders as previously. In 1841 Mickiewicz
noted that the blood feud was still rife, thieves were pursued
and shot by their victims, and families sheltered criminals.[47]
Soon after the victories over Mahmut Paşa's army, the failure
of the headmen to respond to Peter's appeals for the creation
of a common judicial organ indicates that their military
co-operation in self-defence did not imply a willingness to
surrender tribal autonomy. It testifies rather to a readiness
to make concessions to central authority, provided they
imposed no obligatory tax payment and remained unenforcible.[48]
Appreciation of this distinction by the headmen, with the
further knowledge that an executive force could not be formed
without their consent, reinforces the thesis that they supported
the concentration of temporal power in the bishop's hands as
long as it remained nominal. Montenegro did not become a
theocracy in any real sense.

The one non-ecclesiastical sphere in which the bishop's
authority was practically acknowledged and employed was that of
military leadership.[49] Dressed more like a general than a
bishop in time of war, Peter presented a forbidding figure with
his attendant bodyguards.[50] The tribesmen had learned in
conflict with the Turk that fewer casualties were sustained and
more heads, booty and 'glory' won, from the use of the frontal
charge in battle. The elements of speed and surprise implicit
in this were reinforced by terror tactics in the suspension of
severed heads from the neck or shoulder. Tribal honour made
the employment of reserve forces inconceivable, although the
tactics of retreat and ambush were not unheard of. It lay upon
the commander-in-chief to determine the most propitious moment
for attack and co-ordinate the action of tribal units by means
of signals. Not renowned for his formal discipline at other
times, when in sight of the enemy the tribesman was obedient to
his officers. Not coincidentally these were also his local
elders. Lightly equipped and self-supporting, the tribal army
was highly mobile. It never fought far outside Montenegro's
frontiers, so that familiarity with terrain provided initial
advantage over the enemy. It would have been impossible for
the bishop to deny the warriors plunder, which was the primary
material reason for their presence among his troops. The
practice of the taking of trophies in what General Lauriston,
in the voice of civilization, described as 'atrocities
contrary to the spirit of European war'[51] the bishop was unable

219

to suppress. Russian offers to redeem living French prisoners were no more successful, as the tribesman resumed the role of freeman upon the conclusion of hostilities. Humanitas heroica in warfare permitted neither the request nor the dispensation of mercy. The same egalitarianism made the unquestioning obedience to officers of 'civilized' troops when not embattled incomprehensible to the tribesmen.

The primeval qualities displayed by the bishop's flock and clergy in warfare, determined their religious outlook at other times. The ethic of the new covenant was not deeply revered. Preoccupied by the immediate concern for survival, the tribesmen were little more than sentimentally attached to Orthodoxy. The custom by which any man to have taken a life was forbidden holy communion for twenty years, resulted in the majority of tribesmen partaking of it less than annually. What educative instruction was given in Montenegro, however, devolved upon the church, its 200 popes (priests) and 25 monks. The popes were outwardly little differentiated from the rest of the community and practised the same husbandry as their spiritual flock. Few qualifications were required of them apart from the capacity to recite the liturgy and other major rites. Elementary literacy was exceptional among the popes. On the whole Montenegro's monks were less badly educated. Each of the nahije contained at least one monastery, whether inhabited or not, and it was in the stronger ones that basic religious education was offered. The need to import writing materials from Kotor perhaps reflects the conditions under which instruction was given, if not also the level of scholarship. Occassionally a secretary of the bishop would provide secular teaching for the dozen or so boys at Cetinje, but in the absence of a library of any proportions apart from that of the bishop himself, it proved irregular in quality and frequency. Pupils seeking a higher education had to descend to the schools in Dalmatia or, more rarely, travelled to Russia to obtain it. The level of literacy, otherwise indeterminable, can be gauged from Vuk Karadžić's 'Serbian Dictionary' of 1818 finding twelve subscribers in Montenegro. The monasteries received a certain, if modest, income from their estates, acquired in feudal times in bequests of the Crnojević dynasty and tilled by the monks, as well as from the exploitation of fishing rights in Lake Scutari. The combination of this income and the financial assistance received sporadically from the Russian Synod enabled the church to subsist. At no point in its history has the clergy formed a privileged estate in Montenegro.

Because of the marked imbalance between the sexes through-out the rest of Montenegro, women constituted an indispensable part of the work force. A tribesman would not tolerate the insult of a woman of his household or brotherhood by an out-sider, but neither were her exertions generally appreciated. Horses were not kept by most of the tribes on account of the mountainous terrain, and if a donkey were not available, the role of porterage fell to the women. The custom was for the man of the household to lead and keep watch, bearing rifle and chibouk (pipe). Pregnancy, being a condition in which a woman of childbearing age often found herself, did not diminish her manual labour in tillage, pasturage or domestic activity. Childbirth commonly took place in field or forest, customarily without complaint, and a return to normal activities was expected within a few days. Children were suckled for three years, a fourth with the permission of the church, and exceptionally until the child reached the age of six.[52]

The wealth of individual brotherhoods consisted in flocks of sheep and goats, and cattle rather than in pasture or arable land. Kine did not thrive and swine were not generally kept: the one because of the quality of pasture, the other on account of their relative immobility.[53] Oxen were valued for draught purposes, sheep primarily for wool and meat, goats for their milk and meat. Maize and to a lesser extent wheat and rye were cultivated throughout the tribal lands, although the unpredict-ability of climate and distractions of tribal or other skirmishes rendered harvests variable in yield. A further agricultural problem was posed in the early nineteenth century by the appearance and rapid spread of burdock, from North Albania or from Dalmatia, when held by the French, through Kotor. The spread of the weed was being witnessed in Bosnia and north-west Serbia in the same period. The potato, originally introduced from Russia by Peter in 1786, was considered a delicacy and was often traded by tribesmen from the uplands for pomegranates from the coastal belt. The primary aim of pastoral and agricultural activity was self-sufficiency. Food and clothing were almost wholly produced within the brotherhood. The local scarcity of flax led to shirts being little worn. In the 1830s even the towel, if ever common, had disappeared from most districts. The only purchased item of men's attire was the cap.

A handful of shops in Rijeka and Vir and weekly stock and grain markets in the same villages comprised Montenegro's only domestic trading facilities. Without developed urban settlements until 1878, Montenegro had no established trading or merchant class or craftsmen. The tribesmen seeking to obtain essentials such as salt, powder and shot, flint, cartridges. and oil for the lubrication of weapons, the comparative luxuries of honey, figs, candles and wax, more rarely fine textiles and manufactured goods, and in times of need, grain, descended to the thrice-weekly market in Kotor. Trade with the Moslems of surrounding territories was yet less developed, since the personal safety of both parties was at best dubious in intercourse. The Austrian market held a further advantage in that there were no quarantine regulations governing the transit of cattle or other animals on the hoof through Kotor. Montenegro's other exports, again through the enterprise of brotherhoods, consisted of dairy products, dried meat and fish (mostly bleak, caught in enormous numbers in the northern tip of Lake Scutari in the last quarter of the year). The men of Crmnica conducted a lively but local trade in tiles with the men of Scutari. Freedom of access to each of the markets in neighbouring territory varied in accordance with prevailing political conditions. The absence of developed domestic markets in Montenegro and the consequent reliance on adjacent ones, were exploited by both Austrian and Ottoman authorities to exert pressure on Cetinje in times of crisis.

The level of sanitation and standard hygiene were, predictably, abysmal. No doctor was resident in Montenegro during, or for twenty years after Peter's reign. The nearest doctor was to be found in Kotor. Enigmatic references in contemporary documents to 'nervous winter fever', 'creeping summer fever', 'the fury', 'plague' and 'scabs', would indicate that malaria, dysentery, rabies and smallpox were endemic. Reference to 'the possessed' (zgranuti koji besne)[54] being chained and whipped by monks illustrated the normal treatment of epilepsy. No less effective was the tradition of sending the cap of a patient too weak to be carried, to be prayed over by the bishop. The use of balms, herbs and other popular remedies had attained a high level of sophistication among the pastoral tribesmen, experienced in the treatment of surface and bullet wounds. The patient was invariably denied water, liberally

supplied with brandy and, after the extraction of shot, had
wild mint applied to the wound to prevent the development of
gangrene. The remark of Karadžić, himself a cripple, that the
Montenegrins 'dispatch to the other world the odd man who might
have been kept alive, albeit crippled, by learned European
doctors'[55] contains more than a grain of sympathy and under-
statement.

* * * * *

In the early nineteenth century the Montenegrin way of
life was 'miserable and barbaric',[56] following a circular
course of poverty, need, conflict, the consequent neglect of
productive means and further misery, made tolerable only by a
specific code of honour. The conglomerate of brotherhoods and
tribes shared interests which both conflicted and overlapped.
Given the conditions in which pre-feudal forms had been re-
adopted and survived, Montenegro's social structure was not
anachronistic. By acquiescing in the concentration of nominal
temporal power in the bishop's hands and the establishment of a
weak central authority, the headmen intended to ensure the
maintenance of the status quo. The system was not to be dealt
a single death blow either by the reformist zeal of Bishop
Njegoš (Peter II) or the determined ambition of Nicholas I.
The appearance of conditions in which private capital could be
accumulated and the interests of the individual begin to dis-
place communal consciousness, marked the genesis of the
dissolution of the tribe from within.

The first and pre-eminent work on Montenegrin society in the early nineteenth century and since reprinted in Serbo-Croatian in numerous editions as Crna Gora i Crnogorci is Vuk St. Karadžić, Montenegro und die Montenegriner (Stuttgart and Tübingen 1837). Less reliable, though still providing valuable information, are S. Milutinović Istorija Černe-Gore od iskona do novijega vremena (Belgrade 1835); M. Medaković, Povjestnica Crne Gore od najstarijih vremena do 1830 (Zemun 1850) and D. Milaković, Istorija Crne Gore (Zadar 1856). Interesting for its anecdotes but far from scholarly in its historical accuracy is Lj. Nenadovic, O Crnogorcima (Belgrade 1878).

The first serious studies in Serbo-Croatian of Montenegrin history in the nineteenth century are: V. Djordjević, Crna Gora i Rusija 1784-1814 (Belgrade 1914), a fundamental and penetrating reappraisal of Montenegro in the first half of the reign of Peter I; I. Jelić, Krvna osveta i umir u Crnoj Gori i sjevernoj Albaniji (Belgrade 1926); R. Petrović, Zakonik Petra I vladike crnogorskog (Cetinje 1929) and D. D. Vuksan, Poslanice mitropolita crnogorskog Petra I (Cetinje 1935).

Major works published in Serbo-Croatian in the last thirty years include J. Jovanović, Stvaranje crnogorske države (Cetinje 1947); D. Lekić, Spoljna politika Petra I Petrovića Njegoša (Cetinje 1950); P. I. Popović, Crna Gora u doba Petra I i Petra II (Belgrade 1951); D. D. Vuksan, Petar I Petrović Njegoš i njegovo doba (Cetinje 1951); M. Djurović, Osnovica i oblici zelenašenja u Crnoj Gori (Istorijski zapisi, II, Cetinje 1953); B. Pavićević, Stvaranje crnogorske drzave (Belgrade 1955); M. Djurović, Trgovački kapital u Crnoj Gori (Cetinje 1958); V. Čubrilović, Terminologija plemenskog društva u Crnoj Gori (Belgrade 1959) and Periodizacija istorije Crne Gore u novom veku (Belgrade 1963); I. Radosavljević, Medjunarodni položaj Crne Gore u XIX vijeku (Belgrade 1960); Lj. Ćirić-Bogetić, Komunice u Crnoj Gori u XIX i početkom XX veka (Titograd 1966) and with M. Djordjević, Iz političke istorije jugoslovenskih naroda (Belgrade 1975).

Studies in Russian include V. Bronevskii, Zapiski morskogo ofitsera, 2 parts, (St. Petersburg 1818 and 1819); E. P. Kovalevskii, Chetyre mesyatsa v Chernogorii (St. Petersburg 1841); P. Rovinskii, Chernogoriya, vol. i (St. Petersburg 1888) and I. S. Dostyan, Opisanie Chernogorii nachala XIX v. v doneseniyah S. A. Sankovskogo (Moscow 1972).

Studies in French and English include Vialla de Sommières, Voyage historique et politique au Monténégro, 2 vols. (Paris 1820), based more on hearsay than observation; P. Coquelle, Histoire du Monténégro et de la Bosnie (Paris 1895); F. S. Stevenson, History of Montenegro (London 1914); M. E. Durham, Some Tribal Origins, Laws and Customs of the Balkans (London

1928) and M. Djilas, Njegoš (New York 1966).

1. For the sake of euphony, the Serbs of Serbia will be referred to as Serbians, the Serbs of Montenegro as Montenegrins. The designation 'Montenegrin' does not denote a specifically national but geographical characteristic. The Montenegrins were distinct from the Serbians in custom and social organization and, under their own metropolitan, were ecclesiastically autonomous, but in their ethnic origins, language and pre-Ottoman history were closely related to them. Gentile Illyrian elements and their aboriginal tribal forms had been assimilated almost completely after the arrival of the South Slavs in Dioclea.

2. The Montenegrins regarded and treated as Turks all their Moslem neighbours, whether of Turkish, Serbian or Albanian origin. Religion was taken as the sole determinant of nationality: the Serbs were all Orthodox; the Moslem 'Turkish' faith was compounded of adherents of various languages and nationalities. That the neighbouring pasaliks were themselves almost independent of Istanbul was of little moment to the Montenegrins.

3. A. Ferguson, Essay on the History of Civil Society (Basel 1789) 257.

4. In post-war Yugoslav historiography the view has been adopted that not only was 'the state' as against 'the tribe' in the ascendant in the late eighteenth century, but that the tribe itself was in dissolution. While it is understandable that the League of Historians should contend that a sense of Montenegrin statehood was an early phenomenon, its appearance, except as an ideal of the bishop's, is not clearly discernible until the 1830s. In the period with which this article is concerned, the bishop's state purpose and tribal particularism were clearly opposed. It is noteworthy that during the campaigns against the French in Dalmatia (1806-7; 1812-13) the Montenegrins fought in tribal units.

5. The Serbs, as the Croats, of the Bay of Kotor were decidedly untribal in outlook, being a sea-faring community which had been subject to Venetian, Austrian and French influences (see V. St. Karadžić, Boka Kotorska, 1836, in 'Kovčežić', 1849).

6. Crna Gora i Rusija, 24. The 1,700 sequins paid by the men of Njeguši were harac, not a fine or penalty (globa) as later historians have asserted.

7. 'Što se ne šće u lance vezati, to se zbježa u ove planine', Gorski vijenac (Vienna 1847).

8. The bishop (vladika) was also metropolitan (mitropolit) of Montenegro and the Highlands. The Orthodox Church there was independent of any higher authority of this world after the abolition of the Patriarchate of Peć in 1767. (Crna Gora i Rusija, 125).

9. Crna Gora i Crnogorci (Belgrade 1969) 273. There are no precise data concerning the number, let alone the scope of the economic activities of the

225

Montenegrins. It is noteworthy that the tribute-paying Serbians reckoned their population in heads (glave), while the Montenegrins calculated in rifles (puške). The long rifle was taken as the unit, as the number of pistols carried by individuals varied from tribe to tribe.

10. Stvaranje crnogorske drzave, 192-3.

11. Crna Gora i Rusija, 226. Brda (in 1805 about the same size as Katuni) 3,200; Katuni 3,900; Lješani 2,900; Rijeka 3,000; Crmnica 4,000: 17,000 in all.

12. Losses were soon compensated for by the high birth-rate. The demographic density of Montenegro was out of proportion to its technical capacity to control flock and crop fluctuations and their consequences as well as epidemic diseases. Whenever the population grew beyond a 'ceiling', the probability increased of sudden catastrophes that would drastically reduce it. Population growth was controlled by an equilibrium mechanism which consisted of a high and highly fluctuating death-rate that checked a high but more stable birth-rate. Abnormal peaks of the death-rate or emigration removed the 'surplus' population. (See C. M. Cipolla, The Economic History of World Population (London 1965).

13. Crna Gora i Rusija, 223.

14. The evidence is clear, though naturally unstressed in Yugoslav historiography, that there were Montenegrin raids to seize flocks, cattle,. ammunition and other booty in the Orthodox and Catholic populated Bay of Kotor in 1799 and 1805, and from the Highlands into Orthodox districts of the Herzegovina in 1800 (Crna Gora i Rusija, 53 and 231). Karadžić suggests as the motives for these raids not the desire for conquest but for murder and plunder, 'held in high esteem as heroic deeds'. (Crna Gora i Crnogorci, 314).

15. The migration of Montenegrins to Ottoman territory has not been generally acknowledged by Yugoslav scholars. The allegiance of the uskoks of the disputed north-west Highlands was notoriously unpredictable. Welcoming their knowledge of Highland terrain, the Turks allowed them to bear arms and organize punitive expeditions into Montenegro (Crna Gora i Crnogorci, 316-7). In 1878 the Serbian writer Ljubomir Nenadović noted in O Crnogorcima that in the 1850s 4,000 Montenegrins were resident in Istanbul and had adopted the less provocative appellation of 'Croats'. Their 'elder' and unofficial consul rejoiced in the title of 'Hrvat-baša' /Hırvat başı/.

16. L. T. Hobhouse, G. C. Wheeler and T. Ginsberg, Material Culture and Social Institutions of the Simpler Peoples (London 1930) 16.

17. Njegoš, 31.

18. The ownership of cultivated land began to be concentrated in the mid-nineteenth century.

19. Some Tribal Origins . . . , 215.

20. Crna Gora Rusija, 223.

21. 'Milija zabava nego i kakva igra ili veselje' (Crna Gora i Crnogorci, 299).

22. A novel recent Yugoslav view is that the 'old society' was in a state of 'dezintegracija' in the eighteenth century. (Iz političke istorije . . ., 59).

23. The absence of gunsmiths was not a serious handicap. Practically all the elaborate arms and the ammunition of the tribesmen were purchased or taken as plunder in Dalmatia, the Herzegovina and North Albania. In Serbia also, rifles with ornate butts were known as arnautski or Albanian.

24. The occasion on which tribesmen played bowls with the heads of four French soldiers in Novi in 1806 and commented on their relative lightness would indicate previous experience. (Crna Gora i Rusija, 261).

25. Two Montenegrins taken prisoner by the French committed suicide rather than be exhibited in Paris: one broke his neck, the other starved himself to death. (Zapiski morskogo ofitsera, 270).

26. 'Slavno mrite, kad mrijet morate' (Gorski vijenac).

27. M. Miljanov, Primjeri čojstva i junaštva (Cetinje 1901).

28. Manslaughter within the brotherhood was considered the most heinous crime, more grievous even than incest, and occurred only rarely. Karadžić relates a case among the Cuce of a man who had two sons, one of whom killed the other. The father unquestioningly shot the surviving son, and then himself. (Crna Gora i Crnogorci, 301).

29. Smaller social groups in danger of extermination would be aided by sympathetic adjacent ones after the conclusion of a pact.

30. In 1834 the value of a life was assessed at 132 sequins, 4 zwanziger and 1 para. The last coin would be broken, and its two halves attached to documents of reconciliation. In the event of murder within a brotherhood, when recompense was impossible, the offender was cast out (a punishment worse than death) or stoned (a disgraceful end normally reserved for traitors or women taken in adultery).

31. Girls could be betrothed, but not married, under the age of twelve. The oldest daughter was always first married; betrothals could not be honourably severed. The dowry was paid by the groom's household.

32. Crna Gora i Crnogorci, 341.

33. Peter I attempted, in vain, to eradicate the abduction of girls and women in his codex of 1798, article 11, through the punishment of offenders, as of murderers, by banishment from Montenegro and the division of their property. This penalty is almost identical to that included in the Dalmatian 'Statute of Poljica' (article 113) in 1605. Abduction was an age-old problem in Dalmatia and its hinterland. (See A. Ferguson, 'The

227

Statute of Poljica', British Croatian Review, iv (1977) 18-44). Harsh
penalties had almost completely eradicated abduction in the Serbia of
Karadjordje and Miloš.

34. Istorija Crna Gore, 238.

35. Povjestnica Crne Gore . . . , 74.

36. Crna Gora i Rusija, 31.

37. G. Thomson, Aeschylus and Athens (London 1946) 41.

38. Attempting to bolster the prestige of the Petrović dynasty, early
Montenegrin historians pre-dated its episcopal inheritance: the revered
'Petrović' Bishop Danilo (1697-1737) was a Šćepćević.

39. Conscious of this, after the extinction of the Venetian Republic Vienna
attempted to make the governor its own creature.

40. See Njegoš, 72-3 and 80-5.

41. The office was suspended by the headmen's assembly, 1818-20. Bishop
Njegoš had little difficulty in effecting its abolition, 1832.

42. No police, guard or standing bishop's bodyguard were formed until
Njegoš' reign.

43. Stvaranje crnogorske nacije, 156.

44. For the complete text, see A. Popov, Puteshestvie v' Chernogoriyu
(St. Petersburg 1847) 281-301. For a partial translation of, and
commentary on the code, and a comparison between it and the Canon of Lek,
see Some Tribal Origins . . . , 76-88.

45. A departure from customary law.

46. It was thereafter treasonable for the governor to maintain covert links
with the Austrian authorities in Kotor.

47. Some Tribal Origins . . ., 81. The system of tribal justice received
its first serious blow in 1855 with the Code of Danilo.

48. One of the first uses to which the newly-formed national army was put,
was the enforcement of tax payment by the Bjelopavlici in 1854 and the Kuci
in 1856. (Iz političke istorije . . . , 62-3).

49. A common phenomenon in tribal society: military leadership being a
specialized occupation, the tendency is for it to become hereditary.
(Aeschylus and Athens, 41).

50. Zapiski morskogo ofitsera, 263.

51. Chernogoriya, 868.

52. Crna Gora i Crnogorci, 344.

53. Boar were nonetheless shot when chanced upon and were widely distributed
only in Moslem-held land.

54. Crna Gora i Crnogorci, 344

55. Ibid.

56. Crna Gora i Crnogorci, 314.

10

ROMANIAN SOCIETY IN THE DANUBIAN PRINCIPALITIES IN THE EARLY 19th CENTURY

DENIS DELETANT

Situated on the periphery of the Ottoman Empire, the political status of the Danubian Principalities of Moldavia and Wallachia differed considerably from that of the Greek, Serb and Bulgarian lands, which were under the direct rule of the Sultan. Although conquered by the Turks, Moldavia and Wallachia never formed an integral part of the Ottoman Empire but were ruled by native princes until 1716 when the latter were replaced by Phanariot Greeks sent from Istanbul. The Principalities were obliged to pay an annual tribute to the Sultan and to supply large quantities of grain, but Turks were forbidden to settle there. Thus the aristocracy was largely native.

The years that bridge the eighteenth and nineteenth centuries were seminal for the development of a Romanian national consciousness. The traditional view of the period of Phanariot rule (1716-1821) in the Principalities is one of intellectual bankruptcy, unbridled corruption, gross exploitation of the land by foreign and native dignitaries, and a complete lack of political stability.[1] Indeed, between 1749 and 1821 there were twenty-five changes on the throne in Wallachia, and twenty-three in Moldavia.[2]

The Phanariot princes have usually been depicted as the representatives of an alien Greek civilisation that stifled any development of a native Romanian culture. Yet the reign of Nicolae Mavrogheni (Nikolaos Mavroghenis), hospodar of Wallachia 1786-1790, saw the printing of one of the earliest Romanian grammars at Rîmnic in 1787,[3] while in December 1817 Ioan Caragea (Ioannis Karatzas), hospodar of Wallachia 1812-1818, sanctioned the foundation of St. Sava, the first college in Wallachia in which Romanian was the language of instruction.[4] The performance of plays in Bucharest in 1818 was a Greek initiative[5] and the example of the Greeks prompted young Romanians to translate plays from French, German, and Classical Greek, which were performed by the pupils of St. Sava;

229

this, in fact, constitutes the first record of a Romanian theatre in Bucharest.[6]

Certainly, during the Phanariot era the dominance of Greek language and culture in the Principalities was never challenged.[7] Greek was the native language of the princes and of several of the leading boyars, and books were printed in Greek at Bucharest and Jassy where the Academies, founded by the later Phanariot princes, were veritable centres of Greek culture.[8] William Wilkinson, British consul at Bucharest from 1814 to 1818, has this to say about education: 'Public schools have, since several years, been established both at Bucharest and Jassy. They are supported at public expense and attended by masters for the Wallachian, ancient and modern Greek languages, writing and arithmetic. The number of students at each school amounts at the present moment to about two hundred. They are the sons of inferior boyars and tradesmen. The children of the principal boyars receive their education at home from private tutors, commonly Greek priests, who are not natives of the Principalities.[9] Even in 1830 the sons of Romanian boyars were still being educated by Greek tutors.[10] The Greek character of cultural activity in the Principalities was strengthened by the presence of numerous Greek monks in the monasteries of Moldavia and Wallachia, and by the printing of service books in Greek. The majority of merchants, who based their activities upon Vienna, Budapest, Sibiu, Braşov, Odessa and Bucharest, were Greeks and the lingua franca of the commercial world in the Balkans was their language. The presence of a large Greek community in Bucharest explains why Rigas Velestinlis was drawn to the city between 1791-4.[11] The Greek merchants brought to Bucharest the Greek newspapers and pamphlets published in Vienna, together with news of the French Revolution and its aftermath, and in Moldavia and Wallachia they were the principal source of information about developments in Western Europe. It was from the Greeks in the Principalities that a large proportion of the membership of the Philiki Etairia, founded in 1814 in Odessa, was to be drawn.[12]

A revealing testimony to the intensity of Greek influence in Wallachia is provided by the Wallachian boyar Constantin (Dinicu) Golescu. In drafting his account of his travels in Europe which was published at Buda in 1826 in Romanian, he writes: 'when I left Braşov, I began to record what I saw in Romanian, but after a few days I was forced to use Greek for I often saw things for which we have no words in Romanian. In doing so, I wondered whether the language in which I was writing was my native tongue, and I was forced to admit that my native language is Greek, with the further admission that in our country /Wallachia7, all the sons of noblemen usually write in Greek'.[13]

The impact of the French Revolution on the Principalities does not appear to have been very great. This despite the fact that the second half of the eighteenth century had seen the growth of French influence there. As French was the language of diplomacy, the Phanariot princes felt the need to employ French secretaries. French was used at court and Frenchmen were engaged by the princes as tutors for their children.[14] The example of the prince was followed by the boyars, both Greek and Romanian. The princes also helped to introduce French literature to the Principalities. Constantin Mavrocordat (Konstantinos Mavrokordatos), hospodar of Moldavia on four occasions and of Wallachia on six during the period 1730 to 1769, assembled a large library of French books. Jean-Louis Carra, secretary to Grigore Ghica (Grigorios Ghikas) the Third, hospodar of Wallachia 1774-1777, tells us that the works of Voltaire were very popular in the Principalities although the Patriarch of Constantinople had banned them as seditious Catholic literature.[15] French books, periodicals and journals reached Bucharest and Jassy via Vienna, brought mainly by merchants.[16] A Bucharest bookseller's catalogue for 1797 lists Histoire de la Convocation et des Elections aux Etats généraux en 1789, Histoire politique de la révolution en France, De la souveraineté du peuple.[17] One year earlier Charles Fleury, the first permanent representative of the French Republic, arrived in the Principalities.[18] In March 1797 a Vice-Consul by the name of Parant was sent to reside at Jassy. The principal concern of the French government was to counter the spread of Russian and Austrian influence in the Balkans but, in spite of sporadic efforts to initiate political action, the French consuls in Bucharest and Jassy were largely ineffective. To judge from letters, reports and appeals[19] to the Great Powers from Wallachian boyars, the French Revolution made little impact upon the Romanians.

The opposite was the case with the Greeks in Wallachia who were inspired by the Revolution to organize a number of politico-literary societies in Bucharest. Romanian boyars, too, were associated with Rigas Velestinlis during the period 1791-94.[20]

231

In contrast with the lack of political influence, there was a steady growth of French cultural influence on the Romanians, the principal agents of which were émigrés of the French Revolution. The practice of employing French secretaries amd teachers, the respect for the language and literature of France, and the curiosity to learn from eye-witnesses what had happened in Paris led both Greek and native boyars to open their doors to the émigrés. With the turn of the century each year brought a new contingent whom the boyars engaged to instruct their children. Konstantinos Ypsilantis, hospodar of Moldavia 1799-1801, made Gaspar-Luce, le comte de Belleval his Foreign Minister. When Ypsilantis was deposed in 1801, his successor retained him. In 1804 Ypsilantis, now hospodar of Wallachia, welcomed the Marquis Beaupoíl de Sainte-Aulaire as the teacher of his children, one of whom, Alexandros, was to become leader of the Philiki Etairia in 1820. The majority of émigré teachers came to the Principalities during the opening years of the nine-teenth century.[21] Their pupils were to become the leading protagonists of the cultural and political developments in Moldavia and Wallachia during the third and fourth decades of the nineteenth century - Vasile Alecsandri, Grigore Alexandrescu, Nicolae Bălcescu, Ion Cîmpineanu, Ion Ghica and Mihai Kogălniceanu. Speaking of the activity of these teachers, Ion Ghica himself wrote: 'The transition from education in Greek to that in French and Romanian had begun some time before, during the period of the French Revolution, with Laurençon, Ricordon, Colçon, Mondoville etc., all of whom were émigré counts and marquesses who had become teachers.'[22] The effect of the émigrés' teaching was that boyars filled their libraries with French books, especially those of French classical literature of the seventeenth and eighteenth centuries. This literature was the principal intellectual nourishment of young Romanians at the turn of the nineteenth century and through it, ancient Greece and Rome became known to Romanians. Although many translations were made from French into Greek during the last quarter of the eighteenth century, few were made from French into Romanian. Only after 1820 did translations into Romanian become much more common. Many of the books translated were moralizing works, sentimental novels, and examples of French classical literature.[23]

From the second decade of the nineteenth century it became fashionable for boyars to send their sons to Paris to

232

study. Before 1827 seven Romanians had enrolled at the University of Paris. In 1820 the governing body of the Wallachian
schools sent four young men to study, first at Pisa and then in
Paris. On their return to Bucharest, they became teachers at
the Romanian college of St. Sava.[24] By the early 1830s the
French language and culture had replaced Greek as the principal
foreign influence in Moldavia and Wallachia. Contemporary
visitors to the Principalities stress the mimicry of French
manners and fashions by boyars and their families. This gallo-
mania was mirrored in the language and style of writers of this
period and facilitated the adoption by the Romanian language of
a host of French neologisms.

The ascendancy of French culture over Greek in the
Principalities must be seen in the context of political and
cultural developments in not only Moldavia and Wallachia, but
also in Transylvania. A strong impetus was given to the spread
of French influence by the Transylvanian School (Şcoala
ardeleană). In emphasizing the idea of the latinity of the
Romanians and their language, the Transylvanian School provided
not only the impulse for creating a national consciousness among
the Romanians, but also the realization that Frenchmen and
Romanians shared the same heritage. This realization contributed
in the Principalities to the consolidation of French influence.
In Transylvania itself, the Romanians, living in a completely
different milieu to their compatriots in Moldavia and Wallachia,
had less knowledge of France.

The Transylvanian School is the name given to a movement
centred around the activity of those Romanians in Transylvania
who led their nation during the last quarter of the eighteenth
century and the first quarter of the nineteenth. The majority
of these Romanians were members of the Uniate clergy who had
attended institutions of higher education in Rome or Vienna.
The Uniate, or Greek Catholic, church in Transylvania had been
established in 1699 as a result of a partly successful attempt
on the part of the Roman Catholic hierarchy of Hungary to convert the Orthodox Romanian clergy of Transylvania to Catholicism
In promoting the Union with Rome, the Catholic hierarchy's main
objective was to spread the faith.[25] The Emperor Leopold I
saw the Union as a means of increasing the power of the Catholic
minority in Transylvania and thus curbing the influence of the
Calvinist Hungarian nobility. The Roman Catholic Church took
good care to educate the Uniate priesthood above the level of

the Orthodox priests in Transylvania and maintained an extensive proselytizing activity. Uniate schools were opened in Transylvania for the new Romanian converts and bursaries founded at seminaries in Vienna and Rome for Uniate priests. In Rome the priests were inspired by the monuments of the Roman Empire and awakened to their own Latin ancestry and on their return to Transylvania they propagated amongst their countrymen the idea of the Roman origin of the Romanians and the Latin character of their language. The writings of such Uniate priests as Samuel Clain, Gheorghe Sincai and Petru Maior on the origins of the Romanians were major contributions to the awakening of the Romanian national spirit. The Romanians could claim to be the direct descendants of those Romans that had settled in Dacia and as such to be the inheritors of a great imperial civilisation. This Latin pedigree entitled them to consider themselves of nobler stock than their Hungarian and German neighbours in Transylvania. Politically and socially disenfranchised, the work of the Transylvanian School provided the historical justification for the demand for equal rights with all other nations in Transylvania and the establishment of a national assembly in which the Romanians should be justly represented: These demands were embodied in a petition to be presented to the Emperor Leopold II in 1791 entitled Supplex Libellus Valachorum and signed by the two Romanian bishops of the Orthodox and Uniate church, the only acknowledged representatives of the Romanians in Transylvania.[26]

The apostle of the Transylvanian School in Wallachia was Gheorghe Lazăr. A Transylvanian by birth, he arrived in Bucharest in 1816 and addressed himself to the Council for the administration of schools in Wallachia (Eforia) with a proposal to teach in Romanian. The Wallachian schools were at that time conducted in Greek; nevertheless the Prince, Ioan Caragea, gave his approval and in March 1818 Lazăr opened the first institute of higher education in the Principalities in which Romanian was used as the language of instruction. The seat of this institution was the St. Sava school, founded by Constantin Brîncoveanu, hospodar of Wallachia 1688-1714, which was being used as a boarding house by the Greek and Albanian bodyguard of the Prince. Alongside courses in the Romanian language and mathematics, the ideas of the Transylvanian School were expounded by Lazăr, and, on his death in 1823, by Ioan Heliade Rădulescu around whom Romanian cultural life was to revolve for a generation.

234

In Moldavia Lazăr's counterpart was Gheorghe Asachi. In 1820 he established a college at Socola, a suburb of Jassy, where instruction was to be given in Romanian. He recruited his five teachers from Transylvania where he had travelled for six months with this express purpose. Four of these teachers were former pupils of Uniate schools and colleges.[27]

The Latinist ideas expressed by the Transylvanian School were echoed by the teachers at the St. Sava college throughout the 1820s and 1830s. The representatives of Romanian cultural and political life in Wallachia during the period 1830-1860 were, for the most part, pupils at the college. The creation of a Romanian national consciousness in the Principalities was the product of the influence of the Transylvanian School and of that of French culture. Scholars disagree as to the relative importance of each of these currents. Some consider that French influence may not have been so intense had it not coincided with the impact of the Transylvanian School.[28] Others feel that the intemperance of the philological and historical reasoning of those associated with the School caused it to lose prestige and that French influence was strong enough to stand on its own feet.[29] Greek culture was no longer in a position to rival French after 1821 for following the revolts of Alexandros Ypsilantis and Tudor Vladimirescu of that year, the Phanariot princes were replaced by native Romanian ones, with the result that Greek influence in education and literature began to wane. Greek culture, unlike French, could not be associated in any way with Romanian aspirations and was supported artificially in the Principalities by the Phanariots. The collapse of the Phanariot regime in 1821, coinciding as it does with the spread of French influence and of the ideas of the Transylvanian School, heralds a new era in Romanian history – the beginning of a Romanian national revival in the Principalities.

Although we have, thus far, traced cultural developments in the Principalities up to 1821, we have, as yet, said little about society there during this period. The population of the Principalities at the beginning of the nineteenth century is given by one contemporary source as one million for Wallachia and five hundred thousand for Moldavia.[30] Society was divided into three classes in each Principality; the boyars, the merchants and tradesmen, and the peasants.[31] Wilkinson claims that there were nearly thirty thousand boyars in Wallachia at

the turn of the eighteenth century.[32]   Although they were
nominally the public officers of the hospodar, they were in fact
defenders of their own interests as landlords.[33]   Two thirds of
the land in the Principalities was owned by the boyars and the
Church, while the remaining third belonged to the free peasants,
called răzeşi in Moldavia and moşneni in Wallachia. A French
observer tells us that of 1,713 villages in Moldavia, 25
belonged to the Prince, 215 to various monasteries, 927 to
boyars and 546 were free.[34]

The boyars were exempt from direct taxation. Those of the
first rank lived in great wealth from the income of their
estates. 'Money is their only stimulus; and the means they
employ to obtain it are not the efforts of industry, nor are
they modified by scruples of conscience. Habit has made them
spoiliators; and in a country where actions of an ignominious
nature are even encouraged, and those of rapacity looked upon
as mere proofs of dexterity and cunning, corruption of principles
cannot fail to become universal.'[35]

Only the hospodar could admit to the boyar class or make
grants of land. The Phanariot hospodars came with their
relatives and creditors whom they appointed to high offices
which automatically conferred the rank of boyar. The right to
bestow boyar rank constituted an important source of income for
the prince and consequently, he made frequent use of it. The
hope of obtaining lucrative positions induced many boyars to
indulge in bribery of the prince on a grand scale.

The Phanariot hospodars were obliged to pay an annual
tribute to the Porte which they raised from taxes and the sale
of favours. It was the custom for public officers to give a
share of their profits to the hospodar and this, together with
the sums he received for conferring boyar rank, secured him a
considerable private income. The metropolitan and diocesan
sees were also in the gift of the prince. Their revenues were
derived from landed property bequeathed to the sees by boyars
and others, and from an annual capitation tax levied on the
lower priests.[36]   Each hospodar when appointed demanded a
payment from the existing metropolitan and if he could not
meet the sum required, he was replaced. Thus in 1819 the
metropolitan of Wallachia, Nectarie, was replaced by Dionisie
Lupu whose appointment cost him five hundred thousand lei. The
bishop of Rîmnic had to pay the prince 418,000 lei to retain his
position. The new metropolitan recovered his outlay by levying

contributions from every priest. The archdeacons also levied a fixed sum from the priests they ordained.[37] The lot of the lower clergy differed little from that of the peasant. They were exempt from some taxes but if they acquired land, they were subject to the robot (clacă) and to pay métayage (dijmă).

Approximately one third of the land in the Principalities was the property of the Church. This land was often sparsely populated, as can be seen from the breakdown of the numbers of villages in Moldavia where of 1,713 only 215 belonged to the monasteries. The latter had extended their estates as a result of gifts and bequests from princes and boyars. The monasteries themselves fell into two categories - the national and the dedicated. The abbots of the former were generally Romanian while those of the latter were Greek. The dedicated monasteries belonged to the convents of Jerusalem, Mount Athos and to the patriarchates of Constantinople and Alexandria and yielded a considerable income. Benjamin Barker, the agent of the British and Foreign Bible Society at Izmir, in a report dating from 1835, gives the number of native monasteries in Wallachia as 133 and of dedicated monasteries as 69.[38]

A special category of landowners was formed by the independent tenant farmers (răzeşi in Moldavia and moşneni in Wallachia). They were free peasants who worked their own land but were subject to various taxes and dues.

The merchant class was cosmopolitan in character. The nature of their occupations in Bucharest is described by Barker: 'The population of Bucharest is generally computed to about 80,000 souls, composed of Wallachians, Moldavians, Bulgarians, Greeks, Armenians, Jews, Germans, Hungarians, Russians, Transylvanians, a few French and Italians, and many gypsies. The shopkeepers are the merchants of the place, and they are principally Greeks, Bulgarians, Armenians, Jews and a few Moldavians. The Germans, Hungarians and Transylvanians are generally artisans and mechanicks, and the Russians coachmen and hardware merchants. The Jews are also Painters, Tinkers and distillers of spirits. The Wallachians may be divided into two distinct classes, Nobles and Plebians. The former living by the rents of their estates and salaries from government as civil and military officers, and the latter by their earning as labourers, water carriers, Brick layers, Porters and other menial occupations.'[39] Jassy, the capital of Moldavia, is said to have a population of '40 to 45,000 souls, of which more than 12,000 are Jews, from Poland, Galicia, Bessarabia, etc. The rest of the inhabitants are Moldavians, Bulgarians, Greeks, Armenians, and a few Hungarians, Germans, Russians and Poles.' The most prominent merchants were Greeks, as indeed were the bankers and money-lenders. The Germans, of whom there were about eleven thousand in 1820, were, for the most part, tailors, shoemakers and carpenters. There were many jewellers and money-lenders amongst the Armenians while the majority of Jews were engravers, glaziers and tinsmiths.[40] Most of the merchants and tradesmen were foreign subjects and enjoyed the protection of a consulate.

'There does not perhaps exist a people labouring under a greater degree of oppression from the effect of despotic power and more heavily burthened with impositions and taxes, than the peasantry of Wallachia and Moldavia.'[41] A vivid description of the peasant's lot comes from the pen of a Wallachian boyar, Constantin (Dinicu) Golescu: 'Anyone who enters the so-called villages will see neither church nor house nor fence around the house, nor cart, nor ox nor cow nor fowl nor patch sown for the family's food - in a word, nothing; only some rooms in the earth which are called bordeie . . . And then, if one went into those bordeie of theirs, it would be impossible to find on their persons or in the house anything worth ten lei . . . And when these men, by good fortune, got wind that a zapciu, polcovnicu, captain, or an agent of the ispravnic or of the Prince was coming to their village, they fled with their wives and the children that were able to flee . . . For they knew that if they were caught, there would be a demand for money, and as they had no money, they would receive lashes on their backs.'[42]

The great mass of the peasants in the Principalities during the first half of the eighteenth century were serfs. In Moldavia they were known as vecini[43] and in Wallachia the term rumâni came to be applied. As Prince of Wallachia in 1746 Constantin Mavrocordat emancipated the rumâni, and as hospodar of Moldavia in 1749 he emancipated the vecini, giving them the right to buy their freedom for ten piastres. His emancipation decree mentioned the fact that 'some landlords have been in the habit of selling serfs like slaves, treating them like gypsies . . .'.[44] Nevertheless, the emancipated peasants were still subject to the clacă and dijmă. Although they could no longer be treated like the enslaved gypsies, bought and sold like goods and moved from one place to another, they were still bound

to the village which they could not leave. The _robot_ was
fixed at twenty-four days service per year in Moldavia in 1749
and at twelve days per year in Wallachia in 1780.[45] However,
in 1766 Prince Grigore Ghica issued a decree that was to worsen
the lot of the peasant in Moldavia. Whereas the peasant's service had, till then, been measured by the actual time spent in
doing it, this decree now fixed the quantity of labour which,
according to its nature, each peasant must perform in one day.[46]
The amount of labour was designated _nart_ and was in some cases
three times as much as that which a peasant could normally do in
a day. In 1777 the Prince added to the decree various obligations which amounted to five more days of fixed labour or _robot_.
By 1805 it had been estimated that the _boyars_ had obtained
privileges from succeeding _hospodars_ which brought the total
servitude dues from the peasants to 36-40 days yearly.[47] In
Wallachia the peasant appears to have fared better. Although
the _robot_ had been fixed at twelve days, contemporary evidence
suggests that in the last quarter of the eighteenth century and
the first of the nineteenth the obligations of the peasant were
nearer to six than to twelve days. Moreover, there is no
record that a _nart_ was ever fixed for the _robot_ in Wallachia.[48]

The economic exploitation of the peasants was the goad
with which Tudor Vladimirescu incited them to revolt in
Wallachia. When the plans were made for a national rising of
the Greeks under the banner of the _Philiki Etairia_ to break
out on Romanian soil in 1821, Vladimirescu seized the opportunity to instigate a revolt of the native peasants.[49]

Vladimirescu himself was a member of the _Philiki Etairia_.
Born about 1780 in Oltenia, he distinguished himself as an
officer in the Russian army during the Russo-Turkish war of
1806-1812. He is said to have been initiated into the _Etairia_
in Bucharest by Iordakis, Alexandros Ypsilantis's chief lieutenant, and to have signed a bond with Iordakis to 'pretend to
provoke disorders . . . and to use any cunning which may lead
to attaining the common end.'[50] The _Etairia_ also found
sympathy among the most prominent Wallachian _boyars_. Some of
them saw in the _Etairia_ an opportunity to discredit the
Phanariot _hospodars_ in Turkish eyes for they wanted the prince
to be chosen from among the native _boyars_. A Romanian rising
in Wallachia, timed to coincide with the revolt instigated by
the _Etairia_ in Moldavia, would embarrass further the Phanariots.
At the end of January 1821 Vladimirescu was given a written

promise of aid by three of the leading boyars, Grigore
Brîncoveanu, Barbu Văcărescu, and Grigore Ghica, who in the
following year became the first native hospodar of Wallachia
for over a century. He had been chosen by them, they said, to
raise the people with arms.[51] He was also receiving substantial
sums from the coffers of the Etairia.[52] His proclamation to all
Wallachia, issued on 29 January, was not in the spirit of the
Greek aspirations of the Etairia. The populace of Wallachia was
rising against the oppressive rule of the government and was
justified because the Sultan wished his loyal subjects to live
well:[53] 'These dragons, our ecclesiastical and political chiefs,
who are devouring us alive, how long shall we let them suck our
blood, how long shall we remain their slaves?'[54] To reassure the
Turks he wrote to Dervish Paşa, the commandant of Vidin: 'Our
rising is directed only against the boyars, who have devoured
our rights.'[55] He issued instructions to his followers not to
touch any property other than 'the ill-gotten wealth of those
tyrant boyars who would not support the rising',[56] clearly an
attempt to put pressure on the boyars to join the movement.
While neither this proclamation nor the letter sent to the
Porte via the commandant of Vidin reflect the Etairia's objectives, there is no doubt much truth in the claim of a contemporary that 'if Tudor had told the Oltenians the aim of the revolt,
namely that it was against the Turks in favour of the Greeks,
he would not have succeeded; but being a good politician, he
knew where to touch them.'[57]

On 6 March Alexandros Ypsilantis crossed the Prut into
Moldavia, accompanied by a small band of followers. His confidence in Russian support led him to tell the Prince, Mikhail
Soutzos, himself a benefactor of the Etairia,[58] that 70,000
Russians would be following him. A proclamation of 8 March,
made by Ypsilantis at Jassy and addressed to all Greeks,
stated that a great power would protect their rights to freedom.
He called upon them to 'free the fatherland Greece, and raise
the Cross where the Crescent once stood'.[59] That same day he
issued an appeal for volunteers to help 'in the resurrection
of Greece'[60] while the Prince of Moldavia wrote to the Tsar
for his support.[61] At the end of the month he received the
Tsar's refusal to intervene and offer of asylum in Russia for
members of the Etairia.[62] Soutzos promptly accepted the offer
and abdicated on 10 April. Ypsilantis had crossed into
Wallachia on 25 March at the head of a force of little over

2,000 men. He reached the outskirts of Bucharest on 6 April
but was prevented from entering by Vladimirescu, who had
reached the city on 28 March. Most of the boyars had fled to
Transylvania several days previously on learning of the activities of both rebels. At a meeting of the two leaders it would
appear that Vladimirescu refused to identify himself with the
Greek cause but, at the same time, he promised not to betray it;
he himself was fighting only against abuses, not against the
Turks.[63] Unable to reconcile their aims, it was not long before
both men became mutually suspicious. Three separate forces of
Turkish troops entered Moldavia, Wallachia and Oltenia
respectively on 13 May to crush the revolt. Vladimirescu,
perhaps, sought a direct understanding with the Porte for when
he was visited by Iordakis, Ypsilantis's lieutenant, on 21 May,
letters addressed to the paşa of Silistra by Vladimirescu were
produced and the latter was promptly arrested. He was taken to
Ypsilantis's headquarters at Tîrgovişte the next day and
executed. With Vladimirescu removed from the scene the Turks
were able to devote their attention to Ypsilantis. His forces
were easily routed at Drăgăşani on 19 June and he himself fled
to Transylvania where he was arrested. His next few years were
spent in Austrian prisons.

The events of 1821 destroyed Turkish confidence in the
Greeks and, as a result, they put an end to the Phanariot
regime in the Principalities. In the following year native
princes were appointed in Wallachia and Moldavia, a propitious
start to a decade that witnessed a rapid development of
Romanian national consciousness. This development found
expression in the activity of two men in particular: Constantin
(Dinicu) Golescu and Ioan Heliade Rădulescu. The former was one
of the most enlightened boyars of the age. His travels in
Western Europe prompted him to write a travelogue entitled
Insemnare a călătoriii mele (A Note on my Travels), published in
Buda in 1826. In his account Golescu highlighted the political,
social and cultural backwardness of the Principalities and, in
doing so, attempted to popularize advanced political theories
and to encourage a system of education based on Romanian in
Wallachia. He himself in May 1826 founded a school in his
native village Goleşti. His principal idea was to found a
society for the promotion of literary and linguistic studies
and he outlined the aims of such a society in his Insemnare.[64]
In 1826 he founded, with Heliade, Societatea literară (The

Literary Society). Its members met in Golescu's house at
Goleşti; although there is no record of the names of the members,
it is probable that they included Dinicu's brother Iordache, the
poets Iancu Văcărescu and Barbu Paris Mumuleanu, and Eufrosin
Poteca, a teacher at St. Sava.[65] The society disbanded early in
1828 because of the outbreak of the Russo-Turkish war which
brought the Russian army to Wallachia. According to Heliade,
the aims of the society were the development of education in
Romanian, the foundation of Romanian newspapers, the publication
of translations, and the creation of a national theatre.[66] One
of these aims was realised in 1829 when Heliade, with funds from
Golescu, launched the first Romanian newspaper to appear in
Wallachia, Curierul rumânesc ('The Romanian Courier').

Heliade, like most of his contemporaries, had been
instructed by Greek teachers during his youth. He left the
Greek Academy in Bucharest in 1818 to attend Lazăr's courses in
Romanian at the newly opened St. Sava school, and from 1820
to 1828 he taught there. In 1828 he had his grammar of Romanian,
Grammatica românească, published at Sibiu at the expense of the
boyar Scarlat Rosetti. In this work Heliade called for the
adoption of a phonetic rather than an etymological orthography
for Romanian. Phonetic spelling implied the reduction of the
cyrillic alphabet in which Romanian was written, through the
renunciation of those letters which did not correspond to a
Romanian vowel or consonant. This simplification of the
cyrillic alphabet may be seen as the first step towards its
replacement by the Latin alphabet, a transition that Heliade
regarded as inevitable.[67] In the same work Heliade advocated
the adoption of neologisms from Latin and the Romance languages
to enrich Romanian. In 1830 Heliade bought one of the few
private printing-presses in Wallachia and installed it in his
house in Bucharest. From the end of 1830 not only was the
journal Curierul rumânesc printed here, but also much of the
literature, both original and in translation, that was to appear
in Wallachia during the following decade. Heliade, as teacher,
grammarian, translator, literary editor and publisher, was the
embodiment of the Romanian cultural revival in Wallachia.

His parallel in Moldavia was Gheorghe Asachi.[68] The son
of a priest, he studied in Lemberg and Vienna. In 1814 he gave
the first courses in Romanian at the Greek Academy in Jassy, an
activity he was to continue for a number of years. In 1820 he
gave new life to a seminary at Socola, on the outskirts of Jassy,

242

which had opened originally sixteen years earlier, where
Romanian was to be the language of instruction. In 1828 he
opened a Romanian 'Lancastrian School' at the Three Ierarchs
monastery in Jassy. The appearance on 1 June 1829 of the first
Romanian journal in Moldavia, Albina românească ('The Romanian
Bee'), was the work of Asachi who edited several Romanian
publications before his death in 1869. His role as a patron of
Romanian literature in Moldavia was as significant as that of
Heliade in Wallachia.

The removal of the Phanariots in 1821 and the accession of
native princes in both Moldavia and Wallachia created a more
favourable climate for the manifestation of western ideas, the
penetration of which exhibited itself not only in the cultural,
but also in the political, sphere. In 1822 a group of second
and third rank boyars, with the approval of the new native
prince of Moldavia Ion Sturdza, drew up plans for a new
constitution for the principality which provided for a representative assembly, individual freedom, a national printing-press
to publish books in Romanian, and a system of education with
teaching in Romanian.[69] However, the 'privileges' of this
constitution were to be accorded only to the boyar class; the
artisans and peasants were excluded. Sturdza, under pressure
from the first rank boyars, was forced to reject the proposals.

Whatever the constitutional plans of the more enlightened
boyars in both Principalities, political developments in
Moldavia and Wallachia were determined by the policies
pursued by the Great Powers regarding the Eastern question.
Successive Russo-Turkish wars during the last quarter of the
eighteenth century and the beginning of the nineteenth had led
to an erosion of Turkish authority in the Principalities and a
consequent growth of Russian influence there. The convention
of Akkerman (1826) and the Treaty of Adrianople (1829) merely
confirmed the position of authority Russia now had in the
Principalities while the Sultan's power was restricted to
appointing the princes and receiving the annual tribute. The
Russian army occupied Moldavia and Wallachia in 1828 at the
outbreak of the Russo-Turkish war and remained there until
1834 when all war reparations had been paid. Supporting such
an army placed a great burden upon the economies of both
Principalities and the behaviour of the military authorities
alienated any sympathy the Russians may have enjoyed from the
local inhabitants. Nevertheless, Russian domination also

brought General Paul Kisseleff who was appointed by the Tsar President Plenipotentiary of the <u>Divans</u> of the two Principalities in November 1829. During the exercise of his office, which lasted until April 1834, he was intent on improving political and social conditions in the Principalities, and to this end he introduced administrative, judicial and health reforms. After the war of 1828-1829 the populations of Moldavia and Wallachia were threatened by plague and starvation. Kisseleff organized a medical service to control the plague and by the end of 1829 the epidemic had been stamped out. Grain was imported from Odessa to combat starvation. Kisseleff also established a national guard and definite taxes were brought to the knowledge of the taxpayers. These measures were incorporated in the <u>Règlement Organique</u> which served as a constitution in both Moldavia and Wallachia until 1859. The <u>Règlement Organique</u> was drawn up by two committees, each made up of four Moldavian and four Wallachian boyars under the chairmanship of the Russian consul General Mintchiaky. The text was amended by Kisseleff, after which it was examined by the Imperial Cabinet. It was promulgated in Wallachia in July 1831, and in Moldavia in January 1832.

The Règlement, however, also strengthened the <u>boyars</u>' position immeasurably. The peasants were deprived of land that they possessed before the application of the <u>Règlement</u>, and the various rights that they enjoyed on the land were curbed.[70] As J. C. Campbell has written: 'The younger nationalists, growing in strength in the next fifteen years, would become bitter opponents of the <u>Règlement</u>, for the controlling position which it gave to Russia offended their national pride, and the exclusion of all but the <u>boyars</u> from political power offended their newly acquired doctrines of liberalism and democracy.'[71]

The period 1800-1830 witnessed in the Danubian Principalities the beginning of the national regeneration of the Romanian people. This regeneration was promoted by the enlightened youth of the <u>boyar</u> class: Ion Heliade Rădulescu, Gheorghe Asachi, Constantin Golescu, Ion Cîmpineanu and later Vasile Alecsandri, Nicolae Bălcescu, Mihai Kogălniceanu were all from lower or higher ranking boyar families. It was the <u>boyar</u> class which claimed a limited national independence through such constitutional proposals as those put forward in Moldavia in 1822, and through its request for native princes following the collapse of the revolts of 1821. It was the <u>boyar</u> class that

244

made such claims since it was the only class that was recognized politically. The merchant class, because of its cosmopolitan character, was not a political force during this period, while the peasants were among the most exploited in Eastern Europe. Only members of the boyar class were in a position to engage French tutors, to travel outside the Principalities, to afford books and thus disseminate Western ideas. The national regeneration was the result of the fusion of French cultural influence, conveying Western ideas, with the influence of the Transylvanian School. The impact of these currents was confined to small groups of educated boyars whose activity manifested itself in the newly created schools, the literary societies and in the printing-press. Yet by 1830 the two avenues of influence had still to merge into a doctrine of nationalism. Education and literature was still, to a great extent, Greek in character. The earliest expression of Romanian literary consciousness was in poetry and such poetry that existed at this period was largely of French inspiration. The Romantic movement, with its cultivation of the national past, produced an emphasis on patriotic sentiment in the literature of this period.

From the political point of view, nationalist sentiment was still in an incipient stage. The failure of Ypsilantis's revolt in 1821 demonstrated that the Romanians had little sympathy for the cause of Greek nationalism. Vladimirescu's rising was social in origin and directed initially against the economic oppression of the peasants by the boyars, irrespective of their ethnic origin.[72] Tudor Vladimirescu was inspired by the same ideas of liberty and equality that was epoused by Ypsilantis and his followers; only the former's pretentions to the throne of Wallachia, coupled with the fact that Ypsilantis had been disowned by the Tsar, led him to disavow the Greek cause[73] and turn his revolt into a 'national' one. Although his followers drifted away after his murder, a legend soon grew up around him which turned him into a national hero for his people. He had associated the peasants in his revolt, unlike later nationalists, and has thus become a cult for the Romanians.

1. For a survey of Phanariot rule see M. Zallony, Essai sur les Fanariotes (Marseille 1824).

2. P. Eliade, De l'influence française sur l'esprit public en Roumanie (Paris 1898) 98.

3. Observaţii sau băgări de seamă asupra regulelor si orînduielelor grammaticii rumâneşti; see I. Bianu and N. Hodoş, Bibliografia românească veche 1508-1830, ii, 1716-1808 (Bucharest 1910) 318-322.

4. V. A. Urechia, Istoria scoalelor iv (Bucharest 1892) 195-196.

5. I. C. Filitti, Frămîntările politice şi sociale în principatele române de la 1821 pînă la 1829 (Bucharest 1932) 16-17.

6. I. Massof, Teatrul romînesc i (Bucharest 1961) 86.

7. Ion Heliade Rădulescu (1802-1870), one of the leading figures in the Romanian national revival, tells us in his Dispoziţiile şi încercările mele de poezie of 1838 that, as a boy, he learned to read Greek before Romanian; see I. Heliade-Rădulescu, in C. Măciucă ed., Pagini alese (Bucharest 1965) 109.

8. A. Camariano-Cioran, Les Academies princières de Bucharest et de Jassy et leurs professeurs (Thessaloniki 1974).

9. W. Wilkinson, An Account of the Principalities of Wallachia and Moldavia (London 1820) 130.

10. I. Ghica, Opere ed. I. Boman i (Bucharest 1967) 260.

11. P. Eliade, op. cit., 202-208.

12. Of the Etairia's membership, a total of 425 out of 1,027 who reported their area of initiation into the society were recruited in the Principalities and the cities of south-western Russia; 244 of the 425 were from Moldavia and Wallachia; see G. D. Frangos, 'The Philike Etairia: A premature National Coalition' in Richard Clogg ed., The Struggle for Greek Independence (London 1973) 94.

13. D. Golescu, Însemnare a călătoriii mele (Bucharest 1971) 93.

14. P. Eliade, op. cit., 146-164.

15. J-L. Carra, Histoire de la Moldavie et de la Valachie, avec une dissertation sur l'état actuel de ces provinces (Jassy 1777) 196.

16. J. C. Campbell, French Influence on the rise of Roumanian Nationalism (New York 1971) 13.

17. E. Hurmuzaki, Documente privitoare la istoria românilor xix pt 1 (Bucharest 1922) 815 and J. C. Campbell, op. cit., 15.

18. G. Lebel, La France et les Principautés danubiennes (Paris 1955) 219.

19. Contained in E. Hurmuzaki, Documente privitoare la istoria românilor, 30 vols. (Bucharest 1887-1908).

20. P. Eliade, op. cit., 206; G. I. Ionescu-Gion, Bucurestii in timpul revolutiunii franceze (Bucharest 1891) 15-23.

21. For a list of them see P. Eliade, op. cit., 27.

22. In a letter to Vasile Alecsandri; see I. Ghica, op. cit., 260.

23. For an admirable study of the influence of moralizing works upon Romanians see A. Duţu, Les livres de sagesse dans la culture roumaine (Bucharest 1971).

24. E. Close, The Development of Modern Rumanian (Oxford 1974) 27.

25. K. Hitchins, The Rumanian National Movement in Transylvania 1780-1849 (Cambridge, Massachusetts 1969) 15.

26. R. W. Seton-Watson, A History of the Roumanians (London 1934) 188-191.

27. G. Adămescu, Istoria seminarului Veniamin Costache (Bucharest 1904) 55-56.

28. P. Eliade, op. cit., 277-318.

29. J. C. Campbell, op. cit., 27.

30. W. Wilkinson, op. cit., 60. F. G. Laurençon, Nouvelles observations sur la Valachie (Paris 1822) 21 gives the population of Wallachia as 1,100,000 - 1,200,000.

31. Ibid., 60.

32. Ibid., 55.

33. D. Mitrany, The Land and the Peasant in Rumania (London 1930) 23.

34. C. Perthusier, La Valachie, la Moldavie et de l'influence politique des Grecs du Fanar (Paris 1822) 28.

35. W. Wilkinson, op. cit., 131.

36. Ibid., 68.

37. A. Oţetea, Tudor Vladimirescu şi mişcarea eteristă în tările romăneşti 1821-1822 (Bucharest 1945) 63.

38. E. D. Tappe, 'A Bible Society agent in the Rumanian Principalities', The Slavonic and East European Review xlii, (1964) 391.

39. Ibid., 391.

40. F. G. Laurençon, op. cit., 22-4.

41. W. Wilkinson, op. cit., 155.

42. D. Golescu, op. cit., 85-6. The passage quoted is reproduced in full in English translation by E. D. Tappe in D. Warriner ed., Contrasts in Emerging Societies (London 1965) 144-5.

43. I. L. Evans, The Agrarian Revolution in Roumania (Cambridge 1924) 7-8.

44. A. Oţetea, op. cit., 34.

45. D. Mitrany, op. cit., 20.

46. Ibid., 19.

47. Ibid., 20.

48. Ibid., 20.

49. For a brief account of both risings see E. D. Tappe, 'The 1821 Revolution in the Rumanian Principalities' in Richard Clogg ed., The Struggle for Greek Independence (London 1973) 133-55.

50. Quoted from E. D. Tappe, op. cit., 138.

51. A. Oţetea, <u>Tudor Vladimirescu şi revoluţia din 1821</u> (Bucharest 1971) 8.

52. Ibid., 202.

53. Ibid., 205.

54. A. Otetea, <u>Tudor Vladimirescu şi miscarea eterista</u> . . . 144.

55. Ibid., 147.

56. A. Otetea, <u>Tudor Vladimirescu şi revolutia din 1821</u> . . . 206.

57. E. D. Tappe, op. cit., 139.

58. R. W. Seton-Watson, <u>A History of the Roumanians</u> (Cambridge 1934) 194.

59. <u>Documente privind istoria Romîniei. Răscoala din 1821</u> iv (Bucharest 1960) 131.

60. Ibid., 133.

61. Ibid., <u>Documente</u> . . . i (Bucharest 1959) 421 note 2.

62. Ibid., 421-22.

63. E. D. Tappe, op. cit., 146.

64. D. Golescu, op. cit., 65-6; 92-3.

65. B. Close, op. cit., 4.

66. Ibid., 3.

67. <u>Grammatica romănească</u> (Sibiu 1828) xvi.

68. See note 27.

69. J. C. Campbell, op. cit., 31.

70. D. Mitrany, op. cit., 33.

71. Op. cit., 40.

72. See note 55.

73. See E. D. Tappe, 'The 1821 Revolution in the Rumanian Principalities' 146.

INDEX

251